# COMMENTARY ON
# THE NEW LECTIONARY
## Volume 1

BY THE SAME AUTHOR

*The Liturgy of Penance* (Faith Press, 1966)
*The Feast of Pentecost* (Faith Press, 1967)
*Christmas and Epiphany* (Faith Press, 1967)
*Greater Things Than These* (Faith Press, 1974)

CONTRIBUTIONS

'Charisms and Confirmation' in *Crisis for Confirmation*, ed. Michael
Perry (SCM Press, 1966)
'Catholics in the Church of England' in *Catholic Anglicans Today*, ed.
John Wilkinson (Darton, Longman and Todd, 1968)
'The Changing Liturgy of Penance' in *Penance: Virtue and Sacrament*,
ed. John Fitzsimons (Burns and Oates, 1969)

# COMMENTARY ON THE NEW LECTIONARY

## VOLUME 1

*A scriptural and liturgical guide to the two-year cycle of readings for Sundays and Holy Days*

JOHN GUNSTONE

LONDON SPCK

*First published in 1973*
*Second impression 1974*
*S.P.C.K.*
*Holy Trinity Church*
*Marylebone Road*
*London NW1 4DU*

*Printed in Great Britain by*
*The Camelot Press Ltd, Southampton*

SBN 281 02782 X

TO

*The Barnabas Fellowship*

WHATCOMBE HOUSE

Did we not feel our hearts on fire
as he talked with us on the road and
explained the scriptures to us?

# CONTENTS OF VOLUME 1

# ACKNOWLEDGEMENTS

Acknowledgements are due to the Faith Press Ltd, Leighton Buzzard, for permission to use material from two of my books, *The Feast of Pentecost* and *Christmas and Epiphany*, published in 1967, and to the Church Literature Association, 199 Uxbridge Road, London W.12, for permission to use material from two booklets, *Lent* and *Holy Week and Easter*, published by them in 1969. Acknowledgement is also made to Mayhew-McCrimmon Ltd for permission to reproduce the theme titles for Epiphany 5 and 6 and Trinity 21 and 22 from *In Life Eternal* by Margaret Stevens.

Quotations from the New English Bible 2nd Edition © 1970 are made by permission of the Oxford and Cambridge University Presses.

# INTRODUCTION

This book is a scriptural commentary and liturgical guide to the new lectionary now in use in various Christian Churches. The scheme of lessons was originally published by the Joint Liturgical Group in Britain as *The Calendar and Lectionary*, edited by R. C. D. Jasper (Oxford 1967). The Church of England authorized its use with the Series 3 Order for Holy Communion in 1973, and the Methodist Church, the United Reformed Church, and the Churches of Christ in this country have also adopted it. In the Anglican Communion it is in use in the Church of Ireland and the Church of the Province of South Africa. At the time of writing other Christian bodies are considering it for use in their own churches. It is, then, an ecumenical project of considerable significance. When the Churches read and expound the same passages of scripture on Sundays and Holy Days across the world, they are demonstrating a unity in the proclamation of the gospel of Jesus Christ which offers many opportunities for united teaching and evangelism.

The Group drew up the lectionary on a two-year cycle with an Old Testament lesson, an epistle, and a gospel for each Sunday and Holy Day. In selecting the readings, they worked on the principle of letting one of the lessons guide them in the choice of the other two. This reading is called 'the controlling lesson', and is distinguished in this commentary by an asterisk placed to the left of the reference at the heading of the passage to be commented on. During the pre-Christmas period (nine weeks) the OT lesson is the controlling one, from Christmas to Whitsunday it is the gospel, and for the rest of the year it is the reading from the Acts or the epistles. With this structure in mind, they composed a lectionary trying to keep in balance the Church's traditions and present-day needs.

The ministry of the word of God has its own long tradition in Christian worship which cannot be ignored if we are to hear what the Spirit is saying to the churches in our day. The reading and exposition of scripture is intimately linked with the evolution of the Christian year, so this book begins with a brief survey of how the calendar and lessons developed, especially with reference to the eucharistic liturgy. This should give preachers and readers something of the 'feel' of the days and the seasons. Over the centuries time has been sanctified by the way in which the Church has been led to reflect on different aspects of the work of our redemption through the year. Though tradition must never be a burden, yet respect for it as a living heritage can give us a glimpse of that vision which the author of the Letter to the Hebrews had when he spoke of 'all these witnesses to faith around us like a cloud'. A particular passage was read on a certain day because it spoke to our forefathers in the faith on that occasion. On that same day it may well speak to us also. Our past is part of ourselves, and tradition is still one of the ways in which the Holy Spirit guides us as we move forward on our pilgrimage to 'the city which is to come'. The first section of this book, The Christian Year and the Lectionary, may help us to assess the value of the past in this respect.

Each passage of scripture is then given a short commentary. I should stress that these commentaries are not intended to be sermons. Rather, I hope that they will do something that biblical commentaries are intended to do when a sermon is being prepared. At this point I must say that I owe an enormous debt of gratitude to those scholars whose understanding of scripture is far deeper than mine can ever be; their books have supplied so much of what is in this volume. It has been impossible to acknowledge in footnotes where each explanation or suggestion about a word or a passage originated, much as I would have liked to do this.

When the Church of England Liturgical Commission first published the new lectionary in The Calendar and Lessons for the Church's Year (S.P.C.K. 1969), the title of theme was printed over each Sunday's readings. The Commission said, however, that 'the thematic titles provided are no more than indications of emphasis. They are not intended to dictate to the biblical material, and should not be allowed to do so' (p. 11). The titles were omitted when the lectionary was published in 1973. Using the lessons over a period of four years in a parish church, I discovered that although the theme titles were sometimes helpful in preparing for the ministry of the word on a particular day, often other themes sprang out of one or more of the readings. The Holy Spirit seemed to be leading me to a different topic on that day. And this, I am sure, is how a lectionary should be used. It is to give guidance for everyone in the Church in scripture reading, but the local and individual application of a reading cannot be dictated. In writing these commentaries, therefore, I have tried to avoid putting too much stress on the theme which links a set of lessons. Where the unifying subject is strong, as for example on Lent 4, the transfiguration of Jesus Christ, there is no need to point it out. Where it is weaker, it is better that the reader and the preacher should be led to it or to some other theme without any prompting from me. A table of the themes appears in Vol. 2, together with an index of lections and commentaries. The former may be useful when drawing up services based on a particular topic, the latter when using other lectionaries which include the same passages of scripture.

No attempt has been made to provide a commentary on the readings from the Psalms or Canticles, though in some places reference is made to them.

I have used the New English Bible as the basic text, though where it seemed helpful I have referred to the Revised Standard Version and the Jerusalem Bible. The quotations from the passage commented on are printed in heavy type. Other quotations are between inverted commas. Where only the chapter and/or the verse numbers are given, it means that they refer to the book of the Old or New Testament from which the passage has been taken.

This book will not, I imagine, ever be read from cover to cover in a short space of time. It is more likely to be picked up for reference week by week. I have therefore tried to make each set of commentaries for a particular day self-explanatory, with some repetition and occasional references to other parts of the book. The length of the commentary depends on what a lesson contains and what I felt might be useful to make notes on. I did not see any virtue in trying to standardize the length of each commentary. I am conscious that the passion narratives in Holy Week have been treated more sketchily than other passages. This is because a full-length treatment of them would have increased both the size and the cost of the book. So I have made notes on the passion according to Mark, read on the Monday, Tuesday, and Wednesday before Easter in Year 1, and only added a few comments on the passions according to Luke and John, where I thought that some special characteristic of their presentation should be drawn to the reader's attention. Brief commentaries are provided for Tables 2 and 3, the Holy Days and other occasions in the Church of England's new lectionary. Notes have also been added for the optional extensions to some of the lessons provided by the Church of England Liturgical Commission. The chapter and/or verse numbers of these are in brackets in the commentary. Finally, for the sake of completeness, I have included a commentary on what was in the Joint Liturgical Group's proposals the Old Testament lesson, the epistle and the gospel for 'the Seventh Sunday before Christmas'. This was omitted by the Liturgical Commission, who promoted the material for the next two Sundays and made new provision for Trinity 25 the Fifth Sunday before Christmas, but other Churches who have based their lectionaries on the original scheme of lessons may not have done this.

The new lectionary is part of that great movement to enable the people of God in the latter part of the twentieth century to respond to God in worship and living. We can no longer rely solely on the past. It is true that through liturgical scholarship we have recovered the simplicity and directness of the early Church's worship—which is why a knowledge of the past is as important in the revision of a lectionary as it is for, say, a eucharistic prayer—but in applying what we have learnt to the needs of today and the possibilities for tomorrow, we require the creativity and inspiration of the Holy Spirit. Only then will Christian congregations worship in spirit and in truth.

It is helpful to remember that every act of worship is essentially an assembly of the people of God to hear the word of God and to respond to him by participation in the Christian cultus, and in their daily lives. The presentation of the word of God is based on the reading of select passages of scripture. These can be expounded in the normal manner through a sermon or a discussion (if the congregation is a small one in a house group) and their meaning demonstrated with the use of further non-scriptural readings, visual aids, dramatic and musical presentations, and so on. But all additional material should be presented in such a way that it enables the congregation to 'hear' the word of God in Isaiah's sense of 'hearing'.

But it is equally important to exercise care and sensitivity in the choice of other material with which congregations can articulate their response to that word. The receiving of Holy Communion (if the word of God is being presented in a Eucharist) is, of course, the climax of that response, and its implications are worked out in the course of ordinary living during the days following the act of worship; but the people must be given words to say or to sing so that they can lift up their hearts and minds to God in praise for what he has done, is doing, and is going to do. For what we hear in the scripture readings are the words of eternal life, and our response to those readings in worship is powerfully effective in building up our faith. The clergy and those who plan worship are the servants of God and of his people in this respect as well—they must be led by the Holy Spirit, not only to write the sermon, but also to select the right psalm, canticle, or hymn which will enable the congregation to respond to God for what they hear in the ministry of the word. And this is especially vital in those gatherings for worship where there is no opportunity for any spontaneous response.

At the beginning of the service, therefore, the congregation must be helped to prepare to receive the word of God. The purpose of the first hymn is not to give the congregation something to do while the choir, the minister, and his assistants enter the church; it is to create in them a feeling of expectancy and an assurance of acceptance by God and by each other. New rites like Series 3 provide seasonal sentences as overtures to the main theme of the day. There is no reason why another key phrase or sentence from the readings should not be used for this purpose. The Roman Catholic *missa normativa* suggests in a rubric that the celebrant or some other suitable person should briefly introduce the subject of the readings so that the congregation may listen or follow the lessons in their Bibles more intelligently. A pause after each reading encourages the members of the congregation to reflect upon what they have heard. The hymn, canticle, or psalm between the readings (if there is one: it is not always necessary, even at sung services), provides the congregation with words with which to meditate further on what has been read. The new lectionary suggests psalms and canticles for the different readings. If they cannot be sung without distracting the congregation from the meaning of their words, then it is better to say them, chorally or antiphonally, sitting. Nothing should be allowed to hinder the Holy Spirit as he stirs in those listening to the word of God.

The Second Vatican Council declared that 'like the Christian religion itself, all the preaching of the Church must be nourished and ruled by the scriptures'. Every preacher who uses this book should, I believe, remember this declaration each time he begins to write his notes for a sermon. He will want to comment on one or more of the readings to draw the congregation's attention to those verses or events to which the Holy Spirit has led him as he prayed and prepared for his part in the ministry of the word. The things that Jesus said and did, as revealed in the gospel for the day, will be especially precious to him, and the manner in which he speaks of Christ will stir within the hearts of his hearers a deep love for the Saviour. He will also discuss the mysteries of God with a reverence and humility that convey the awe of the believer in the presence of the Most High. It may be right from time to time not only to expound and comment on the readings, but also to explain why they have been read on a certain day or during a particular season for centuries. That may give the congregation a sense of their oneness with the Body of Christ across the ages. I hope this book will help the preacher to fulfil that aspect of the ministry of the word. The application of scripture to a group or congregation can only be done by the man on the spot, since he knows the attitudes, the backgrounds, and the problems of those he is addressing.

After the sermon the people's response to the word of God still continues. The theme of the readings can be recalled at appropriate points in the service, even in the final hymn. Thoughts and words from the lessons can be included in those parts of the intercessions which have to be composed locally or said spontaneously. The *missa normativa* has a whole series of proper prefaces which link the readings to the eucharistic prayer. Where it is permitted, as in some of the eucharistic prayers of the Episcopal Church of America, home-made proper prefaces can be written based on the ministry of the word. If silence is kept after communion or at a later part of the service, then it is sometimes effective if the key phrases and sentences of the lessons are read out meditatively for the congregation. This develops the purpose for which material is provided in the seasonal sentences after the communion in Series 3.

The ministry of the word, then, is very much more than writing a sermon based on the readings of the day. It is the exercise of those gifts of the Holy Spirit which enable an individual and a team to prepare for and to lead an act of worship in such a way that God's word can be 'alive and active', sifting 'the purposes and thoughts of the heart' among those who assemble for it. It is a ministry through which the Church of Jesus Christ is built up in the Spirit as each congregation recognizes corporately and as individuals that they may 'boldly approach the throne of our gracious God, where we may receive mercy and in his grace find timely help'. For the response of the people is nothing if it is not the response of the Holy Spirit within them, drawing them through the word of God into the presence of God. Then, equipped as 'a chosen race, a royal priesthood, a dedicated nation, and a people claimed by God for his own', they are enabled so to live that they 'proclaim the triumphs of him who has called you out of darkness into his marvellous light'.

# THE CHRISTIAN YEAR AND
# THE LECTIONARY

Certain passages of scripture are traditionally associated with particular days or seasons in the Christian year. To understand why this is so, it is necessary for us to review briefly the evolution of the calendar as it affected the Church in the West. The readings set for the Sundays and Holy Days in the old missal of the Roman Catholic Church were the basis for the epistles and gospels in the Book of Common Prayer—the variations being due partly to differences in the lectionaries in use in western Europe in medieval times, and partly to some amendments by sixteenth- and seventeenth-century revisers in the Church of England. We can therefore assume for the purposes of this essay that the Book of Common Prayer and all the Prayer Books which have descended from it share in the lectionary of western Christendom, and that is why we have to pay attention to the development of certain liturgical traditions in Rome when that lectionary was in the process of formation. The period during which this formation took place was roughly the fourth to the eighth century.

The most important development was the emergence of Easter as the Christian Passover. This set the pattern for the rest of the liturgical year. We shall therefore discuss first the appearance and significance of the Easter cycle of feasts—Easter Day itself, Holy Week, Lent, and the great Fifty Days, in that order. Then we shall turn to the origins of Christmas and Epiphany and see why they came to be observed in our calendar. Finally we shall deal more briefly with a few of the other Holy Days and special occasions which have lessons assigned to them in the new lectionary.

## THE EASTER CYCLE OF FEASTS

Until about the middle of the fourth century, the Christian calendar was a very simple affair. It was marked by a weekly assembly for the Eucharist, and a christianized version of the Jewish Passover; and that was all.

If the absence of festivals in the calendar appears somewhat puritanical to us today, we have to remember that the first generations of Christians associated feast days with the pagan practices of the people among whom they lived. It is calculated that by the beginning of the third century, about one hundred and seventy-five festivals were held every year in Rome.

Many of them had a religious significance, and they were occasions for savage games in the circuses, immoral plays in the theatre, and excesses of various kinds. The Church had no inclination to copy these! That is why Paul warned the Galatians about 'special days and months and seasons and years'. Observances such as these belonged to the time when they were 'slaves to "gods" which in reality do not exist'.

The weekly assembly for the Eucharist can be traced back to the New Testament. It took place on 'the first day of the week'. In Jewish society the sabbath was the only free day, so Jewish Christians probably began observing the day of resurrection with a Eucharist by prolonging the sabbath into the night of Saturday-Sunday. By custom a day began at sundown the previous evening. What we would reckon as the end of the sabbath, Saturday night, was in New Testament times the beginning of the next day, the first day of the week. The incident at Troas, when Paul addressed a gathering until well past midnight and then broke bread, suggests something like this. The author of the Book of Revelation refers to 'the Lord's Day', and by the second century its observance was a well-known feature of Church life.

'On the day which is called the Sun's Day', wrote Justin (d. 165), 'there is an assembly of all who live in towns or in the country ... because it is the first day, on which God put to flight darkness and chaos and made the world; and on the same day Jesus our Saviour rose from the dead.'

## EASTER DAY

The origins of Easter are more obscure. It was hardly possible for Christians to ignore the significance of the Passover when it arrived in the spring of each year; the redeeming work of God is focused on this festival, and paschal themes are interwoven within the context of the Church's teaching and devotion. Paul wrote, 'Our Passover has begun; the sacrifice is offered—Christ himself' (he was probably referring to the paschal nature of the eucharistic assembly, not to the celebration of the feast in the year he was writing his letter to the church in Corinth), and the author of the fourth Gospel drew his picture of the mission of the Word made flesh within the framework of three successive Passover festivals. The first Christians, being Jews, must have brought the observance into the new Israel with them.

Be that as it may, the first real evidence for the Church's observance of Easter comes from the middle of the second century, when a controversy arose about the day on which it was to be kept. The churches in Asia observed it on the same day as many Jewish communities, the fourteenth

Nisan (March–April), whether this fell on a Sunday or a weekday. Elsewhere Christians kept the feast on the Sunday following the fourteenth Nisan. The details of the controversy need not concern us here, but we notice that from this time references to the *Pascha* begin to appear in Christian letters, treatises, homilies, and liturgical material.

Because of its roots in a Jewish observance, the celebration of Easter has always been a Saturday-night-and-Sunday-morning affair. It was during the night that the paschal mysteries of the Old Testament had taken place (the escape from Egypt and the crossing of the Red Sea) and it was during the night of the first day of the week that the Lord had risen from the dead. Christians kept the Passover, therefore, with a vigil which began at sunset on the Saturday and ended with a Eucharist in the early hours of Sunday morning. During the vigil the catechumens were baptized. It was felt that the sacrament of participation in Christ's death and resurrection was most fittingly administered during the paschal night, and this association with Christian initiation gave the formularies for the vigil, especially the readings, their baptismal theme.

Yet Easter in the early Church was not just a commemorative occasion. The Christian Passover celebrated the Lord's death and resurrection as a here-and-now reality. It was effective in the lives of those who repented and turned to him. The vigil, the baptisms, and the Eucharist represented, in one paschal mystery, the totality of God's saving work in Jesus Christ through the Holy Spirit; and that salvation was offered to the individual on the paschal night. The commemoration of Christ's Passover as a series of historical events was a later development in the Church's life.

In fact, the attitude of early Christians to the vigil and the feast was eschatological rather than historical. They kept Easter expecting the Lord to appear. In the parable of the wise and foolish virgins, the bridegroom came at midnight: the paschal vigil seemed to be the most likely moment in the year when this promise would be fulfilled. So the Church watched for the second coming of Christ on this night and, when the Bridegroom did not appear in his glorious *parousia*, her members met him in the paschal Eucharist instead.

Many different passages of scripture were provided for use during the Easter vigil in the early lectionaries—the story of creation in Genesis 1, the cleansing of Jerusalem in Isaiah 4 (leading into chapter 5, 'I will sing for my beloved a love-song about his vineyard', used as a canticle) and Moses' charge to the people about the book of the covenant, Deuteronomy 31. These passages were chosen because they unfolded the meaning of the baptismal rites which were performed later in the night. But two readings had a special significance. One was Exodus 14, the crossing of the Red Sea—the culmination of the original Passover when God saved his people from the Egyptians. The other was 1 Cor. 5 quoted above, 'Our Passover has begun; the sacrifice is offered—Christ himself'. Both these readings are set among the lessons for Easter Day in the new lectionary. The Eucharist at the end of the vigil had as its gospel the Matthean account of the resurrection. When the observance of the vigil was brought forward to Holy Saturday, another Eucharist was provided with either the Marcan or the Johannine account of the resurrection as its gospel. These three accounts are also set for Easter Day in the new lectionary. The other readings, Isa. 12.1–6, 1 Cor. 15.12–20, and Rev. 1.12–18, preserve the eschatological character of the feast and remind us that the resurrection of Christ points us forward to the second coming, the last judgement, and the resurrection of Christians.

## HOLY WEEK

The controversy about the observance of Easter in the second century also provides us with evidence that the Church prepared for the festival by keeping a fast. Irenaeus, Bishop of Lyons (d. 200), mentioned it in a letter which he wrote to Victor, Bishop of Rome, remonstrating with him for the harsh way he had treated the Asian Quartodecimans: 'Some think they ought to fast one day, some for two, others for still more; some make their "day" last forty hours. . . . In spite of that, they all lived in peace with one another, and so do we: the divergency in the fast emphasizes the unanimity of our faith.'

By the following century the fast had been lengthened to include the week before Easter. The Syrian *Didascalia Apostolorum*, which was supposed to contain the teaching of the twelve apostles, directed that a moderate fast should be kept from the Monday to the Thursday until the ninth hour (3 p.m.) by taking only bread, salt, and water, and that a stricter fast should be kept on the Friday and the Saturday immediately before the paschal vigil. In a letter to Basilides, Bishop of the Churches in Cyrenaica, Bishop Dionysius of Alexandria (d. 264) complained about those who did not keep the six days' fast with equal rigour. Unlike Irenaeus, he evidently did not appreciate the ecumenical principle that unity does not necessarily entail uniformity!

Since the Easter vigil became the major—if not the only—occasion when baptism was normally administered, the catechumens prepared for their initiation by keeping a fast during the days immediately before it.

By pious custom, their sponsors and some of the congregation used to keep the fast with them. This gave the week before Easter the tradition of a corporate fast. Besides this, a weekly fast was kept on Wednesdays and Fridays in some parts of the Church (another inheritance from sectarian Judaism), so a pre-paschal fast would seem only like an annual extension of it.

It was not in any sense commemorative. It was simply a period of preparation for the greatest festival in the year. Yet as early as the third century there was in the *Didascalia Apostolorum* an attempt to explain the significance of the six days' fast observed in Syria in terms of the Passion events: you fasted on Monday because of Judas' betrayal, on Tuesday because of the arrest after the last supper, on Wednesday because of the detention in the house of Caiaphas, on Thursday because of the examination before Pilate, on Friday because of the crucifixion, and on Saturday because of the burial in the selpulchre. Already Christian devotion was beginning to assign historical happenings to particular days; and in the following century this process crystallized.

The historicization of the liturgical year began in Jerusalem because of the circumstances in which the Christians of that city found themselves after the peace of the Church. The emperor Constantine (d. 337) visited the Holy Land and sponsored an ambitious scheme to build churches over the sacred sites associated with the life, death, and resurrection of Jesus Christ. As a result of this scheme, the Church in Jerusalem possessed at the end of the fourth century a number of magnificent basilicas which were the object of wonder and devotion among Christians throughout the empire.

The most important of these churches was a building—or rather a complex of buildings—over the sites of the hill of crucifixion and the sepulchre. From the main street of the city, which roughly coincided with the north-south section of the present Via Dolorosa, the visitor entered a richly furnished basilica known as 'the Place of Witness', the *Martyrium*. Beyond this church at its westward end he passed through doorways into a courtyard containing a baptistry and an outcrop of rock believed to be the original Golgotha. The courtyard then merged into a splendid rotunda called 'the Resurrection', the *Anastasis*, built over the cave where the body of Jesus was supposed to have rested. All that remains of the Martyrium-Anastasis is the Church of the Holy Sepulchre which incorporates a later version of the rotunda; but present-day pilgrims are usually taken to the back of a sweetshop in the Via Dolorosa to see one of the ancient columns which once formed part of the entrance to the

Martyrium. The adjoining Russian Excavations also contain certain remains.

Other basilicas were built on the site of the house with the upper room, the church of the Apostles or *Sion*, in the Garden of Gethsemane where Jesus taught the disciples, the *Eleona*, and on the summit of the mount of Olives, the Church of the Ascension or the *Imbomon*. A church was also constructed at Bethlehem—but we shall notice its importance when we came to discuss the Christmas cycle of feasts.

As people began to make pilgrimages to the Holy Land to visit the sacred sites and the churches, the bishop and the clergy in Jerusalem organized themselves with commendable ingenuity to cater for the spiritual needs of the pilgrims. In the manner of modern tourist agents, they set about providing devotional treats for the travellers with services in the different churches at which passages of scripture were read and prayers offered uniting the worshippers with the saving events associated with that particular place. These services took on a historical and dramatic character during the days before and after the celebration of Easter, and there were special commemorations of the entry of Christ into Jerusalem, the Last Supper, the agony in the garden, the trial and crucifixion, and the burial.

One of these pilgrims at the end of the fourth century was a nun from Spain called Egeria. She remained in Jerusalem throughout Lent and Eastertide and afterwards wrote an account of what she had seen and done for the benefit of her sisters in religion at home. Much of her journal has survived and from it, together with some other material, it is possible to discover in some detail how Jerusalem observed 'the paschal week'. 'Here', said Egeria, 'they call it "the Great Week".'

On the eve of Palm Sunday there was held in Bethany a service commemorating the supper in the house of Simon the leper. Then on Palm Sunday afternoon the people assembled in the church on the mount of Olives for longer devotions. Towards evening there was read to them the gospel of Christ's entry into Jerusalem and a procession moved off towards the city. 'All the children in the neighbourhood, even those who are too young to walk, are carried by their parents on their shoulders', wrote Egeria, 'all of them bearing branches, some of palms and some of olives, and thus the bishop is escorted in the same manner as the Lord was of old.' In later years the role of the bishop was made even more like that of Christ: he rode into the city seated upon a donkey!

During the following weekdays services of readings, hymns, psalms, and prayers were held in the Anastasis. The last office, which began about

4 p.m., included the lighting of candles from a lamp burning before the sepulchre, blessings, and prayers. On Maundy Thursday there was a Eucharist in the late afternoon in the Martyrium at which the account of the last supper was read as the gospel, and then the congregation went out to keep an all night vigil on the mount of Olives, with readings and prayers to commemorate the agony in the garden of Gethsemane, which lies at the foot of the hill.

On the morning of Good Friday the congregation returned to the Martyrium-Anastasis for a special service during which a relic of the Cross—found, it was said, by Constantine's mother Helena, when the Anastasis was being built—was produced in a silver casket for veneration. Egeria described the cremony: 'When it (the relic) has been put on the table, the bishop, as he sits, holds the ends of the sacred wood firmly in his hands, while the deacons who stand around guard it. It is guarded in this way because the custom is that the people, both the faithful and the catechumens, come one by one, and bowing down kiss the sacred wood and pass by. And because, I know not when, someone is said to have bitten off and stolen a piece of the holy wood, it is guarded in this way.' At midday the people assembled round Calvary for a three hours' vigil, ending at 3 p.m. with the reading of the death of Christ from the fourth Gospel.

On the eve of Easter a vigil was kept in the Anastasis; it included the reading of Matt. 27.62–66, the Jews' request to have Christ's tomb sealed, and the singing of Psalm 88.4, 'I am counted as one of them that go down into the pit', which was interpreted as Christ's prayer as he descended into hell. Then the congregation moved into the Martyrium for the keeping of the paschal vigil, during which the bishop, his clergy, the catechumens, and their sponsors went into the baptistry for the rites of initiation. Finally the Eucharist was celebrated.

Behind these ceremonies and readings, of course, was the intention of re-enacting and sharing in the events of the passion from the entry into Jerusalem to the resurrection, on the day and at the hour when they originally happened; and when the clergy and the pilgrims returned to their own homes, there was an irresistible urge to repeat the services for the benefit of those who could not make the long journey to the Holy Land. Out of this the universal observance of Holy Week grew. In Spain and in Gaul the pattern of the Jerusalem ritual was copied in elaborate detail, and a harmony of the gospels was compiled so that the story of the passion could be read in its fullest dramatic extent.

But the Church in Rome was more conservative. Some ceremonies, such as the Palm Sunday procession, were not introduced until the middle ages. The older tradition in Rome was to point the congregation to the whole mystery of the passion during the week, not to the events narrated in a quasi-chronological order. Leo the Great preached on the passion on Palm Sunday, Wednesday, Good Friday and Easter Day. The reading of the passion according to Matthew on Palm Sunday and that according to John on Good Friday is attested in the first lectionaries.

The Church in Rome achieved a dramatic effect another way. When a passion narrative was read, other lessons were selected to provide a kind of script for the *dramatis personae* involved. The first readings assigned to the Tuesday in Holy Week in the old lectionaries are a good example of this:

I had been like a sheep led obedient to the slaughter; I did not know that they were hatching plots against me and saying, 'Let us cut down the tree while the sap is in it; let us destroy him out of the living, so that his very name shall be forgotten' (from Jer. 11.18–20)

'Let us lay a trap for the just man. . . . He knows God, so he says; he styles himself "servant of the Lord". . . . He boasts that God is his father. . . . Let us test the truth of his words, let us see what will happen in the end; for if the just man is God's son, God will stretch out a hand to him and save him from the clutches of his enemies. . . . Let us condemn him to a shameful death, for on his own showing he will have a protector' (from Wisd. 2.12–22)

Jesus knew that his hour had come and he must leave this world and go to the Father. . . (from John 13.1–32).

The special character of Good Friday and Holy Saturday as a two days' intensive fast in preparation for the paschal vigil was recognized from early times. Augustine, Bishop of Hippo (d. 430), called the three days the *sacratissimum triduum crucifixi, sepulti, suscitati*. But Maundy Thursday at first did not have any particular importance. The pope used it as an opportunity for blessing the oils for the rites of initiation to be performed during the paschal vigil; he also absolved those who had been doing penance during Lent to enable them to take their full part in the ceremonies of the next three days. The formularies for these services have survived in the older Roman sacramentaries. In time, the service for the reconciliation of penitents was performed in the stational churches which specialized in penitential discipline, and the pope added to his duties an evening mass in commemoration of the last supper. Eventually this Eucharist also spread to the stational churches in the city and then to all churches where the Roman rite was followed. Maundy Thursday was the last day in Holy Week to receive its distinctive commemoration; and when it did, the gospel of the feet-washing and the accompanying discourse (John 13.1–15) was transferred from the Tuesday to this day. The passion according to Mark was read on Tuesday instead.

There were no Eucharists on weekdays in the Roman Church until the sixth century. The liturgy of the day consisted simply of readings, a homily, and prayers. This ancient liturgy was retained in the Roman rite on Good Friday. The climax of the lessons is the passion according to John and the so-called 'solemn prayers' are the primitive form of offering intercessions to God. The ceremony of the adoration of the cross and the chanting of the Reproaches were imported from the East and added to this ancient liturgy about the seventh century. The custom of receiving communion from the reserved sacrament was also an importation from the East. The Church of England practice of keeping Good Friday with the service of Antecommunion, therefore, is true to the most ancient traditions of the western Church.

When we turn to the new calendar we find that these traditions of Holy Week have been preserved. The readings make it possible for churches to adapt the traditional ceremonies. Palm Sunday has the passion according to Matthew, which has been read on that day for centuries, together with the account of the entry into Jerusalem by the same evangelist, which can be used instead or for a separate processional service. The passion according to Mark is read in a *lectio continua* on the first three days of the week in Year 1, that according to Luke in Year 2. The Old Testament lessons present prophecies and types of the passion as the old lectionaries did. The songs of the Servant of God from Isaiah are read on Palm Sunday Year 2 and on the first three weekdays in Year 1; on the other weekdays are a passage from Lamentations, the sacrifice of Isaac, and the bronze serpent in the wilderness.

In the epistles we follow the first Christians as they meditated on the great saving events of the week. Maundy Thursday is a commemoration of the last supper, with Pauline instructions on the Eucharist for the epistles, 1 Cor. 11.23–29 in Year 1 and 10.16–17 in Year 2, and the traditional gospel John 13.1–15, the feet-washing, alternating with Mark 14.12–26, the last supper. Exodus 12, the first Passover, is the Old Testament lesson for Good Friday and the passion according to John is still read on this day as these passages have been since antiquity. A set of lessons has been provided for Easter Eve.

## LENT

While the pre-paschal fast was evolving into Holy Week, its effect was also stretching back to the sixth and seventh weeks before Easter. This, too, influenced what passages of scripture were appointed for these weeks. Much work has been done by liturgists in recent decades to reconstruct the evolution of the Lenten lectionary in Rome in the period from the fourth to the eighth century. Early lists of readings in codices of scripture (*capitula*), epistle books and gospel books, and complete lectionaries have been important sources for the investigation. The oldest list of epistles for the Roman rite comes from a Fulda codex containing the Pauline letters, written between 540 and 546 for Victor, Bishop of Capua. In England the *Lindisfarne Gospels* are an important source. According to G. Morin its annotations reveal the readings of the ancient liturgy of the Church in Naples.

Five elements influenced the choice of readings during Lent.

1  THE CATECHUMENS  The first element was the preparation of the catechumens for their baptism at Easter. Even when the number of adult baptisms declined and the baptism of infants became normal, the ancient rites were still performed, though in a truncated form. The most important of these were the 'scrutinies'—services during which the evil powers which, it was believed, possessed all neophytes, were exorcised and the Creed and the Lord's Prayer were formally 'handed over'. In the latter half of the fourth century there were probably three such scrutinies in Rome. Each service was associated with a passage from the fourth Gospel —the Samaritan woman at the well (John 4.5–42), the man born blind (John 9.1–38), and the raising of Lazarus (John 11.1–45). These pericopes taught the meaning of baptism in terms of the water of life, an enlightenment, and a death-and-resurrection respectively. A continuous reading of the fourth Gospel from Christmas to Easter was a feature of the early Roman lectionary,[1] and it is possible that the three passages formed part of this sequence and were used on or near the Sundays of a three-

---

[1] Traces of this continuous reading of the fourth Gospel can still be seen in the choice of the pericopes for Christmas Day, Christmas 2, Epiphany 2, Lent 4, Passion Sunday, Good Friday, Easter Day, and Easter 1 in the Prayer Book. These readings were, of course, taken from the Sarum missal.

week Lenten fast which was observed in Rome in the fourth century.[2]

By the end of the fourth century the Lenten fast had been stretched to six weeks, making forty days from Lent 1 to what is now Maundy Thursday, then the day before the *sacratissimum triduum* of Good Friday, Holy Saturday, and Easter Day. Leo the Great (d. 461) regarded the forty days' Lent as a venerable institution—'the greatest and most sacred of the fasts' —so it must have been well established by the beginning of his pontificate in 440. More scrutinies were added to the pre-baptismal ceremonies. A pericope about the casting out of the dumb demon (Luke 11.14–26) was one of the readings associated with these, perhaps when salt was placed on the lips of the candidates. The feeding of the five thousand (John 6.1–14) may also have come into the lectionary of Lent at about this time, to teach the significance of the Eucharist. The healing of Naaman (2 Kings 5.1–14) was among other passages chosen to demonstrate to the catechumens the healing power of baptismal water.

2 THE FORTY DAYS' FAST   The second element to influence the choice of readings was the desire to emulate the forty days' fast of Jesus Christ in the wilderness. The Pauline passage, 'Now is the acceptable time' (1 Cor. 6.1–10), and the story of the temptations in the wilderness (Matt. 4.1–12) were being read at the beginning of Lent during Leo's pontificate. During the Wednesday and the Friday of the week following Lent 1, the accounts of Moses' forty days on mount Sinai, Elijah's forty days' fasting journey to mount Horeb, and the forty days' fast of the people of Nineveh, were included in the lectionary to emphasise the symbolic meaning of the number of the days. Then on Lent 2 the gospel of the transfiguration (Matt. 17.1–9) brought together with Jesus Christ the figures of the two men referred to in the previous week's readings, Moses and Elijah; purified by the fast, they were able to share with Christ the glory of God. This was the goal which the ministry of the word set before Christian congregations at the commencement of the fast.

Certain trends began to lengthen the pre-paschal season. Sundays are not fast days in liturgical tradition, so that a six-weeks' Lent contained only thirty-six days on which a fast could be kept (six weeks minus the Sundays but including Good Friday and Holy Saturday). Gregory the

---

[2] It is believed that the three passages were read on the fourth, fifth, and sixth Sundays in Lent before they were moved to the Wednesdays and Fridays of the fourth and fifth weeks in Lent, where they are to be found in the old Roman lectionary. They have been restored to the third, fourth, and fifth Sundays in Lent in the new Roman lectionary, Cycle A.

Great (d. 604) was content to teach his people to offer this tithe of the year to God; but shortly afterwards four days were added to provide forty fasting days before Easter, so that Lent was now reckoned from the Wednesday of the seventh week before the festival. Christ's instructions about fasting and almsgiving (Matt. 6.16–21) have been read as the gospel for the first day of Lent, Ash Wednesday, from the time that this particular day appeared in the lectionaries.

In the east ascetical zeal lengthened the pre-paschal fast to fifty, sixty and even seventy days, and the Sundays within this longer season acquired the names of 'the Sunday in the Fifty Days, . . . in the Sixty Days, . . . in the Seventy Days' (*Dominica in Quinquagesima*, . . . *in Sexagesima*, . . . *in Septuagesima*). The practice was never adopted in Rome, but the names attached themselves to the three Sundays before Ash Wednesday, giving them a quasi-Lenten character. Paul's exhortation to asceticism ('Every athlete goes into strict training'—1 Cor. 9.24–27) has always been read on Septuagesima Sunday. In planning a pre-Easter season of nine weeks, therefore, the Joint Liturgical Group brought this development to its logical conclusion.

3 THE PENITENTS  The third element to influence the selection of lessons for Lent was the practice of imposing penances on those who were separated from the community because of some grave sin, and who wished to be readmitted to communion at Easter. Once a sinner had confessed his fault to the bishop or to the priest-penitentiary appointed for the purpose, he was enrolled in the ranks of the penitents at the beginning of Lent. At first, this was a simple service during which the bishop laid hands on him and the congregation prayed for him. Later it was elaborated with additional ceremonies such as the sprinkling of ashes and the imposition of a sackcloth. In the old Roman missal the gospels for the Monday and the Tuesday of the first week in Lent (the beginning of the penitential season when it was only six weeks in length) seem to have been chosen to teach the penitents and the people the effect of sin and the intention behind the Church's disciplinary action: one was the separation of the sheep from the goats (Matt. 25.31–46), the other was the cleansing of the temple (Matt. 21.10–17). The penances undertaken by the sinners included fasting and almsgiving, mentioned in the readings at the beginning of Lent.

As in the case of the catechumens, congregations tended to identify themselves with the penitence of the sinners and to use the forty days as a season of general confession and sorrow for sin. This strengthened the penitential character of the pre-paschal fast. Later, when the ceremony of the ashes came into use for all worshippers, it was as if the whole Church enrolled herself corporately into the ranks of the penitents.

4   THE PASSION   The fourth element to affect the choice of readings was the stress on the passion of Christ as the cost and means of redemption. This element is associated with the evolution of Holy Week, which we have already outlined, but we notice here that by the middle ages the last two weeks of Lent acquired the name of 'Passiontide', probably because in the chronological pattern of the Lenten season these two weeks were near the climax of the sufferings of our Lord. The fifth Sunday in Lent was given a pericope from the epistle to the Hebrews on the sacrificial nature of Christ's obedience (Heb. 9.11–15) and a reading from the fourth Gospel describing how the Jews attempted to stone Christ because he said, 'In very truth I tell you, before Abraham was born, I am' (John 8.12–20). 'Types' of the passion in the songs of the Suffering Servant of Yahweh and the story of Daniel also came into the lectionary for these two weeks. Passiontide has been suppressed in the latest Roman calendar.

5   THE STATIONAL CHURCHES   The stational churches in Rome were a fifth element in the choice of the Lenten readings. During the pre-paschal season the pope visited the different churches in the city each day to demonstrate the unity of the Christian community, and the old Roman missal still carries notices of these stations. On days when a large congregation was expected, the great basilicas were used, such as St John Lateran, which has been the stational church for Lent 1 since the time of Anastasius I (d. 401). On other days the pope went to the smaller churches.

The Thursdays in Lent, the last to be given their own synaxes, received readings chosen because they could be linked with the stational church in which the pope celebrated mass that day. For example, the station for the Thursday of the third week in Lent was SS. Cosmas and Damian, a church founded by Felix IV (d. 530) in a hall which once housed the city archives. Cosmas and Damian were two early Syrian medicos or wonder-workers, whose cultus developed in the fifth century and who were invoked as the patron saints of the medical profession. They were known as 'the holy money-less ones' because it was believed that they practised medicine without charging fees. For the Lenten mass in this stational church, therefore, the story of the healing of Peter's mother-in-law and of the sick in Capernaum was set as the gospel (Luke 4.38–44).

The Joint Liturgical Group drew up the new lectionary for the period between Christmas and Whitsunday so as to trace through the gospel readings Jesus Christ's ministry from his nativity to the sending of the Holy Spirit. But the traditions associated with Lent were so powerful that the chronological order of the events in the synoptic Gospels was not followed completely. The temptation in the wilderness, a reading of great significance for the penitential season as we have seen, had to be included at the beginning of Lent even though the lesson would then be read five or six weeks after the gospel of the baptism of Christ (itself traditionally associated with Epiphany, for reasons which we shall discuss shortly). The Joint Liturgical Group, therefore, chose the gospels round the general theme of 'The King and the Kingdom', recalling some of the most significant events in our Lord's ministry. This enabled the Group to include in the lectionary some of the readings traditionally associated with Lent.

So we find that after passages depicting Christ as teacher, healer, and worker of miracles on the three Sundays before Lent, Ash Wednesday has retained its old gospel, Matt. 6.16–21, 'When you fast . . .' in Year 1, with a parable about true repentance, Luke 18.9–14, the Pharisee and the tax-gatherer, in Year 2. The temptation in the wilderness is still the gospel for Lent 1, Matt. 4.1–17 in Year 1, Luke 4.1–13 in Year 2. (The lectionary takes advantage on a number of Sundays of the two-year cycle by setting the parallel account from a synoptic Gospel for the same Sunday the following year.) The ancient scrutiny lesson, Luke 11.14–26, the casting out of the dumb demon, is provided for Lent 2 Year 1 with its parallel, Matt. 12.22–32, for Year 2. The confession of Peter at Caesarea Philippi, the first prediction of the passion and the resurrection, and the 'take up his cross' saying, Matt. 16.13–28 and Luke 9.18–27, listed for Lent 3 Years 1 and 2 respectively, is not a Lenten reading in the old Roman missal (the first half of this pericope is the gospel for the feast of SS. Peter and Paul, June 29), but it fits in well with the themes of the pre-Easter season we have been examining. The story of the transfiguration is read on Lent 4, Matt. 17.1–13 in Year 1, Luke 9.28–36 in Year 2, and on Lent 5 our thoughts are turned towards the victory of the cross by reading John 12.20–32, the sayings of Christ about 'the grain of wheat' and 'when I am lifted up', in Year 1 and Mark 10.32–45, a prediction of the passion, the reference to the crucifixion as 'the baptism I am baptized with', and 'the Son of Man did not come to be served but to serve, and to surrender his life as a ransom for many', in Year 2. The parallel of the first of these in Matt. 20.17–28 was the ancient gospel for the Wednesday in the second week in Lent (where Christ's invitation, 'Behold, we are going up to Jerusalem', gives a depth of meaning to the observance of Lent); the second formed part of the gospel for the Saturday before Palm Sunday.

Before we leave the pre-Easter season, it is perhaps worth mentioning that some other ancient Lenten readings are included in the new lectionary. Moses' and Elijah's encounters with God on mount Sinai are read on Lent 4 instead of during the first week of Lent. The healing of Naaman, 2 Kings 5.1–14, is the Old Testament lesson for Sexagesima Year 2. 1 Cor. 9.24–27, the old epistle for Septuagesima, is now read on Ash Wednesday Year 1. The Passion Sunday epistle on the sacrificial nature of Christ's obedience, Heb. 9.11–15, is still in its traditional place in Year 2. Some of the other old Lenten lessons have been moved to different parts of the calendar. The parable of the sheep and the goats, Matt. 25.31–46, which once impressed on sinners the implications of their penances, is now fixed for the first Sunday in Advent Year 2. Of the three ancient scrutiny lessons from the fourth Gospel, the story of the Samaritan woman at the well is divided between Epiphany 4 and 6 of Year 2 (John 4.7–14, 19–26) and the Michaelmas Ember Day, John 4.31–38. The cleansing of the temple, John 2.13–22, is the gospel for Epiphany 2.13–22; the former Lenten reading about the cleansing, Matt. 21.10–17, which was read on the Tuesday of the first week in Lent to warn penitents of the possible consequences of their sins, is now the gospel for the feast of the Dedication or Consecration of a Church!

## THE GREAT FIFTY DAYS

The early Christian Passover—the fast, the vigil, the baptisms, and the Easter Eucharist—ushered in a glorious season of fifty days when penitential acts such as fasting were suspended and praise to the risen Lord in acclamations like the *Alleluia* dominated the Church's worship. The Bridegroom had not come at midnight during the Easter vigil, but Christians were still able to meet him sacramentally in the Eucharist, joining the newly-baptized in their first communion. And then for seven weeks they rejoiced in their union with God through the risen Christ. Turning back to the early church we find the spirit of this great festive season in the words of Tertullian (d. 220):

It is the time when the Lord's resurrection was made widely known among the disciples, when the gift of the Holy Spirit was inaugurated, and when the hope of the Lord's second coming was revealed. It is the time when, after his ascension into heaven, the angels told the apostles that he would return as he had gone up into heaven, that is, at Pentecost. And when Jeremiah said, 'I will gather them together from the farthest parts of the earth on a feast day', he meant by that the Pasch and Pentecost, which is truly a festal day.

Tertullian called it the *laetissimum spatium*, 'the most joyful season'. Nowadays we know it as Eastertide. But at least until the beginning of the fourth century the period was given the title of 'Pentecost'—the Greek word being used in Christian circles to refer to the whole of the fifty days rather than the last day of the season, our Whitsunday.

From its scriptural background as a 'week of weeks'—the ritual season of the Jewish grain harvest—the great Fifty Days symbolized the fulfilment of all that God had promised through Jesus Christ, 'the first fruits of the harvest of the dead'. Later, the unity of this festive season was broken up as individual days were kept as commemorations of the ascension of Christ and the sending of the Holy Spirit; but in its primitive form Pentecost represented in the cycle of the year what the Lord's Day represented in the seven-day cycle of the week. Athanasius (d. 373) called the season (in the Latin version of his letters) the *magna dominica*, 'the great Sunday'. It was when Lent and Holy Week took on a more commemorative character, that the great Fifty Days began to lose their unity. Certain days within them acquired an importance of their own.

1  The Easter octave was established. In Rome the newly-baptized were expected to attend church each day for the week after their initiation for further instruction. This was made possible because in the christianized Roman Empire Holy Week and Easter Week were made public holidays. The neophytes wore their white baptismal robes until the first Sunday after Easter, which became known as the *Dominica in albis deponendis*, 'the Sunday for the laying aside of white robes'. The themes of the resurrection and baptism dominated the choice of the readings on these days with pericopes from the fourth Gospel and from the sermons in the Acts of the Apostles. On the octave day, Easter 1, the gospel was John 20.19–31, which included the appropriate words, 'A week later his disciples were again in the room. . . .'

2  In the process of elaborating the ceremonies in Jerusalem, special services were arranged to commemorate the ascension of Christ in the church of the Imbomon and the gift of the Holy Spirit in the church at Sion. The chronology of Acts 1 and 2 set the pattern: the fortieth day after

Easter became Ascension Day and the fiftieth day after Easter, the last day of the ancient season of Pentecost, now became the Sunday of Pentecost. Whitsunday thus came to be regarded as a feast day in its own right and was given an octave.

3 The Rogations were instituted in the fifth century and when the practice of observing them spread in the west they interrupted the continuity of the great Fifty Days.

Yet the unity of the great Fifty Days has survived. We still call it Eastertide. We still sing 'Alleluia' more frequently during these weeks than at other times of the year. And the lectionary still recalls the triumphant character of the season with readings from the fourth Gospel, Acts, and Revelation.

The unanimity with which the different liturgical traditions selected their Eastertide lessons from these three books is remarkable. Not only in the Roman rite but also in the Milanese, Spanish, and Byzantine rites, the fourth Gospel, Acts and Revelation are all used during the great Fifty Days. We can understand the choice when we remember what the ancient Pentecost stood for: these three books more than any others in the New Testament see through the veil to what lay within the incarnate life of our Lord, and they herald the fulfilment of what God has done in Jesus Christ through the power of the Holy Spirit. John shows us that from the moment of his baptism Jesus was the paschal Lamb and that his work would be completed by 'the Advocate, the Holy Spirit whom the Father will send in my name'. Acts portrays the apostolic Church advancing in the triumph of the paschal proclamation and in the dynamic of the Spirit from Jerusalem to Rome. And the Apocalypse unfolds for us the secret plan of God which will become a reality on earth because 'this is the hour of victory for our God, the hour of his sovereignty and power, when his Christ comes to his rightful rule'. It was in response to such readings that the early Church kept 'the most joyful season'.

Much of this Eastertide joy echoes in the lessons for the great fifty days in the new lectionary. Many of the gospels are taken from the fourth Gospel, those for Easter 1 Year 1 and Easter 2 Year 2 and Easter 5 Year 1 being in the places they occupied in the past. There is a reading from Revelation on Easter 2 Year 1. But the opportunities offered by a two-year cycle have been taken to give the first four Sundays after Easter different overall themes on alternative years. In Year 1 the gospels are accounts of the resurrection appearances, giving Eastertide a rather more historical flavour than it had before when it was regarded more as a season of joy;

23

the epistles in Year 1 point to the triumphant eschatological consummation of Christ's resurrection victory. In Year 2, following the lead of the Prayer Book gospel for Easter 2, a series of four 'I am' passages from the fourth Gospel point to the eternal Christ and his abiding reality to the Christian and to the Church. The remaining Sundays retain their main themes, though Easter 6, the Sunday after Ascension Day, seeks to bring home the truths of the ascension more adequately for the benefit of Sunday worshippers. The season ends with the feast of Pentecost, which is also used in the new lectionary to open up the next section of the Church's year.

## THE CHRISTMAS CYCLE OF FEASTS

When we come to discuss the Christmas cycle of feasts we leave the Christian inheritance from Judaism with its Passover and Pentecost celebrations and move into the pagan Hellenistic world within which the members of the early Church lived. In that society men and women worshipped many kinds of deities and believed that their destinies were governed by the powers whose mysterious will they could trace in the sun, moon, and stars. The sun especially fascinated their imagination and even roused their devotion:

> Glory of the earth and sky,
> The sun is the same for all.
> Glory of light and darkness,
> The sun is the beginning and end.

The ancient hymn tells us something of this devotion to the blazing orb of the heavens. So much depended on its light and warmth. People's lives were caught up in the annual rhythm of sowing and harvesting, and a bad year meant starvation for thousands. No wonder that the day when the sun began its journey back into the northern hemisphere—the winter solstice—was one of great rejoicing!

In the early Christian era the inhabitants of the Roman empire worshipped not so much the sun itself as the god or gods that they believed it manifested. To the devotees of Apollo or Mithras, Dionysus or Aion, the winter solstice was a sign of divine birth or rebirth, an advent or coming of the deity to dwell among his followers. Signs of this were eagerly awaited. Folk were spiritually hungry. When Paul and Barnabas healed the cripple in Lystra, the people of the town thought it was a sign that the gods had come among them, and the priest of Jupiter brought out the dedicated oxen and prepared to offer a sacrifice. It was only with difficulty that the apostles convinced them that 'we are only human beings, no less mortal than you' (Acts 14.15). For everyone, therefore, the winter solstice was a day of profound significance. All over the empire ceremonies and legends were connected with the occasion. In Rome they lit bonfires and listened to the mysteries unfolded by wise men from the east. In Alexandria they processed round the temple of Koré and at midnight celebrated the virgin birth of her son, Aion. In the Nile and in other rivers there were ritual washings and blessings of the water for purification and fertility. In Cilicia and at Jerash rumours went round of wells and springs flowing with wine as a sign of future richness and joy (Epiphanius, a fourth century Bishop of Salamis in Cyprus, claimed that he had tasted some!).

Since the sun was the focus of so much devotion and superstition, it served to draw men of different faiths together in a kind of ecumenical celebration on the day of the winter solstice. The authorities saw advantages in encouraging this. In A.D. 274 the emperor Aurelian proclaimed the day as a public holiday and erected a temple to the sun-god, *Sol*, in Rome. It was a shrewd political move. By it the emperor united the many races and religions under his rule in a universal festival and proclaimed himself patron of all his peoples' deities. The day was immensely popular, with all-night dancing and junketing as the joyful crowd watched for the dawn that heralded a new birth of light and life.

There was, however, one complication. In the western part of the empire they calculated the day by the Julian calendar, and according to that the winter solstice fell on 25 December; but in the eastern part of the empire they used the venerable calendar of Amenemhet I of Thebes (*c*. 1996 B.C.), and according to that it fell on 6 January. The long-term effect, as far as we are concerned, is that when the Church took over the pagan festival and baptized it for her own purposes, she found herself celebrating two days instead of one.

To say that the Church took over the pagan festival is perhaps misleading. It was not a conscious movement. In the first centuries the Church's preachers and writers assimilated and used Hellenistic ideas and words to proclaim and expound the Gospel—we see the process beginning within the New Testament itself (a few instances are noted in the commentary). The same kind of thing happened in Christian devotion. The gospel was the news of salvation to men who looked for light in a world darkened with sin, pain, and death. When the Christian saw his pagan neighbour looking to the shining light of *Sol* as a symbol of joy, peace, and eternity, he told him that as a Christian he worshipped another and greater sun—the one foretold by the prophet, 'the sun of righteous . . . with healing in his wings' (Malachi 4.2). He told him of Jesus Christ, whom Zechariah had heralded as 'the morning sun from heaven' (Luke 1.78) and whom the evangelist had proclaimed as 'the real light which enlightens every man' (John 1.9). What their pagan neighbours celebrated on 25 December and 6 January, therefore, the members of the Church believed that they could also celebrate—but more hopefully and joyfully, for in Jesus Christ what all men looked for had been fulfilled.

This is one reason why the two dates came to be linked with the coming of Jesus Christ into the world. But there was also another reason. In those same centuries the Church's theologians were struggling to maintain against various heresies the truth of the incarnation, and a day celebrating the manifestation of God in Jesus Christ, when the Word became flesh, offered a wonderful opportunity of proclaiming the basic doctrine of the Christian faith. Phrases were added to the creed to underline the divinity of Christ:

> God from God, Light from Light,
> begotten, not made,
> one in Being with the Father.

The Church urged men to cast aside the pale shadows which they followed in vain and to turn to the one true God,

> who was manifested in the body
> vindicated in the spirit,
> seen by angels;
> who was proclaimed among the nations,
> believed in throughout the world,
> glorified in high heaven.

(1 Tim. 3.16)

Originally the Church celebrated on 25 December and 6 January the early events in the gospel narratives through which Jesus Christ revealed his true nature to men, from the birth at Bethlehem to the miracle at the wedding in Cana. The earliest title of the feast was the *Apparitio Domini*, 'the appearance of the Lord'. It was only gradually that 25 December came to be associated exclusively with the birth of Jesus and the adoration of the shepherds, and was called the feast of the Nativity. 'Christmas' is an English title: 'Christ's mass'.

This link between the birth of Christ and 25 December was possible because no one knew on what day of the year the Saviour was born. A few have wondered if 'the sixth month' in which, as Luke recorded, Mary miraculously conceived the Son of God, could have been the sixth month of the Jewish year, *Elul*, August-September, thus fixing the nativity in May-June, but most commentators have taken the phrase to refer to the sixth month of Elizabeth's pregnancy. And there have been many other suggestions based on a mixture of scriptural guesswork and allegorical arithmetic. Clement, Bishop of Alexandria (d. *c.* 215), wrote that some believed 20 May to have been the day, but that his own calculations led him to favour 18 November. Hippolytus (d. *c.* 236) thought that Christ must have been born on the day of the week on which God made the sun —the fourth day, a Wednesday—and *De pascha computus*, written in north Africa about 243 argued that, as the first day of creation must have coincided with the vernal equinox, 25 March, our Lord's birthday must be the fourth day after that, 28 March.

But by the beginning of the fourth century the dates of the winter solstice were accepted as Christian festivals of the appearing of Jesus Christ; in the second quarter of that century a list of Roman martyrs was composed at the top of which were the words *VIII Kal. Ianu. natus Christus in Bethleem Iudaea*, 'on the eighth day of the Calends of January, Christ born in Bethlehem of Judaea'. The Julian calendar retained the custom of numbering the days according to the lunar month. As the Calends of January were those days in December which follow the new moon, the eighth day was 25 December. This is the earliest evidence we have for the observance of Christmas.

The years from which this list originated—the 330s—also witnessed the end of the emperor Constantine's reign, and this inevitably raises the question whether the emperor himself was responsible for promoting the Christian celebration on 25 December. We know that he promulgated a decree concerning 'the venerable day of the sun' and made it possible for Christians to worship on the weekly Lord's Day. And we know that with his mother, Helena, he was interested in the circumstances of the Saviour's birth, for he arranged for a basilica to be constructed over the grotto of the nativity at Bethlehem. Furthermore, the fact that 25 December was kept as a religious festival by almost every subject in the western empire may well have prompted him to encourage its observance by the Church.

We have already seen how important a source for liturgical studies is Egeria's diary. From her we learn that on 6 January the birth of Christ was celebrated at midnight in the church at Bethlehem. Then, as dawn broke, the bishop and the congregation processed to Jerusalem, singing psalms. 'In Bethlehem throughout the entire eight days', she wrote, 'the feast is celebrated in festal array and joyfulness by the priests and all the clerics there and the monks who are stationed in that place.' At about the same time the pope had instituted a mass in Rome on Christmas morning—a radical move, this, for weekday celebrations were unheard-of in those days. Soon a midnight mass was added and, a little later, another mass at dawn for the Byzantine court officials in the church of St Anastasia near their spacious homes on the Aventine. This is how the three masses for 25 December came to appear in the Roman missal.

In the eastern half of the empire Christians kept 6 January as 'the Birthday' or 'the Theophany' or—more commonly—'the Epiphany'. The word means 'the showing forth' or 'the manifestation' of God in Jesus Christ and not, as the seventeenth-century Anglican revisers of the Prayer Book thought, the manifestation of Christ to the Gentiles. In their reading and teaching they included not only the birth at Bethlehem but also those first events in the Gospels which demonstrated that God was revealing himself in Jesus Christ. Perhaps the pagan customs and legends which the Church found in contemporary society had something to do with it. She wanted to answer what was false with what was true. Wise men had brought their cults from the east: magi had come to Christ, too. There were ritual washings and blessings in rivers: Christ, too, had been baptized by John in the Jordan, when the voice of the Father had been heard from heaven and the Spirit had descended as a dove upon him. There were legends of water changed miraculously into wine: Christ, too, had once changed water into wine at Cana.

When in the west the Church began to keep 6 January as well as 25 December as a festival, and when in the east Christians began to observe 25 December as well as 6 January, the saving events were divided between the two days. 25 December became the celebration of Christ's birth, 6 January became the commemoration of the magi, the baptism, and the miracle at Cana. The antiphon for the Magnificat at vespers on the feast sums up its intention: 'We keep this day holy in honour of three miracles: this day a star led the wise men to the manger; this day water was turned into wine at the marriage feast; this day Christ chose to be baptized by John in the Jordan, for our salvation. Alleluia.' So did Christopher Wordsworth in his hymn:

> Manifested by the star
> to the sages from afar. . . .

Manifest at Jordan's stream,
  Prophet, Priest, and King supreme;
And at Cana wedding-guest
  In thy Godhead manifest. . . .

    (English Hymnal 47, A. & M. Revised 81)

The new lectionary preserves all the traditional scripture readings for these feasts and enhances the use of them by allocating them to the Sundays after Christmas Day and Epiphany. Isa. 9.2–7, 'The people who walked in darkness have seen a great light', which supplied the material for the propers in the old Christmas rites, is the Old Testament lesson for Christmas Day Year 2. Titus 2.11–14, 'The grace of God has dawned upon the world', and Luke 2.1–10, the adoration of the shepherds, the epistle and gospel of the midnight mass, are set for Year 1, and for Year 2 there is the old gospel from the mass for the day which came into the Prayer Book on Christmas Day, John 1.1–14. Isa. 60.1–6, 'Arise, Jerusalem, rise clothed in light', which was read on Epiphany in the missal, is the Old Testament lesson for Christmas 1 Year 1 with Matt. 2.1–12, the adoration of the magi, sensibly brought forward to the Sunday as the gospel for both Year 1 and Year 2. The presentation in the temple, Luke 2.21–40, is commemorated on Christmas 2 Year 1 and the boy Jesus in the temple, Luke 2.41–52, in Year 2. The baptism in the Jordan is the theme for Christmas 3, the Matthean account in Year 1 and the Johannine in Year 2. The wedding at Cana, John 2.1–11, is the gospel for Christmas 5 Year 1. The calendar fills up the other Sundays in both years with events from the early ministry of Christ which proclaim that God is manifesting himself to men and showing them the implications of his coming. Since the circumcision of Christ and the presentation in the temple are now caught up into the Sunday readings, the feasts on 1 January and 2 February are less important, though lessons are provided for them in Table 2 of the new lectionary. The older title of the latter, *Hypapante*, 'the Meeting', indicates its true significance—the Christ-child is brought to the temple to meet the saints of the Old Israel, Simeon and Anna. The use of candles on this day goes back to some Roman pagan ceremony.

## ADVENT

Advent is an entirely western institution. It does not appear in the calendars of the Orthodox Churches. In Rome it seems to have developed from the December fast of Embertide, and in Gaul it served as a second Lent when catechumens were preparing for their baptism on the feast of the Epiphany. The name was taken from the old title of the Christmas period, *De Adventu Domini*, 'Of the Coming of the Lord'. The great figures of Advent are Isaiah, John the Baptist, and the Virgin Mary—those who prepared for and co-operated with the incarnation of the Son of God. Their words and activities have been the subject of the readings in Advent since the time when the season began to appear in the Roman lectionary about the sixth century.

But in the early middle ages another note began to sound during Advent, that of Christ's Second Coming. The last weeks in the year reminded the Church of the end of all things. The famous 'O antiphons' of the Magnificat both look back to Christ's earthly coming and forward to the parousia:

O Day-spring, Brightness of Light Everlasting, and Sun of Righteousness: Come and enlighten him that sitteth in darkness and in the shadow of death.

But in the Church of England other themes were introduced into Advent through the collects and epistles. Advent 2 happened to have Rom. 15.4-13, 'All the ancient scriptures were written for our instruction', as its epistle, and this gave it the character of a 'Bible Sunday'. Advent 3 happened to have 1 Cor. 4.1-5, 'Stewards of the secrets of God', as its epistle, and since this Sunday is near the time when the Advent ordinations are usually held, it has become an occasion for preaching and praying about the Church's ordained ministry.

The Joint Liturgical Group boldly extended the pre-Christmas season to nine weeks (there is precedent, for those who want to look for it, in the longer Advents of the Gallican calendars) and, using the Old Testament lesson as the controlling readings, traced the story of God's work from the creation to the incarnation—creation, the fall, Noah, Abraham, Moses—and then merged this with the traditional themes of the season—the Advent hope, the word of God in the Old Testament, the Forerunner and the annunciation. The Church of England Liturgical Commission has amended this slightly. They have kept the Advent season to four weeks but used four of the five other readings for the last Sundays in Trinitytide; and they have altered one Sunday's readings and rearranged the order of two more. A commentary on the readings dropped by the Commission will be found in Vol. 2, pp. 408-12.

# TRINITYTIDE AND HOLY DAYS

## TRINITYTIDE

The lessons for the Sundays after Trinity reflect the ancient method of reading the Bible in church. The choice of scriptures was left to the bishop presiding over the Eucharist. Sometimes a book of the Bible was read through more or less continuously. The epistles and gospels in the Roman missal and in the Prayer Book seem to have come from a collection of passages which by the seventh century had been attached more or less haphazardly to certain Sundays. This series existed in two forms containing substantially the same passages in nearly the same order but assigned to different weeks. One came from northern Europe, the other from Rome. The differences account for the divergences which used to be found between the readings in the Prayer Book and the Roman Missal. For the new lectionary a completely fresh selection has been made. This has been drawn up with the epistle as the controlling lesson to express the continuing life of the pilgrim Church after Pentecost in the experience of the living Spirit of Christ. Four lessons from Acts in Year 2 describe the life of the apostolic community in Jerusalem following the gift of the Spirit, Acts 2.22–24, 32–36, Acts 2.37–47, Peter before the Sanhedrin, Acts 4.5–12, the Ethiopian eunuch, Acts 8.26–38, and the Gentile Pentecost, Acts 11.4–18. The last discourses of John 13–17 supply some of the gospels, appropriately because they come from an evangelist who was prophetically inspired to teach us the significance of the union of Christ with his Church.

## ROGATION DAYS

The Rogation Days, *Litaniae minores*, were instituted by Mamertus (d. *c.* 475), Bishop of Vienne in Gaul, when his diocese was stricken by volcanic eruptions. He led his congregation in penitential processions in the open air. The practice was copied by neighbouring churches in Gaul and by the sixth century there were canons passed by councils ordering their observance throughout the country. They appeared in service books in the seventh and eighth centuries. Two of the lessons provided in the new lectionary, James 5.16–20, 'Elijah . . . prayed earnestly' and Luke 11.5–13, the friend at midnight, are the original readings for Rogationtide and reflect its character as a period of intense prayer. Intercessions for a fruitful harvest and processions in the fields led to 'beating the bounds' to establish parish boundaries.

## EMBER DAYS

The Ember Days are early fasts attached to certain Wednesdays, Fridays, and Saturdays of four weeks in the different seasons of the year. They were devoted to prayer to implore God's blessing on the new season. They also became occasions for ordinations, held during the Saturday-Sunday vigil at the end of each Embertide. The readings for these days in the new lectionary concentrate on the ordained ministry. The gospel for the Advent Ember Days, Luke 12.35–43, 'Be like men who wait for their master's return', is the gospel for the ordination of deacons.

## SAINTS' DAYS AND COMMEMORATIONS

The practice of commemorating the saints on certain days of the year arose out of the cult of the martyrs. These who suffered for their faith were highly esteemed in Judaism from the time of the Maccabees, and when the Church began to acquire its own list of martyrs, beginning in New Testament times with Stephen and James in Jerusalem and Peter and Paul in Rome, their memory was honoured in that they had suffered like their Lord as a witness (the meaning of 'martyr') to the gospel. The cult began in the east and in Gaul with the records of the sufferings (the 'passions') of Pothinus and his companions at Lyons, Perpetua and her circle at Carthage, and Polycarp at Smyrna. In the letter reporting Polycarp's death in c. 155 it was said that the Church carefully preserved his relics 'in a fitting place' and celebrated the anniversary of his death joyfully. The first mention in the west of a register of martyrs being kept occurs in the correspondence of Cyprian, Bishop of Carthage (d. 258). He instructed his clergy to bury the remains of a confessor of the faith carefully and to note the day of his death. It was out of such lists as these that the martyrologies developed. The practice of commemorating local saints within the eucharistic prayer is an early feature of the Roman and other liturgies.

It was, however, in connection with the dedication of churches in honour of saints and the reinterment of the relics of the martyrs that other dates became attached to the calendar to make the *Sanctorale*. The cult of Peter and Paul began in Rome in the second century (the memorial over the supposed grave of the apostle under St Peter's is dated from about 150) and developed in the third, for their relics were taken to the catacomb of St Sebastian for safety during the Valerian persecution of

258. 29 June may have been connected with this event or, more probably, with the transfer of their relics to the great basilicas built and dedicated in their honour in the fourth century. The Blessed Virgin Mary was honoured in Rome in the following century when Sixtus III (432–40) rebuilt the old basilica of Pope Liberius and inscribed on its walls, 'Virgin Mary, it is to thee that I, Sixtus, have dedicated this new temple. . . .' These words can still be seen in St Mary Major. That church was dedicated on 5 August. Some dates, such as the Annunciation, 25 March, and the Nativity of John the Baptist, 24 June, were calculated from Christmas Day. The new lectionary provides readings for Holy Days which are substantially the same as the Red Letter list of the Prayer Book, except that the feasts of the Visitation of the Blessed Virgin Mary, St Mary Magdalen, the Transfiguration of our Lord, and the Beheading of St John Baptist, have been given the same Red Letter status, following the proposals of the Prayer Book of 1928. The feast of the Circumcision has been given the additional title of the Naming of Jesus. Local commemorations are encouraged and provisions are made for Martyrs, Doctors, etc., in Table 3. The Roman requiem mass had its origins in the ancient practice of celebrating the Eucharist at the tombs of dead members of a family. The readings for the Commemoration of the Faithful Departed can be used at a Eucharist before a funeral or on the anniversary of a Christian's death. The Thanksgiving for the Institution of Holy Communion does what the medieval feast of Corpus Christi was intended to do—namely, to provide an opportunity to focus the Church's teaching and devotion on this sacrament without its being caught up in the observance of Holy Week. Many of the readings in the new lectionary are traditional for these days.

This, then, is the background to the development of the lectionary which now takes form in the new two-year cycle of readings based on the proposals of the Joint Liturgical Group. We begin to prepare for Christmas nine Sundays before the feast (Trinity 23 in the Church of England Liturgical Commission's lectionary) with the story of God's creation of the world and the establishment of his covenant with Abraham and Moses. As a Christian community we are conscious of our ancestry in the old Israel at this time of the year, so it is appropriate that on Advent 3 we should be led to meditate on the word of God in the Old Testament. But the promise of the Second Coming of Christ, born out of the hope that Judaism had for its vindication by God in the last days, breaks into these themes on Advent Sunday, and until Christmas we hold together faith in the parousia with faith that Christ came in flesh; and before us on the two Sundays preceding Christmas we have the example of those who were full of God's grace, John the Baptist and the Virgin Mary.

The rich content of the Christmas cycle of feasts is now spread over the Sundays at the beginning of the new year. Excessive concentration on the Bethlehem story could obscure the fact that what we are celebrating is the epiphany of God in man. Christmas and Epiphany are festivals of God's new creation, the consequences of which are to be seen by those who have the eyes of faith in events such as the visit of the magi, the presentation in the temple, the baptism of Christ, the wedding at Cana, and the call of the first disciples. At this time of the year, therefore, the ministry of the word expounds the initiative of God in revealing himself to men.

The three Sundays before Lent dwell on various aspects of Christ's ministry before we begin, through the liturgy, to make our spiritual pilgrimage to Jerusalem with Christ in the season of Lent. The proclamation of the Kingdom of God and the opposition that it roused in Jerusalem causes us to reflect on our own disobedience. These are weeks of penitence, of self-denial, of recalling all that baptism means and all that God has done in Christ to make regeneration possible for us sinners. The sufferings which we experience in this life are brought to the suffering Servant as he treads the road to Calvary. But it is a glorious and a victorious road. The temptations and the conflicts in the gospels for the first three Sundays in Lent lead to the glory of the transfiguration and the victory of the cross in the gospels of the fourth and fifth Sundays. And so we are brought to the great and holy week in which we participate in the entry to Jerusalem, the last supper, the garden of Gethsemane, the interrogations before the Sanhedrin and Pilate, the horror of the Via Dolorosa and the death on the cross, and the rest in the tomb. The whole content of the passion from the gospels, together with the prophecies and the types from the Old Testament and the reflections and the teachings from Acts and the epistles, lay before us the cost of our redemption, what the Passover of Christians has meant for the Lamb of God.

Then comes the triumph and joy of Easter Day and the great Fifty Days, the ancient Pentecost, in which we rejoice in the accomplishment of God's purposes in Christ and that foretaste of their fulfilment which is ours through the Spirit. Eastertide closes with the glorious celebration of Christ's ascension as King to heaven and the outpouring of the Holy Spirit. This is, perhaps, more than any other time of the year the occasion for the Church to proclaim to the world the mighty work of God in Jesus

Christ and the power of the Holy Spirit, when the fruitfulness of creation (in the northern hemisphere) is a sign of the fruitfulness of God's love for his people.

In the weeks of Trinitytide the emphasis shifts to our fellowship. We reflect on the Church as the temple of the Holy Spirit and ourselves as members of a prophetic, priestly, and royal race to minister in the name of Jesus Christ in God's world. The lessons teach us the many aspects of Christian duty and service. The initiative is still from God, but now we learn more of what God is doing through the Body of Christ and what he is calling us to do. And so, looking to the future, we once more approach Advent, and the yearly cycle of readings begins again.

This is the outline of God's saving and sanctifying purposes to which the scriptures point us as they are read in the new lectionary. And it is the task of the preacher and those who assist in the ministry of the word to help us to understand that word, to apply its message to our lives, and to respond as members of Christ to its demands and encouragements as we live, love, hope, doubt, and believe in today's world. Their ministry is to say what Paul said to the Colossians, 'Since Jesus was delivered to you as Christ and Lord, live your lives in union with him. Be rooted in him; be built in him; be consolidated in the faith you were taught; let your hearts overflow with thankfulness.'

# COMMENTARY
Advent 1 to Easter 3

# ADVENT 1
Fourth Sunday before Christmas

*The Advent Hope*

\* Isaiah 52. 1-10

This passage divides itself into three sections. Verses 1 and 2 are a summons to a celebration, beginning with the Advent call to watchfulness,
1 **Awake, awake**. Jerusalem, former **captive daughter of Zion**, is to adorn herself ready for a festival. She is holy because she is the city chosen
1 by God and freed by him for a new life. **The uncircumcised and the unclean** are the enemies who destroyed the city and the temple, not the whole of the Gentile world. It is possible that this section had some connection with an annual celebration in Judaism.

Verses 3 to 6 are an additional note, forming the second section of this passage. The repetition of **says the Lord** in these verses indicates a variety of original sources from which the texts were taken. The story of Israel's oppression began with Egypt. Then she was subject to the Assyrians. What is God about, allowing her to be taken captive into Babylon, where his name is reviled? Second Isaiah grapples with this problem.

In verses 7 to 10 the prophet's work reaches its climax with the procla-
7 mation of his 'gospel'. It is the **good news** that, in spite of the past, God is still king. Different voices are built into a crescendo of joy. There is the single voice of the messenger, whose feet are lovely because of the news he brings across the mountains which surround the holy city. There are the voices of the watchmen on the ruined walls shouting when they see
8 the Lord **returning to Zion** (NEB footnote). And there are the voices of
9 those inhabitants within the ruins who learn that **the Lord . . . has ransomed Jerusalem**. The last verse affirms that the Lord has shown his strength and brought deliverance to Israel in the sight of all other nations. The belief that other nations, especially those who had oppressed her, would see Israel's final vindication was an important element in the prophetic tradition. Those who had failed God in this life would know it as they suffered the consequences of their failure.

1 Thessalonians 5. 1-11

Jewish apocalyptic ideas about the Day of the Lord, when God would

\* An asterisk denotes the 'controlling lesson' (see p. 1).

bring to an end the present order with its sinfulness and corruption and establish his rule, vindicating his people and eliminating his (and their) enemies, passed into Christian expectation concerning the Second Coming; and it is about this particular topic that Paul was writing in his letter to the Church in Thessalonica. The matter was of importance, for there were teachers among the congregation saying that the Second Coming had happened already and some were anxious about the fate of those who had died. Paul himself was in the full throes of his life's work and, convinced of the imminence of the parousia, wanted to bring the gospel to the Gentiles while there was time.

The arrival of the Day, he said, in words which echo Christ's own teach-
2 ing (Matt. 24.43), will be as unexpected as a thief in the night. But he had no idea when that Day would be and could only repeat what Jesus himself had said (Matt. 24.36). He knew that it would come as suddenly as the labour pains of a pregnant woman—a simile used in Jewish apocalyptic for the messianic woes which, it was thought, would precede the coming of the Day.

Reference to the Day led the apostle's mind, by an association of ideas, to the contrast between daylight and darkness as a symbol of the light in which Christians walk and the sin from which they have been delivered.
5 We are children of light, children of day. We must be wakeful and sober, as those who watch. Since we are children of light, we have nothing to fear from the judgement of God which will occur on that Day. Employing one of his favourite metaphors (borrowed, perhaps, from contemporary Christian catechesis) the apostle urged the Christians to arm themselves with faith, hope, and love, the three virtues which are the subject of the hymn in 1 Corinthians 13. God has destined us all, living Christians as well as the faithful departed, to live in company with him through the sacrifice of Jesus Christ. The Thessalonians can strengthen one another with this belief.

At the time this letter was written, Paul was expecting the parousia within his own lifetime (1 Thess. 4.17). Later his views changed and he decided he would probably die before the Lord came.

## Luke 21. 25–31

In answer to a question about the last times, Jesus had answered—according to the arrangement of his sayings in Luke—that there would be wars and natural disasters, persecutions for Christians, and Jerusalem itself would be destroyed (a prophecy which had been fulfilled in A.D. 70, when the Roman army under Titus seized the city and razed the temple to

the ground. Luke may well have known about this when he wrote.) But these would not necessarily be signs that the end was at hand. Luke's theological insight convinced him that Christ's coming must be delayed in order that all men might hear the gospel. The signs to look for would
25 be cosmic—universal in their implications. **Portents will appear in sun, moon and stars**: the continuity and orderliness of the whole world would be interrupted. **The roar and surge of the sea** was a symbol for a momentary return to that state of chaos which ruled the universe before the Creator called it to order. **On earth nations will stand helpless**:
26 the event would reveal to all men their utter weakness. **The celestial powers will be shaken**: these were believed to control the destinies of men as unfolded in the movement of sun, moon, and stars. Before the last day, however—and here the Lucan eschatological scheme differs from those in other NT writings—there would be the return of the Son of Man. As at the transfiguration and the ascension, the glory of God would be manifested in this mysterious person from Daniel 7, identified in the NT with Jesus at his parousia. The cloud was a symbol of the divine presence, the *shekinah*, in biblical imagery.
28    What are Christians to do when these things happen? **Stand upright and hold your heads high, because your liberation is near.** They can be confident that the consequences of Christ's redemption are universal. In their Redeemer they will be saved from whatever overtakes this world and the men in it at the end of time. Christ told them to be watchful, to look for the signs as they might look for the first buds on the
29 fig-tree (**or any other tree** Luke adds, for the benefit of readers in whose territory the fig-tree might not flourish). The fig-tree is one of Palestine's few deciduous trees; it stands starkly bare in the winter, and only puts on fresh green leaves in the spring—rapidly, for the interval between winter and summer is short, March to mid-May. Like these rapid signs, so also will the portents of the Day of the Son of Man be, telling his
31 followers that **the kingdom of God is near.**

# ADVENT 1
Fourth Sunday before Christmas

*The Advent Hope*

\* Isaiah 51. 4–11

The OT lesson is in two sections (though the exegetical problems associated with these verses, not detailed here, go much deeper than that): the first is an address by God to the people (5–8); the second is an appeal or lament to God by the people (9–11).

First, the Lord directs the nation's gaze towards the coming world-judgement in which heaven and earth and those who dwell in it are to be destroyed. When the end of the world comes, there will be only one

6, 8 security—God's salvation which continues for ever (the phrase, **my saving power shall never wane/shall last for ever**, appears twice in the passage). The law of God, his divine instructions, will be vindicated and he will rule all nations. When the signs of the end appear, his people

8 are to look to him and to the **deliverance** from the judgement which he brings **to all generations.**

Secondly, the people cry to God for help. Their situation is that of the Babylonian exile or something very much like it, when they are surrounded by oppressors. God appears to be silent or inactive, so they appeal to him to awake and to do for them what he did in the past. Verses 9 and 10 link God's work of creation with his work of redemption at the

9 exodus. **Rahab** and **the dragon** are the figures from ancient eastern mythologies which depict the act of creation as the victory of God over primeval chaos, and the waters of that myth are associated with the waters of the Red Sea which also obeyed God's word. The anthropo-

9 morphism implied in the words, **Put on your strength, O arm of the Lord** speaks of an arming with weapons, an important feature in the ancient myths which tell of the struggle with chaos. When God acts for his people, as he did in the past, they will return to Zion with joy and their sorrows will be over. The lament asks God to let the new exodus begin.

## Romans 13. 8–14

The whole of Paul's letter to the Church in Rome was directed towards showing what the love of God has achieved for us in Jesus Christ. Here he stresses that the love of our neighbour is the dynamo that energizes our Christian conduct. The charge to pay all outstanding debts, with

which this passage begins, led him to say that there is one debt which we
8 can never repay—the debt of love to our neighbour. Yet he who loves
his neighbour has satisfied every claim of the law. We are no longer
'in debt' to the law. For example, the apostle said, take any of the commandments which govern our relationships with other people (and he
cited four of them), and you will find that they are all summed up in the
9 one rule, Love your neighbour as yourself. With love as the motive,
10 nothing can affect our neighbours in an evil way: therefore the whole
law is fulfilled by love (NEB footnote).

To emphasize his injunction, the apostle reminded his readers that they
were living in critical times. The Greek word for 'time', *kairos*, is translated in biblical terms as 'the latter days' and refers to the eschatological
era which has been ushered in by the death and resurrection of Jesus
Christ. This critical 'time' is the age of salvation and is coextensive with
the age of the Church on earth. Christians are emancipated from the age
of this world and the kingdom of darkness and are already living in the age
to come and in the Kingdom of God and his Son. Although Paul said less
in this letter about the coming of Christ than he did in earlier writings,
yet his idea was that the lapse of time between the conversion of Paul and
his readers and the moment of writing was a significant proportion of the
total interval between the resurrection and the parousia. The consummation of God's final act of redemption was near.

In the OT lesson the prophet and the people called on God to awake
out of sleep; here it is the apostle who told the people to awake. The 'day'
which is coming is not just the day of judgement: it is 'the age to come'
(as night is 'this age'). The practical consequences of Paul's reveille is the
moral life of the Christian, a putting on of the armour for the conflict
with temptations and evil. It is possible that behind the exhortations
there is a common form of catechetical instruction used by the apostolic
Church to help the converts distinguish between walking in the light and
walking in the darkness, as they put behind them the customs and standards of a pagan society. The armour is none other than Jesus himself.

## Matthew 25. 31–46
One of a series of prophecies and warnings which in Matthew precede the
narrative of the passion. They are set against the background of contemporary Jewish apocalyptic writings, but with some unique and striking
features. One of these is that it is the Son of Man himself who will be
31 judge at the end of time. When the Son of Man comes in his glory is
an image from Dan. 7.13–15 describing the solemn moment of divine

judgement, but in the OT it is God himself who judges. Furthermore, Jesus described the Son of Man as sitting in state on his throne—another function in Jewish apocalypse attributed only to God. Into this picture Jesus brought the scene of the Palestinian shepherd pasturing his mixed flock of light-coloured sheep and dark-coated goats until he has to separate them; the animals represent the righteous and the wicked who remain together in this life until they are separated by the Judge (the basic meaning of the Greek word *krinein* 'to judge', is 'to separate'). The former inherit the Father's blessing, the latter are cursed and sent into the eternal fire—again Jesus used images from Jewish apocalypse.

Another unique and striking feature of the passage is the way in which Jesus identified himself with the needy and underprivileged. When he answered the question, On what grounds will a man be judged on the last day? he answered this entirely in terms of that man's conduct towards his neighbours. He would not be judged on his membership of the Jewish race or his success in keeping the Law of Moses, but on what he did for those around him. The list of needy and underprivileged is taken from Jewish lists commending acts of charity (except that of visiting prisoners). But who are these people? The whole of mankind? This is how the

40 passage is usually interpreted. But Jesus specifically said, **Anything you did for one of my brothers here, however humble, you did for me**: 'brothers' is the normal NT term for fellow-Christians. Jesus called 'brothers' those who, like him, could address God as 'Father'.

# ADVENT 2
Third Sunday before Christmas

*The Word of God in the Old Testament*

\* Isaiah 55. 1–11

God's word has power to achieve all that he has promised, and in this passage he summoned Israel through the prophet to a new condition of salvation. The vendors in the market-place try to sell the essentials of life, water and bread; but God offers freely not just water and bread but

1 the fat of the land, **wine and milk** (NEB footnote). All the people have to do is to listen to God's word and to obey it. The prophecy seems to be addressed to those in exile in Babylon. God intended to make a lasting

covenant with them, the content of which was compared to the favour he once showed David. What was promised for that king personally by God
4 was extended for the whole nation. David was **a witness to all races, a prince and instructor of peoples**; now Israel was going to be blessed in such a way that other nations would see the glory of God revealed in her.
6 **Inquire of the Lord while he is present, call upon him when he is close at hand** is basically a summons to worship, to offer oblations to God, and to pray to him in the temple. But as used by the prophets, it became a summons to worship God by obedience to him in daily life. This involved the abandonment of the ways and thoughts of the wicked, an act of repentance. The ways and thoughts of God are on a different
9 plane: **For as the heavens are higher than the earth, so are my ways higher than your ways, and my thoughts than your thoughts.** The Creator of the world and the Lord of history has plans and designs for procuring Israel's salvation, and his word is as prolific as the fertile
11 cycles of rain and growth in the earth: **the word which comes from my mouth (shall) prevail; it shall not return to me fruitless without accomplishing my purpose.**

(–13)
The prophet assured the exiles that they would return to the land of promise, and that when they did it would be in a joyful procession—the joy of those going home after a long absence. Because the God who would arrange this return is also the Creator, creation itself would share in their
12 joy: **the trees of the wild shall clap their hands.** And all this would glorify the God of Israel.

### Romans 15. 4–13

Commences in the middle of a digression in Paul's discussion in this letter to the Church in Rome. A few verses earlier he had been dealing with the matter of the polarization of the Christian community (everywhere, not just in Rome) between those who were completely committed and well-instructed and those who were weaker in faith: 'Those of us who have a robust conscience must accept as our own burden the tender scruples of weaker men, and not consider ourselves' (15.1). Characteristically, he cited the example of Christ with a quotation from Ps. 69.9, 'The reproaches of those who reproached thee fell upon me' (15.3), to show from prophecy that Jesus put the interests of others first. In justifying this appeal to scripture—and this is where our passage (and the digression) begins—he reminded his readers that scripture is for the instruction and strengthening of Christians that they might be built up in hope. And he prayed that they will be enabled to live together in unity, understanding one another and praising God together.

Returning to his main theme in verse 7, he urged the stronger and 7 the weaker members of the Church to accept one another as Christ accepted us, to the glory of God. Pointing again to the example of Jesus, the apostle said that Christ became the servant of those who were, as far as religion was concerned, the most awkward and scrupulous of people; yet, because he was prepared to accept them as they were, the promises which God had given his people under the old covenant had been fulfilled. Furthermore, Jesus' acceptance of his servant role among 9 the Jews meant that all other nations, the Gentiles, were coming to glorify God for his mercy (an echo of today's OT reading). Paul assembled a number of scriptural texts to demonstrate that the blessing to the Gentiles was not an afterthought on God's part, but prophesied under the old covenant—an important argument in his debate with those Judaising Christians who wanted to make Gentile converts Jews by circumcision as well as Christians by baptism. The texts quoted by the apostle are: Ps. 18.49 (=2 Sam. 22.50), Deut. 32.43 (LXX), Ps. 117.1, and Isa. 11.10. The last text is a messianic prophecy envisaging the Messiah as one raised up by God not just for Jews, but for all peoples.

The passage ends with Paul's brief prayer that God, as the source and goal of Christians' hope, will so fill the apostle's readers with joy and peace through their faith in Jesus Christ that their hope will spill over to others as they are released in the power of the Holy Spirit. The 12 prayer comes out of the last text, There shall be the Scion of Jesse, the one raised up to govern the Gentiles: on him the Gentiles shall set their hope.

## John 5. 36-47

Jesus has a testimony that is higher than that of John the Baptist. This testimony was given by the Father to John the Baptist at Jesus' baptism ('When you see the Spirit coming down upon someone and resting upon him you will know that this is he who is to baptize in Holy Spirit' 1.33). It is also given through the works which Jesus performed, as Nicodemus acknowledged ('We know that you are a teacher sent by God, no one could perform these signs of yours unless God were with him' 3.2). But the Jews were unable to see these testimonies because the word, the whole revelation of God, had found no home in them through their unbelief. In spite of their intense study of the scriptures—and intensive study of the scriptures was a mark of the devout Jews, for there was a rabbinic saying that 'He who has gained for himself the words of the law has gained for himself the life of the world to come'—they were unable to accept Jesus Christ as Messiah. Properly understood, the OT scriptures converge on Jesus who is their focus; but both the works of Jesus and the scriptures only testify to Jesus as one whom the Father has sent when we believe in him. Unbelieving Jews were failing to hear the Father's voice, and their failure corresponded to their unbelief.

From verse 41 Jesus asserted that, although he did not seek honour for himself, their failure to see that he was accredited by the Father was the same as rejecting God himself. They could not be blamed for not seeing God, for no one has done this (1.18), but they could be blamed for neglecting their opportunity of knowing him through his Son, to see whom is to see the Father (14.9). A further evidence of their failure was when a voice was heard from heaven and they misinterpreted it (12.28ff).

They were willing to welcome some self-accredited messiah (as in the case of Simon bar Kochba, leader of the Jewish revolt in A.D. 132–5), and they put their trust in Moses, the one who gave them the Law, but they did not believe in the one to whom the writings of Moses pointed. When the trial judgement came, and their failure was exposed, it would be Moses himself, not Jesus who would accuse them. They had set their hope on the Law of Moses, only to find, as Paul did, that it simply ex-
46 poses men as sinners. **If you believed Moses you would believe what I tell you, for it was about me that he wrote.** Properly understood, Moses was a prophet of the gospel, the good news of God's mercy to the sinner.

YEAR 2

# ADVENT 2
## Third Sunday before Christmas

### *The Word of God in the Old Testament*

\* Isaiah 64. 1–5
The earthquakes on the mountains and the manifestations of fire described in the opening verses of the OT lesson are familiar features of God's epiphany: 'The earth trembled and quaked: the very foundations of the hills shook and were moved, because he was wroth. There went a smoke from his nostrils, and a consuming fire from his mouth: coals of fire issued from his presence.' (Ps. 18.7–8)

The trembling of the nations in the face of God's awful advent is also a regular feature of the theophanies: 'Mount Sinai was all smoking because the Lord had come down upon it in fire; the smoke went up like the smoke of a kiln; all the people were terrified.' (Exod. 19.18–19)

The present passage looks back to the great epiphanies associated with Israel's past. Can we hope, the prophet seems to ask, that they will ever come again?

Yet it is also a prayer that God will come again. There is no such God 4 as the God of Israel who takes **the part of those who wait for him** (a piquant phrase as we approach the feast of the Incarnation). To wait in hope is an attitude of faith towards God which he honours with his support and protection. He accepts completely those whose happy objective in life is to fulfil his will.

The prophet then confessed that, in spite of God's former anger against evil, the people continue to sin against him.

(–12)

8 The confession continues to verse 8, where the mood changes. **But now, Lord, thou art our Father.** Israel, in spite of her sin, had confidence in God—though not so much as children than as creatures in the hands of their Creator: **We are clay, thou the potter, and all of us are thy handiwork.** The confession is taken up again in verse 9 as a lament for the destruction of the temple in Jerusalem and ends with an anxious question put to God: how long?

## 2 Timothy 3. 14–4. 5

Timothy was the son of a heathen father and a converted Jewish mother. He first joined Paul's entourage at Lystra in Lycaonia at the beginning of the latter's second missionary journey. He was already a Christian of some standing, having probably been converted when Paul preached in the neighbourhood a year or two previously. The apostle persuaded Timothy to accompany him, but first circumcised him as a concession to Jewish susceptibilities among Christians (Acts 16.1–3). He remained Paul's constant companion and intimate friend, collaborating with him in several letters (1 and 2 Thess., 2 Cor., Phil., Col., and Philem.) and being entrusted with important missions—to Thessalonica (1 Thess. 3.2) and Corinth (1 Cor. 4.17). The apostle regarded him as his 'colleague' (Rom. 16.21) and 'a dear son and a most trustworthy Christian' (1 Cor. 4.17). When Paul was setting out on his last journey to Jerusalem, Timothy was in the party (Acts 20.4) and he was at his side during his Roman imprisonment. Indeed Paul drew special comfort from his presence and planned to send him on a mission to the Philippian church (Phil. 2.19–24). At the time of the Letters to Timothy, he was an apostolic delegate in temporary charge of the church in Ephesus. He was still relatively young and needed the apostle's guidance and encouragement.

In this passage, Paul is urging him to stand by the truths which he has learned and believed. He learned them from his Christian mother, Eunice, and his Christian grandmother, Lois; he also learned them from the 'sacred writings' (the usual Greek expression for the Old Testament scriptures) from childhood—Eunice may have followed the normal Jewish custom of making her son memorize passages of the Law by heart. These make the Christian wise with the wisdom of God which leads him to salvation through faith in Christ Jesus.

A note of urgency is sounded at the beginning of Chapter 4. Paul was expecting martyrdom before the second advent of Christ. When Christ 4.1 came he would **judge men living and dead**—a phrase that is found elsewhere in the NT and that already sounds like a credal expression, as 2 in the Nicene Creed. **Appearance** is the English translation of the Greek *epiphaneia*, from which 'epiphany' is derived. He urges Timothy to preach the gospel at every opportunity, especially as he foresaw a time when Christians might refuse to listen to it and succumb to a morbid fascination for other cults. As an evangelist, Timothy must be a sound and resourceful teacher of the Christian truth.

The Old Testament was the only canonical scriptures for the early Church in apostolic times and for several generations afterwards. Irenaeus (*c*. 180) was the first to speak of a 'New Testament', though as early as 2 Pet. 3.15f Paul's letters were being ranked as 'inspired wisdom', while for Ignatius (*c*. 110) 'the gospel' was an equivalent authority to 'the prophets'. 'It was not through any human whim that men prophesied of old; men they were, but, impelled by the Holy Spirit, they spoke the words of God' (2 Pet. 1.21).

### Luke 4. 14–21

The ministry of Jesus in Luke begins with his sermon in the synagogue at Nazareth, following the temptations in the wilderness. The passage describes the reading of the scripture and summarizes what Christ said. The service in the synagogue probably consisted of prayer (the Eighteen Benedictions came into use this way), two scripture readings (one from the five books of the Law, the Pentateuch, and the other from the Prophets), a homily and a blessing (Num. 6.22–27)—a framework not unlike the beginning of a Christian eucharist. It was usual for a member of the congregation to be invited to stand and read a lesson from the Prophets and

then to sit and expound it. Jesus had already gained a reputation as a
15 teacher—he taught in their synagogues and all men sang his
16 praises—and when he visited a town, and especially Nazareth where
he had been brought up, it was natural that he should be asked to
speak. He may have welcomed opportunities to teach in the synagogues
in this way, like the apostles after him, and many of his memorable sayings
may have been heard for the first time in synagogues where Jewish communities assembled for instruction and worship.

14    Luke pictures Jesus as a great prophet, armed with the power of
the Spirit, and also as one in whom the scriptures find their fulfilment.
21 The today of God's grace had arrived. The OT passage read by Jesus
(Isa. 61.1–2, with an additional phrase from 58.6) is a familiar one in the
NT: it is used to answer the messengers sent from John the Baptist
19 and it is echoed in the Beatitudes. Its theme is the year of the Lord's
favour. It originated as an oracle which declared that after the Babylonian exile the people of Israel would once again be free to return to
Jerusalem and celebrate 'the jubilee year' (Lev. 25.10). According to the
Law, this was a year for the release from all outstanding debts and certain
social obligations, but by our Lord's time it was interpreted as a prophecy
of the messianic age—as yet unfulfilled, so the Jews believed. The
21 summary of Christ's sermon, Today in your very hearing this text
has come true, makes the stupendous claim that the messianic age has
dawned. Christ announces the OT witness to himself for himself.

# ADVENT 3
## Second Sunday before Christmas

*The Forerunner*

* Isaiah 40.1–11
1 Comfort, comfort my people begins the book of Second Isaiah's
prophecy—from which it gets its title, 'the Book of the Consolation of
2 Israel'. Exiled Israel is soon to know salvation. (Jerusalem is the name
given to the people who are committed wholeheartedly to God); her
bondage is over, reparation has been made for her sin. (The passage
is linked with 52.11.) God's voice—or perhaps the voice of one of his
messengers—announces the beginning of a new exodus, a magnificent

pilgrimage back to the Holy City. The return of Israel from exile will also in some sense be a return of the Lord himself in a theophany which the watchmen in Zion will see (52.7ff). The highway must be prepared for the
5 coming of the King. The **glory of the Lord** is to be revealed and all men will see it.
6   In verse 6 the Lord addresses the prophet. **A voice says, "Cry," and another asks, "what shall I cry?"** It is his call, his commissioning. He is to prophesy that, although mankind is weak and transient like grass, yet the impossible will happen, for the word of God is strong and intransient. Verse 9 continues the prophecy. The revelation of God is announced by a herald who speaks from the mountains, as God did in
9 former times. The **good news** (gospel) is that **your God is here**. The arm of the Lord is a symbol of his power. He will lead his people back like a shepherd and king.
10  **Recompense** is the payment due to a man who labours: the words 'recompense' and 'reward' are closely connected: they picture the Lord as completing his work in restoring his people. The image of the shepherd is, of course, a continuing one through both Old and New Testaments (See pp. 221–4.)

## 1 Corinthians 4. 1–5

Earlier in this letter Paul had had to warn the Corinthian Christians against those who divide the congregation into factions, using the names of other apostles—Apollos, Cephas, or even his own—as party titles. Here he expounds the vocation of an apostle, and, beyond the apostolic office, of all who are called to exercise pastoral care in the Church, in
1 terms of **Christ's subordinates** (at the Lord's beck and call) **and stewards of the secrets** (RSV, JB 'mysteries') **of God**. *Mysteria* is the Greek word for the sacred rites of pagan religions and divine secrets revealed to a few initiates. In this sentence it is used to describe the plan of God for the salvation of the world, hidden from men in the divine foreknowledge until the time comes when it can be revealed to those whom he had chosen and, through them, to the whole of mankind. Christian theology employed the words for the sacraments of Baptism and the Eucharist—the celebration by the Church of God's saving work. The image of a steward is used elsewhere in the NT of Christians in general, but the apostle uses it in this passage for apostles and ministers. Their office is exercised within the Church, God's household (1 Tim. 3.15), and it is essential that such officials should be reliable.

But these are only preliminaries. Paul's main concern in his letter at

this point is to answer criticisms about himself and his work. It does not matter, he says, how he is judged by his fellow men (he may have had at the back of his mind the distinction made by the Jewish rabbis between 'judgements of men' and 'judgement of heaven'). He does not judge himself. He has a clear conscience; but he adds that a clean conscience does not prove that he is innocent, **I have nothing on my conscience . . . that does not mean I stand acquitted.** The only competent
3 judge in these matters is the Lord (= Christ). So, he tells them, wait until the Lord comes again. The parousia will throw light on things that
5 men keep hidden in their hearts and minds. **Then will be the time for each to receive from God such praise as he deserves.**

## John 1. 19–27

The fourth Gospel omits the details of John the Baptist's ministry and focuses on his witness to Jesus Christ. In an earlier verse John has been introduced as 'a man . . . sent from God . . . as a witness to testify to the light, that all might become believers through him'. He preached of Jesus, 'This is the man I meant when I said, "He comes after me, but takes rank before me"; for before I was born, he already was' (1.6, 15). The Jews, usually represented as hostile to Christ by this evangelist, question John on his ministry. He affirms that he is not the Messiah, nor is he Elijah, who was expected to return at the beginning of the messianic age (Mal. 4.5–6, a later addition identifying the 'messenger of the covenant' with the returning Elijah, whose task it would be to restore peace in the community and so avert God's wrath on the day of judgement.) Nor, says John, is he the eschatological prophet promised by Moses (Deut. 18.15).
23 He is the herald of Isaiah, **crying aloud in the wilderness, 'Make the Lord's highway straight'** (Isa. 40.3).

The Jews go on to ask him about his baptism. The ceremony of immersion in water to symbolize purification or renewal was a familiar one in ancient religious practices. Washings of various kinds were a feature of cleansings for ceremonial purposes in Judaism (Num. 19.1ff, Exod. 30.17ff, etc.) and, together with circumcision and the offering of a sacrifice, were included in the rites for the initiation of a proselyte. The Qumran community used lustrations in their rituals. But John's baptism, although it had affinities with these ceremonies, was distinctive for three reasons.
1. It was a sign of moral conversion and purification, not merely of ritual washing. Men must live changed lives; tax-gatherers must not make extortionate claims; soldiers must not bully or blackmail (Luke 3.10–14).
2. It seems to have been offered once only and therefore had the character

of an initiation. 3. It had an eschatological value in that it enrolled the baptized into the congregation of those who were preparing themselves for the coming Messiah and who could expect to be members of the messianic community. Because it had this preparatory nature, the Baptist
27 saw himself in the humble role of a servant: **I am not good enough to unfasten his shoes.** The **I am not** of John contrasts with the 'I am' saying of Jesus which this Gospel records (see p. 217). The figure of John shrinks before the person of the Word made flesh who comes to enlighten the world. John baptizes in water, but the one who comes after him is to baptize in Holy Spirit (1.33; see Epiphany 1 Year 2). Yet, in Jesus' own words, John was 'more than a prophet', for he lived in an age when prophecy had all but died in Israel.

# ADVENT 3
Second Sunday before Christmas

*The Forerunner*

* **Malachi 3. 1–5, 4. 1–6**
  Malachi is the Hebrew for 'my messenger' (NEB footnote). The introduction to his book informs us that he was 'Ezra the scribe'. In 4.5 'the messenger' is identified with Elijah, though in this passage he is almost synonymous with the Lord himself. The situation envisaged is a restored temple, so the prophecy is dated after the exile. The people have said that the Lord does not concern himself with what is right, 'Where is the God of justice?' (2.17), but the prophet tells them that they will learn the truth when he comes. There is some doubt as to whether the advent described in verses 2–4, **Who can endure the day of his coming? . . .,**
2 refers to the coming of the Lord or to the coming of the messenger. But the effects are the same. God's judgements will be made from the temple, which is his dwelling-place and throne-room on earth, and the first to be purified will be the officials associated with it, the Levites. The work of purification will be analogous to the process whereby gold and silver is purified in the fire. Then the offerings of the people will be acceptable as in former times. This act of the community's purification is linked with the day of judgement, described in terms of a court. No individual dare be complacent on that day, for each one will be judged according to his

conduct. The Lord will witness against all wrong-doers and those who have no fear of him.

(4. 1–6)
Malachi joined with his brother prophets in condemning abuses among God's people. He attacked the common evils of his day (perhaps about 400 B.C.)—the oppression of the poor, the laxity of the priests, and the non-payment of temple dues. He warned them that the Lord would return one day and bring judgement upon the godless, burning them up like
2 chaff. **But for you who fear my name, the sun of righteousness shall rise with healing in his wings.** The image may be drawn from the representation of the sun-god as a winged disc, common in the religious art of Egypt, Babylon, Assyria, and Persia. On that day the righteous
3 oppressed would be liberated and would **trample down the wicked.**

Belief that Elijah would also return on the day of the Lord became part of Jewish eschatological expectations. Malachi told the people that when the day of the Lord came, the herald would not be an unknown prophet, but would be none other than Elijah himself, who had ascended into heaven without suffering human death (2 Kings 2.11). Jesus was later to explain that Elijah had come in the person of John the Baptist (Matt. 11.7–14). See also Mark 9.2–13, Matt. 17.1–13 (the transfiguration).

Thus the last book in the canon of the OT ends appropriately with the hope that one of the great prophets of the old Israel would come back to act as herald at the coming of the Messiah.

### Philippians 4. 4–9
Coming towards the end of Paul's letter to the congregation in Philippi, these verses strike a buoyant note of confidence and hope. 'I want you to be happy, always happy in the Lord: I repeat, what I want is your happiness' (verse 4 JB). He urges them to show that quality of toleration and
5 kindness—**magnanimity**—which can be recognized and valued by all men, especially as the advent of the Lord is imminent. The eschatological hope of the apostolic Church was high; they lived like men who expected the immediate and sudden return of their master (Luke 12.36). One of the earliest Christian prayers was *Maranatha*, 'Come, O Lord!' (1 Cor. 16.22, Rev. 22.20). Christians need have no fear, says the apostle, for they can commit themselves in complete trust to the Lord, who is the Lord of their future as well as the Lord of their past and their present.

Thanksgiving is an essential part of Christian prayer. It is in praising God that we demonstrate our assurance in his promises and purpose for

us, no matter how black our personal situation may seem to be. 'Give thanks whatever happens; for this is what God in Christ wills for you' (1 Thess. 5.17–18). By offering thanks to God in all circumstances, we appropriate for ourselves by faith Christ's victory over all evil. Then
7 we know the peace of God, which is of far more worth than human reasoning (NEB footnote). The peace which God gives is the gift of himself to men. In scripture 'peace' is more positive than the absence of strife. It is the restoration of God's order in creation—wholeness, well-being, safety—and it is the dominant characteristic of his kingdom. The peace which Christ has made with men and which he alone can give remains in the world by the operation of the Spirit of Christ (Acts 10.36, John 14.27, Gal. 5.22). This peace guards the affections and ideas of those who are in Christ.

It is notable that Paul's list of virtues is not a specifically Christian catalogue: 'Everything that is true, everything that is noble, everything that is good and pure, everything that we love and honour, and everything that can be thought virtuous and worthy of praise' (verse 8 JB). He may have come to recognize that there was a genuine capacity for moral discernment in the pagan society around him and that things which were counted honourable by good men were in fact worthy of a Christian's
9 honour too. The lessons and the traditions were evidently the moral rules which concerned the life of congregations and individuals, together with the summary of the gospel, which was expressed in the credal statements then in the process of formation. To these were added the facts of Christ's life, death, and resurrection, and the theological interpretation of them which we find taking shape in the earliest Christian letters (1 Cor. 11.23, 15.3ff). When Paul speaks of 'the tradition he received from the Lord' he means the teaching which he had been given through the mediation of the Church.

The passage is typical of a Pauline ending to a letter. The reason for the apostle's joy is his recognition of the way in which the work of God has progressed. The proximity of the Lord's advent is cause for Christian joy—proximity which is not to be thought of now just in terms of time but also in terms of the imminence of the Lord's activity. Christian eschatological thought has shifted, through the influence of Christ's own teaching, from an expectation of the Day of the Lord in Jewish theology to the return of the Lord himself.

## Matthew 11. 2–15

According to Josephus, John the Baptist was imprisoned at Machaerus, east of the Dead Sea, at the southern border of the tetrarchy of Herod Antipas, who had arrested him. Some of his disciples continued to be loyal to him and to assist him in prison, and it was through them that he heard what Jesus was doing. There is a problem in the story. If John had recognized Jesus at his baptism in the Jordan, why should he require further assurance? Some commentators have suggested that John's faith was shaken as a result of his experiences; others that the message from John is merely an occasion for Jesus to assert his messianic role in fulfilment of scripture. At any rate, what Jesus is doing is, for the evangelist, sufficient evidence to show that he is the true Messiah. Christ refers to the messianic signs in Isa. 29.18, the healing of the deaf and blind, Isa. 35.5, the lame, Isa. 61.1f, the good news to the poor. Those who do

6 not find Christ a **stumbling-block**—Jesus means here those, like the disciples of John, who recognize the messianic claims—are blessed. They see that the messianic age has been inaugurated.

Christ now continues to address the people on the subject of John. Did they expect him to be as common as the cane grass which grows on the banks of the Jordan? Did they expect someone in luxurious clothing— a hint of sarcasm directed at Herod? Instead, Jesus declares that John was the mysterious messenger of the prophet Malachi.

Yet, great as John is, his greatness is only comparable with the greatness

11 of the old covenant. **The least in the kingdom of heaven is greater than he**, not through any personal achievement, but because of the privilege which God's gift brings. Jesus' disciples are 'greater' in this sense because they are already in the Kingdom, within its empowering borders. (We can perhaps understand that John the Baptist's personal

12 entry into the Kingdom was after his death.) **Ever since the coming of John the Baptist the kingdom of heaven has been subjected to violence and violent men are seizing it** is a difficult verse to interpret. The NEB footnote gives an alternative: **. . . has been forcing its way forward, and men of force. . . .** Either the Kingdom of heaven is subject to violence in that Jesus and his disciples and all that he teaches is being opposed by men, or the Kingdom of heaven has been progressing and keen and daring men are taking hold of it. In whatever way it is interpreted, the next verse goes on to state that John the Baptist's ministry is the last of a long line of ministries stretching back to Moses and the prophets, who foretold the coming of the Kingdom in the person of Jesus

15 Christ. Jesus emphasizes his saying by crying, **If you have ears, then hear.**

# ADVENT 4
## First Sunday before Christmas

*The Annunciation*

* Isaiah 11. 1–9

1 The oracle of the prophet celebrates the advent of a descendant of David, a new king **from the stock of Jesse,** who will restore the nation to its former glory. With the spirit of the Lord resting upon him, he will rule as the representative of God; anointed for his office, he will be equipped with the spiritual gifts required to govern wisely and well. The charisms are linked in pairs: wisdom, the divinely-inspired insight into the ways of God; resolution and the ability to carry out his decisions; and a piety which gives a deep reverence for the Lord and his will. What was original about Isaiah's prophecy was that it saw the authority of the king conferred not by a single, temporary gift, but by a series of apparently permanent gifts. With these gifts the new David will exercise the regal duty of arbitrating between disputants and administering justice impartially in accordance with the justice of God. He will not rely on appearances or rumours to decide between right and wrong; he will uphold the rights of the weak and destroy those who attempt to oppress them. His power will be such that he can send wicked men to their deaths at a word of command.

The prophet then sees a vision of a return to a paradisal state of affairs, reminiscent of Eden, when the peace of God mediated through the Davidic king will remove all inclinations to violence in nature. Even the most fierce of the wild animals will become so tame that a small child will be able to lead them about in safety. In the midst of this vision is the holy mountain of God, and at the end of our passage the prophet sees the whole land filled—could we say 'baptized'?—with the knowledge of the Lord. The revelation of God to man will be complete.

1 Corinthians 1. 26–31

In the midst of his assertion that what God has done in Jesus Christ is a contradiction of man's ideas about wisdom and power, Paul illustrates God's paradoxical way of working by telling the Corinthian Christians to consider themselves. Look at the kind of persons the Lord has called together in Corinth and the nature of the community that has been formed as a result of the divine call. It ought to be obvious that God has other standards in these matters than man has. If we wanted to make friends and influence people, we would gather round us the worldly wise, the

men who can get things done, and the socially respectable. But the Corinthian church was very different from this. While there were a few well-to-do (a synagogue official, Acts 18.8), there were also slaves (7.21). They may have included the poorer sort of Corinthian inhabitants, for Christianity was noted later for appealing to the lower classes in society. God has, therefore, not only rejected the world's standards but over-
26 thrown them. He has chosen things low and contemptible, mere nothings, to overthrow the existing order may have been rhetorical, but the apostle's meaning is clear: God has humiliated the world's pride and negatived man's wisdom even within the Church. Paul had a special purpose in refuting notions of worldly wisdom, for trouble had been caused at Corinth by some who had made 'mere men a cause for pride' (3.21). He forcibly reminds them that they are in Christ, not through any strata-gem or foresight of their own, but because of what God has done for
30 them. Jesus is our wisdom through God's gift.

In Jewish thought wisdom came to be personified as the mediator between God and man in creation and in communicating to man the knowledge of salvation (Prov. 8.22–31; Wisd. 7.22). 'The Lord created me (Wisdom) the beginning of his works, before all else that he made, long ago'; 'She (Wisdom) is but one, yet can do everything; herself un-changing, she makes all things new; age after age she enters into holy souls, and makes them God's friends and prophets, for nothing is accept-able to God but the man who makes his home with Wisdom' (Wisd. 7.27). Sometimes Paul appropriated the concept of wisdom to Christ's functions, but here he directly appropriates it to Christ himself. True wisdom, he says, is not to be found in eloquence or theological speculations; it is to be found in God's plan for the redemption of the world which, for all its own wisdom, had fallen away from him.
30   Christ is our righteousness—another word which Paul uses to express the mediatorship of Christ. Man cannot be judged as righteous, so righteousness is given to him by God, and in these circumstances his faith is accounted to him for righteousness (Rom. 4.3, Gal. 3.6, both quoting Gen. 15.6). Christ becomes righteousness for man (2 Cor. 5.21) and God as judge views man, not as he is in himself, but as man is in Christ. Man can only draw near to God if he is holy, and he can only be made holy in Christ. Similarly it is only in Christ that he can be redeemed, liberated.

Finally, Paul concludes this passage with a quotation from Jer. 9.23f, 'If any man would boast, let him boast of this, that he understands and knows me'. A man has no standing whatever before God except that which he has been given in Christ.

### Luke 1. 26–38a

The ancestry of Jesus' earthly family is significant, for Joseph belonged to the house of David and Mary was a relative of Elizabeth, who was of Aaronic descent. The family tree foreshadowed the royal and priestly character of Jesus as Messiah.

In early Jewish texts 'the angel of the Lord' meant the Lord himself (Gen. 16.7, etc.), but with the development of the doctrine of angels their distinction from God becomes sharper and they emerge as heavenly messengers, conveying the word of God to men from the transcendent
26 God. **Gabriel** (the word means 'man of God' or 'God has shown himself mighty') was one of the seven archangels in the Hebrew celestial hierarchy.
28 **Most favoured one** is the modern equivalent of the more familiar 'full of grace': grace is divine favour. The supernatural naming of the child recalls the naming of Ishmael (Gen. 16.11), Immanuel (Isa. 7.14), and John the Baptist (Luke 1.13). Verses 32–33 tell the reader that the prophecies of Isa. 9.6ff are being fulfilled, with messianic titles and
32 offices: **Son of the Most High, the throne of David,** and **king of Israel.** The OT associated the messianic descendant of David with sonship of God, since the word of the Lord for David had come to Nathan: 'I will set up one of your family . . . to succeed you . . . I will be his father, and he shall be my son' (2 Sam. 7.12ff); 'He shall call unto me "Thou art my Father: my God, and the Rock of my salvation". And I will make him my first-born: highest among the kings of the earth' (Ps. 89.26–27). The promise of an everlasting reign for the Messiah recalls Mic. 4.7, 'The Lord shall be their king on Mount Zion now and for ever'.
34 Mary's question, **How can this be when I have no husband?** implies that her conception is to be virginal. The birth of Jesus is to be brought about by the power of God the Holy Spirit (just as the Church was born out of that same power at Pentecost). The 'overshadowing' of the Most High is another theophany such as that at the transfiguration, the divine *shekinah*. From the time of Irenaeus, Mary's obedience has been contrasted by Christian theologians with the disobedience of Eve. Like Abraham, Mary accepted the divine call with faith; she assented to
38 God with an Amen, **Here I am.** She recognized herself as the Lord's servant in the role to which her nation had been called. Every word of Mary's is full of messianic interest. God is already with her, 'gracing' her for her task. She is Mary, Miriam. It would be unrealistic to ask if she

understood who the holy child to be called 'Son of God' might be. She only faintly saw what her vocation was to be, but she trusted in God. And, like Hannah, whom Mary resembles (1 Sam. 1.11), her faith was rewarded.

# ADVENT 4
First Sunday before Christmas

*The Annunciation*

\* **Zechariah 2. 10–13**
The prophecies of Zechariah seem to date from a period when the temple in Jerusalem was being built after the Exile, and the concern of the prophet is to assure the people that God is going to return to the Holy City. Although the signs of the times are not auspicious, Zechariah assures them that God will come. The passage is the climax of a series of visions on the advent of God—the third being the man with a measuring-line making plans for the rebuilding of the city. The Lord is coming and is going
10 to make **his dwelling** (the word is significant—see p. 60) among his people. Furthermore, many other nations will become the people of
11 God on **that day,** for the scope of the divine advent is universal. The passage ends with a call to silence in adoration and awe, for God has al-
12 ready begun his progress towards **the city of his choice.**

**Revelation 21. 1–7**
Like the OT reading, the epistle also comes at the climax of a prophecy. John's visions culminate in a picture of the eternal city, the new Jerusalem, coming down from above after the first heaven and the first earth (the present order) had passed away. Part of God's plan was that all evil would be destroyed. The sea was a horror and a wonder to people like the Hebrews, who were never a seafaring people; in Babylonian mythology it represented the chaos which God had to overcome before he created the
1 world. So the saying **and there was no longer any sea** meant that the element of disorder in the universe had been conquered. Notwithstanding God's conquest over the waters at the creation of the world, the sea had remained on earth and in heaven as a symbol of a victory still to be claimed, a barrier between God and man through which the martyrs had to pass in the new exodus.

The bridal image is a common one for the people of God, both the old

Israel and the new, but here the new Jerusalem represents the fulness of the Kingdom of God, the Church triumphant in its ultimate sense. The

3 use of the word **dwelling** ('tabernacle') takes us back to the OT and the sojourn of Israel in the wilderness. There the sacred tent in which God was believed to dwell was called the tabernacle. In later times the Hebrew word for the tabernacling of God, the *shekinah*, was used as a reverential way of referring to God, rather in the same way that we speak of 'the Presence' today. In the prologue to the fourth Gospel the author used it to describe the incarnation of the Word of God: 'The Word became flesh; he came to dwell (to tabernacle) among us, and we saw his glory, such glory as befits the Father's only Son, full of grace and truth' (John 1.14, see Trinity 23 Fifth Sunday before Advent Year 2). The author probably chose the Greek word *eskēnōsen* because it recalled the sound of the Hebrew word *shekinah*. He wished to assert that the presence of God had come down among men. John uses the same word here for **his dwelling** and **he will dwell**.

From one aspect the vision is a picture of the future and of what will happen. Yet from another aspect it is absurd to speak of 'the future' when we are concerned with eternity. Eternity is not 'a long time'; it is a condition which is altogether outside time. When we interpret this prophecy, then, we must remember that we are not just seeing into the future, but also that the truth of what has begun to happen in the past and what is happening in our own day is being revealed to us. The eternal can be dimly discerned in the temporal—its past, its present, and its future.

3     **They shall be his people.** The ancient promise to the Jews is given to those who, refusing to be at home in the old order, have lived as citizens of an abiding city whose designer and builder is God. Along with the sea, other elements in the old order will vanish—tears, mourning, death.

5 **Behold! I am making all things new!** Re-creation, the process by which the old order is being transformed, is continuing all the time. Paul wrote of a new creation in the lives of men and women (2 Cor. 3.18, 4.16–18; Col. 3.1–4, see Easter 3 Year 2). John sees the same transformation taking place on a cosmic scale. **I am the Alpha and the Omega.** The

6 first and the last letters of the Greek alphabet signify the fact that when men and women find themselves in the presence of the living God, they confront the beginning and the ground of their being and the goal of their living. All that man has and all that man is—his salvation and his hope—are gifts of God. What God requires is that man should desire **the**

6 **water-springs of life.** The reward for the one who is victorious is the privilege of divine sonship.

## Matthew 1. 18–23

The Matthean narrative of the nativity begins boldly with the assertion that it tells the story of the birth of the Messiah. There is no delicate unfolding of the truth as in Luke. The virginal conception of the child is explained from the beginning. Jewish betrothal customs meant that a fiancée could already be regarded as belonging to her future husband, but he could release himself from the engagement by an act of repudiation of the marriage contract. Mary's pregnancy, if discovered, would cause

19 a scandal. Being a man of principle, Joseph could not condone it. But in order not to make the matter public, he had decided to repudiate the contract and leave Mary's family free to deal with the shame she had brought on them as best they could. But the angelic visitor informs him that the conception is a miraculous act by the Holy Spirit and that he is not to fear the consequences of completing the marriage. The name

21 Jesus is a form of the Hebrew *Yehoshua*, 'God saves'. The quotation from Isa. 7.14 has 'a young woman' in the Hebrew but 'a virgin' in the LXX.

In this Gospel interest in the nativity story is centred on Joseph, whose genealogy is traced earlier in the chapter back to David. It is Joseph who, as head of the family, receives the annunciation, not Mary. Behind the narrative are the traditions of the miraculous births of the OT—Sarah (Gen. 18.11–14), Rebekah (Gen. 25.21), and Hannah (1 Sam. 1.4–20), when future great men were brought into the world through divine intervention. Angels appear in the NT in moments of such divine intervention. The word means 'messenger' in Hebrew and Greek, but in English denotes a supernatural being.

# CHRISTMAS DAY

*The Birth of Christ*

## Micah 5. 2–4

In one of the OT's most direct prophecies about the Messiah's place of origin, Micah says that the Lord is going to resume his work in Bethlehem, which is where he began it in earlier times when he raised up David. The promised son of David, born of the same Ephrathah clan, would rule over the united kingdom of Israel and Judah, and he would be a true shepherd of the people of God. (The role of the monarch in Israel was traditionally interpreted in terms of shepherding.) And when would this

3 be? Only so long as a woman is in labour shall he give up Israel.

Perhaps Micah is echoing Isa. 7.14–16, when he says that God will do this in a period of time equivalent to a woman's pregnancy. The Hebrews lacked a word for our modern concept of 'time'. The word most frequently used has a sense of 'a period of time' or 'a point of time'. The rule of the 4 new king would be upheld by God and would extend **to the ends of the earth.**

Ephrathah originally denoted a clan related to Caleb (1 Chron. 2.19) that settled in the neighbourhood of Bethlehem. Jesse, David's father, was an Ephrathite (1 Sam. 17.12).

### Titus 2. 11–14

Much of this charge to the apostolic delegate in Crete, Titus, is concerned with the importance of teaching Christian conduct, but at the point in the letter where today's epistle begins Paul, or his editor, moves away from the practicalities of godly behaviour to the fount and inspiration of that conduct, namely, what God has done for his people. It is possible that some of the phrases in this passage had their origin in an early Christian hymn.

God's great gift and blessing has now come and been made known 11 to us, he says. The divine favour has **dawned upon the world.** The Greek word for 'dawned' ('appeared' RSV, JB) comes from the noun 'manifestation' (*epiphaneia*). This was a technical term in the language of contemporary Hellenistic religion for the self-disclosure of a god or semi-divine being (e.g. a king, or, in the imperial cult, the emperor). It could refer to the god's birthday, or to some other occasion when he miraculously displayed himself or his divine power, or to the anniversary of a king's coronation, or to his homecoming from a journey abroad. In 2 Tim. 1.10 it is used to describe Christ's first coming, his incarnation; here and in 2 Thess. 2.8 it is used to refer to the second coming instead of the more usual word, parousia. In his early days Paul had anticipated that he himself would live to witness Christ's glorious return (1 Thess. 2.19, 3.13, 5.23, etc.). If the present passage is genuinely Pauline, then it shows that he later came to realize that as far as he himself was concerned, its date lay in the more distant future.

12    By God's grace we are **disciplined to renounce godless ways and worldly desires.** To be disciplined is to be made into a disciple, a follower. Renunciation of the world, the flesh, and the devil is a preliminary to baptism, when the pagan life—so often recalled in this letter—was firmly 12 set aside. **In the present age** echoes the Jewish belief that the present order is under the dominion of the devil and will be overthrown when God

establishes his kingdom. Used in this context it demonstrates how, for the Christian, the kingdom of God is at hand, even though he must still look
13 forward to its fulfilment in the second coming. **Our great God and Saviour Christ Jesus** is a striking but rare example of the way in which the NT confers divinity on Jesus (and is probably to be preferred to the NEB footnote, which distinguishes between **God and our Saviour Jesus Christ**). 'God and Saviour' is a phrase from contemporary pagan theology.

The reference to Jesus leads into a summary of Christ's work. Jesus
14 **sacrificed himself** in order to redeem us (to ransom us), **to make us a pure people marked out for his own, eager to do good.** The concept of a pure people is basic to both OT and NT. The Israelites were cleansed by the blood of the covenant (Exod. 24.8); the new Israelites are cleansed by the blood of the new covenant ('We are being cleansed from every sin by the blood of Jesus', 1 John 1.7). The phraseology goes back to the LXX version of the OT and denotes that God has redeemed his people from slavery and that they are therefore his own in a very special way. Titus has every authority to teach these things.

### * Luke 2. 1–20

Luke skilfully focuses Israel's history on the birth of Christ. Great men of the past looked forward to the redemption of Israel; Bethlehem is associated with the most famous of Israel's kings. For Luke, the infancy narrative is the fulfilment of God's promise that 'the morning sun from heaven will rise upon us, to shine on those who live in darkness, under the cloud of death, and to guide our feet into the way of peace' (1.78–79)—a promise which has a universal implication, not just a Jewish one.
1    There are difficulties in identifying the **registration . . . made throughout the Roman world.** Such a census did take place in A.D. 6–7 under Quirinius (Luke mentions it in Acts 5.37) but Herod (mentioned in 1.5) died in 6 B.C. It is possible that this particular census was a local one towards the end of Herod's reign; this would have been while Saturninus was governor of Syria and Quirinius was holding a less important post in Syria. Scholars on the whole favour the latter explanation, so that Jesus' birth is dated about 6 B.C. (the error in the difference between that date and our own calendar is because in the sixth century Denis the Small made a faulty computation in taking Luke's thirty years too literally).

At Bethlehem under the church of the Nativity there is a cave which according to Origen has been venerated as the traditional grotto of the nativity since the third century. Before that, the place had been a pagan sanctuary. One explanation of the physical circumstances of the birth is that the house was either the front part of the cave walled in and the manger for the animals was at the back, or that there was a separate house where the occupants used a cave on their premises for animals.

Although the image of a shepherd played such an important part in the OT and NT, at the time of Christ these men were often regarded as the poorer members of the community, contrasted with the more sophisticated members of the city and towns. Bethlehem is about four miles south of Jerusalem. Luke describes how the divine *shekinah*, which had once shone over the temple in Jerusalem, now lightened the Bethlehem fields and the infant in the manger. The message of the angel assures the shepherds that the time of fear is over and the time of rejoicing has been inaugurated.

7      There is a profound significance in being a **first-born**. The most ancient strata of the OT demanded the sacrifice of the first-born (Exod. 22.29), illustrated in the story of Abraham and Isaac (Gen. 22.1–9). In the NT Christ is also *the* first-born (Rom. 8.29, etc.), and offered to the Lord in
11   accordance with the Lord's instructions (Luke 2.21ff). **Deliverer** (Saviour) is a more familiar word. In the OT God is the saviour of his people from their enemies and natural disasters. The name 'Jesus' connects the child with God acting as Saviour. During his ministry there were hopes that Jesus would save Israel from political oppression. But in Acts Luke calls Jesus Saviour in a deeper religious sense (5.31, 13.23) and in Eph. 5.23 Christ is 'the Saviour of the body', the Church. The angel announces him as the **Messiah, the Lord**, or **the Lord's Messiah** (footnote), titles with divine authority.

The song of the heavenly host (cf. the vision of Dan. 7.10) is of special interest because it is thought that it may have originated, like other hymns in Luke 1 and 2, in an early Jewish-Christian hymn.

The haste with which the shepherds resorted to Bethlehem depicts the speed with which the poor and the outcast react to Christ's preaching during his public life; being without hope, they recognise someone in whom they may have hope. When they had seen the child, the shepherds
20   returned **glorifying and praising God for what they had seen and heard**—a typical reaction to divine interventions in OT times.

19     Mary **treasured up all these things and pondered over them** in the same way that Jacob meditated about Joseph's dream (Gen. 37.11) and Daniel about the vision of the son of man at the throne of God (Dan. 7.28). The reaction of the disciple who is faced with a mystery that he does not fully understand is to reverence it because he knows it is of God.

# CHRISTMAS DAY

## The Birth of Christ

### Isaiah 9. 2–7

The theological basis of the monarchy in Judah was the covenant that God made with David (2 Sam. 7.16, 'Your family shall be established and your kingdom shall stand for all time in my sight, and your throne shall be established for ever.') These promises were reaffirmed at the accession of a new king, and the people hoped that each new monarch would make the dynastic ideal an actual fact. It was from this theology of the monarchy that the messianic hope developed.

The passage, then, can best be seen against the background of a royal enthronement. When the successor came to the throne, he was given the religious and ceremonial titles of his ancestors. On the coronation day he was hailed as an adopted son of God (Ps. 2.7, and other 'royal psalms') and to him were ascribed the virtues of Moses and the patriarchs, the courage of David, the wisdom of Solomon. More importantly, he was seen as a new fulfilment of God's promise to David. Even though he was still a child, the titles were bestowed upon him.

It is in this setting that the prophet sees the possibility of an ideal king, a new David emerging. The theophany of God at his accession would be as a light in the darkness. (Although the verbs of this passage are in the past tense, they really speak of a 'prophetic perfect', affirming the certainty of something hoped for.) The joyful people would be like victorious warriors dividing the spoil, since oppression would be lifted from them, as in Gideon's day (Judg. 6–8). The grisly debris of the battlefield would be cleared. The ideal king would be born as a child to grow up and to put into effect the royal titles of his proclamation.

It was not a prediction of the Messiah in the strictly Christian sense, but the Church is entirely justified in seeing as fulfilled in Jesus this prophecy of a great and good king who would rule in justice and righteousness.

### 1 John 4. 7–14

The epistle's discussion on faith and love reaches its climax in this passage which affirms that love is what our redemption is all about. Indeed, this is what God is all about. But love is not, in John's mind, something neutral; it is an activity which demonstrates its nature by what it does. God **sent his only Son into the world** because of his love for us. This love, then, means giving up what is most dear, or thinking about

others more than about ourselves. All this is lifted to a divine plane above
10 personal reactions and feelings. **The love I speak of is not our love for
God, but the love he showed to us in sending his Son as the
remedy for the defilement of our sins.** We believe what it is, and we
describe it by recounting the message of our salvation; but we cannot
define it. God acts for love, and is himself love; and it is in the act of
loving one another that the divine presence is manifested in us. The gift
of the Holy Spirit is the assurance of his indwelling, and he bears witness
to the sending of the Son as the Saviour of the world.

Alongside the belief that 'God is light' (1.5) we must then set the belief
that 'God is love'. John does not mean that light is God or that love is
God: rather, he means that loving is the most characteristic activity of the
Godhead, such love as was demonstrated on the cross. His desire is that
Christians should treat one another as God has treated them.

### John 1. 1-14

1 **When all things began, the Word already was, or, the Word was at
the creation** (NEB footnote). John saw the work of Christ as the beginning
of a new Genesis and introduced his Gospel in the same terms ('In the
beginning God created heaven and earth', Gen. 1.1, NEB footnote).

The use of Word, *logos*, was particularly inspired. To the Jew the
*logos* of God meant the manifestation of divine wisdom, power, and love.
God manifested himself through his Word at creation ('God said, "Let
there be light", and there was light', Gen. 1.3) and revealed himself
through his Word to his prophets ('Hear the word of the Lord', Isa. 1.10).
Among those whose Greek vocabulary took a particular meaning through
the influence of the Stoic philosophers, on the other hand, the *logos* was
the rational principle that permeated and governed the universe. In the
years immediately before the formation of the NT, Hebrew Wisdom
literature under this influence interpreted 'the Word of the Lord' in
personal terms, almost identifying it (or him) with divine Wisdom: 'All
things were lying in peace and silence, and night in her swift course was
half spent, when thy almighty Word leapt from thy royal throne in heaven
into the midst of that doomed land like a relentless warrior' (Wisd. 18.14-
15). John must have chosen the term *logos* deliberately because of its far-
reaching implications to both his Jewish and his Gentile readers.

1    **The Word dwelt with God, and what God was, the Word was.**
John affirmed the pre-existence, the personality, and the divinity of the
3 Word **No single thing was created without him.** In the Genesis story
of creation the Word brought light and order and goodness out of chaos;

66

in the Johannine theology of redemption the Word brought light and union with God to a world darkened by sin and death. That is why
5 Christ is the light that shines on in the dark, and the darkness has never mastered it (or, 'understood it': the Greek word has this other meaning as well).

There is a reference to the ministry of John the Baptist as 'the lamp, burning brightly' (5.35), but he was only the forerunner of the light absolute, enlightening every man born into the world (NEB foot-
9 note). The created world did not recognize the Word of God, although it
11 owed its existence to him; his own people (the Jews, the most likely meaning of his own realm) did not receive him. But to all who did
12 receive him, to those who have yielded him their allegiance ('con-fessed Jesus to be the Son of God' JB), he gave the right to become children of God. The implications of this rebirth were discussed more fully with Nicodemus and related to baptism by water and the Spirit (3.1–8, see Trinity 23 Year 1).
14 So the Logos took human nature and came to dwell among mankind. The OT expectation found its fulfilment. In ancient days God taber-nacled, 'pitched his tent' (Gk) with his people; now the Word pitched his tent among men by becoming a man. 'They shall live under the shelter of my dwelling; I will become their God and they shall become my people' (Ezek. 37.27). John saw this prophecy fulfilled, not in the establishment of a new sanctuary in Jerusalem, but in the incarnate Lord, who is the true temple (2.21).

There is no account of the transfiguration in the fourth Gospel. From the first verses of his book John shows that the glory of God was mani-fested in all that Jesus did, even in his death on the cross, and it was this glory which the disciples witnessed.

# CHRISTMAS 1

## The Birth of Christ

### Isaiah 60. 1-6

1, 4 The passage hinges on two imperatives, **Arise** and **Lift**. In the first the mourning people were summoned to raise themselves from their prostrations to see the glory of God shining over them; in the second they were shown that the light that shines on them is a centre upon which the peoples of all nations are converging.

Verses 1-3 contain a magnificent picture of the fulfilment of the biblical promise to Israel. The motif of the Lord's epiphany to his people is an old one, but the elements of warfare and of natural phenomena which accompanied the manifestation of God in other OT passages are missing. All that remains of the latter is the light of God shining in the darkness, the sign of God's presence at the Exodus, but now employed in a way that resembles the NT use of darkness and light—particularly John's—rather than the OT. God's advent is not identified with the people's return to Jerusalem, as it is elsewhere in this collection of prophecies. Instead, other nations come to Jerusalem as a result of God's saving act.

Verses 4-6 demonstrate the universal scope of God's work in the vision of the kings and their peoples making pilgrimage to the holy city in mighty caravans across the deserts of Syria and Sinai (Midian and Ephah from north Arabia; the descendants of Sheba, like their famous queen, from southern Arabia) and from across the sea (the maritime
4 powers of Phoenicia and Greece). With them come **your sons** and **your daughters**, Hebrews of the dispersion, bringing the riches of the nations with them. The foreigners themselves will be heralds of the Lord's praise.

### (-22)

The nations are described in the vision as merely the carriers of all that is brought to glorify Zion in the new age. Massive fleets of ships bring the Israelites of the dispersion home to populate the city, and precious metals to adorn the temple—a building of greater magnificence than Solomon's. After being in servitude to another race, the prophet promised
10 the people, **Foreigners shall rebuild your walls, and their kings shall be your servants.** The caravans from other nations will be so numerous
11 that **your gates shall be open continually.** By acknowledging that
14 Jerusalem was **the City of the Lord, the Zion of the Holy One of Israel**, they would renew her honour.

Thus Jerusalem will become the place of salvation. Her walls and gates

18 will be given new names—**Deliverance** and **Praise**—and the light of
God will shine on her always.

## Hebrews 1. 1–4

The opening verses of the letter to the Hebrews set out a summary of the
redemptive acts of God which the Bible described. They form one of
those great NT passages which embrace the work of God in Jesus Christ,
and they can be compared with John 1.1–14 and Phil. 2.5–11. Behind
these verses is the belief that what we know about God, man, and the
universe, is what God has chosen to disclose to us—and no more. Our
knowledge of God is not primarily the result of our quest for truth: it is
the result of God's intention that the truth should be known. While that
knowledge comes partly from the world around us, God has chosen a
special way to communicate to us the truth about his nature and his
purpose, and this way involved a particular community at a particular
moment in their history in order that, through them, he might reveal his
truth to the rest of mankind.

The passage begins, then, by stating that, having made himself and his
intention partially known to and through the old Israel, the community
chosen for that purpose, God has now finally disclosed all that men need
to know to be at one with him, and he has also done what needed to be
done in order to establish that relationship with himself through Jesus
Christ. God himself, his mind, his purpose and his nature, have been
expressed in terms of human personality. The entrance of Jesus Christ
onto the stage of history is mankind's most decisive hour; it is the culmination of God's revelation of himself and the key to all knowledge of
him. It is, therefore, the most significant moment since creation.

1    The **forefathers** to whom God spoke are the Israelites of the old
covenant, seen from the Christian viewpoint as those who preceded the
new People of God, the Church. The **prophets** through whom he spoke
included men like Abraham, Moses, Aaron, and Elijah. They had different
glimpses of the truth—Hosea the extent of God's love, Isaiah the splendour of his glory. No prophet was shown all of the truth, but each in his
own way and according to his experience of God was shown part of it. The
author of Hebrews demonstrates this in the later verses of chapter 1
where he quoted a series of four testimony-texts from the OT. Yet the
revelation was incomplete because they told of a promise not yet fulfilled.
The full revelation could come only through someone who was himself
one with God.

That revelation was given by Jesus—not just in what Jesus taught, but also through the whole act of God in Christ from the incarnation to the ascension. The writer distinguishes between the revelation that had gone before and that which had been given in Jesus Christ, and he also points to Christ's unique place in the universe. What the writer means by

2 Son—'the one who is a son', to give a literal translation of the Greek— he now goes on to say:

He is **heir to the whole universe**. Jesus is identified with the Messiah, who is made heir in Ps. 2.1–9,

'I shall give thee the nations for thine inheritance:

and the uttermost parts of the earth for thy possession'. Cf. Isa. 11.1–10.

Jesus spoke of himself as the heir in the parable of the vineyard (Mark 12.1–10), implying his unique relationship to God and his authority over the vineyard, Israel. Thus Jesus inherits, on behalf of the new Israel, the assurance of God's presence and power which were promised to the

2 old. **Through him he created all orders of existence.** Jesus is identified with the creative power of God. In the OT the creative act of the Word of God (Gen. 1.3) or the Wisdom of God (Prov. 8) came to be regarded in the intertestamental period as personal emanations of God which could be paralleled with the *Logos* of Greek philosophy, the immanent Reason which created and directed the universe. The pre-existence of Jesus is indicated by his own self-consciousness and identification of himself with the Father. If Jesus was what he claimed to be, and if he had the power that only God can have to heal, to forgive, and to change men's lives, it follows that he must have been eternally present with God. The Wisdom-Logos idea made possible the communication between God and man. The interest of Christian teachers was not theological or philosophical but missionary. In using terms like 'Logos' or 'Word' (John 1.1–4,14), or in other ways identifying Jesus with the creative and sustaining power of God in the universe (Heb. 1, Col. 1.14–17), the NT writers were endeavouring to adapt the concept of the Messiah and all that he meant in Jewish tradition to the language and ideas that were familiar in the Greco-Roman world into which the gospel spread.

3    He was **the effulgence of God's splendour**. The radiance and reflection of God's glory is his divine nature as it is manifested to man. The light and the power and the holiness of God are visible and comprehensible to man only to a degree; beyond that they are past his understanding.

3    He was **the stamp of God's very being**. The image is that of a stamp on a wax seal or a die from which a coin is cast. Christ's character is such that we see in him the image of God perfectly demonstrated in human terms.

3   He **brought about the purgation of sins.** The rest of the epistle gives an elaborate explanation of Christ's death and resurrection and ascension in terms of the most important of all the ritual sacrifices described in the OT, the offering of the Day of Atonement. Here the first words are written to introduce the great theme. It is not individual sins that have been done away, but the effect of sin: the author is to explain what Paul calls justification in cultic terms.

3   He **took his seat at the right hand of the majesty on high.** The symbolic phrase (Ps. 110.1 and Mark 16.19) suggests the royal authority of the one who sits while his subjects stand or kneel. It is the attitude of one whose task is accomplished and whose relationship with God the Father is unique. The Son is both priest and victim, and in virtue of his completed sacrifice he has been exalted to take the highest place in heaven which is his by right. His session is at the throne of God.

4   He **was raised . . . far above the angels.** His superiority is over all spiritual beings as well as over mankind.


\*  **Matthew 2. 1–12**

Although the Gospel of Matthew has a strongly Jewish bias, it begins and ends with reference to the worldwide mission of the Church. At the end of the Gospel Christ's disciples are commissioned to go into all the world; at the beginning the birth of Christ is reverenced both by Jews (Joseph and Mary) and by Gentiles (the magi).

Bethlehem, 'the house of bread', is situated about four miles south of Jerusalem. Herod the Great was a puppet king of Palestine who was maintained by Roman authority from 40 to 4 B.C. According to Matthew's dating (and as implied by Luke's) the birth of Jesus took place before 4 B.C. Astrologers (Gk. *magoi*, Latin *magi*) originated from a tribe of the Medes who became a priestly caste among the Persians. In this sense the magi were wise men, observers of the stars. The word later acquired a more sinister meaning of 'magicians' or 'sorcerers' (Acts 8.9, 13.6,8),

2   though this is obviously not meant here. **The rising of his star** was associated with the birth of great men—e.g. Alexander the Great. The

4   **chief priests** were the families from which the high priests were chosen; the **lawyers** were the experts in the Law, frequently Pharisees, though not always. With the high priests and the elders they constituted the Grand Sanhedrin in Jerusalem.

The gifts of the magi represented the wealth of Arabia, but the early Christian fathers saw in them symbols of royalty (gold), divinity (incense) and the passion (myrrh). The adoration of the magi fulfilled the prophecies that homage would be paid to the God of the Jews by the nations (Isa. 49.7, 60.6; Ps. 72.10–15).

The desire for a saviour was not confined to Jewish circles. There is a good deal of evidence to show that in a world distracted by social up-heavals and civil wars, the men and women of the centuries either side of the birth of Christ longed for a release from the uncertainties they experienced in daily life. There was a move away from the formal and conventional worship of the Olympian gods to the cults from the East which professed to offer divine guidance and protection in return for moral and ritual purification within a close brotherhood of initiates. Thus the Son of God came as a saviour to men awakening to their need on a universal scale, not a narrowly Jewish one.

# CHRISTMAS 1

*The Wise Men*

### Isaiah 49. (1–6)

The second of the four songs of the servant of the Lord in Second Isaiah. The servant of God proclaimed the true faith and suffered to atone for the sins of his people, but God exalted him in the end. Who was the Servant? Some commentators have suggested he was an individual closely related to one of the sources of Second Isaiah; others have seen him as the personification of the people of Israel themselves, or a group of them; **you** 3 **are my servant, Israel through whom I shall win glory.** The problem may never be solved; both suggestions are to be held together, since they point forward to the identification of the servant with Christ, and of Christ with his Church—an identification which is so intimate that Paul could speak of 'helping to complete, in my poor human flesh, the full tale of Christ's afflictions still to be endured, for the sake of his body which is the church' (Col. 1.24).

God called the servant from his birth—indeed before it, as in the cases of 1 John the Baptist and Jesus Christ, for he **named me from my mother's womb**—and equipped him with the ability to speak words that pene-2 trated like a **sharp sword** and ranged far and wide like a **polished arrow. Concealed me under the cover of his hand** may indicate that the first part of his life was hidden until he came out into the open to prophesy; it could also mean that he enjoyed the protection of the Lord.

His task was to glorify God. He set aside the disappointment of his previous failure. Though men had thought that his work had miscarried,
4 God was going to accept it and vindicate it: **my cause is with the Lord and my reward is in God's hands.** His new task was to restore Israel as in the days of promise after the return from exile in Babylon, but with
6 a greater responsibility: **I will make you a light to the nations.** The Gentile world was to be included in God's saving work.

**7-13**

7 A proclamation of deliverance, typical of the prophet. **The Holy One** is not just a gracious God but the God who acts for the redemption of his people—**the Lord who ransoms Israel.** The oppressed and despised nation would be lifted up in the sight of all other nations by God so that they, too, would recognize him as Lord. The redemption was spoken of by the prophet as if it had already happened: **in the hour of my favour**
8 **I answered you, and I helped you on the day of deliverance.** These are the hours when God turned in favour to his people and the day on which he intervened to deliver them. The time of servitude was over.

Verses 8 to 12 spell out the details of the deliverance. The land will be established again, fertile and in temperate heat, and the captives will be set free. Like sheep under a shepherd, the people will find their way home—even those from as far away as Syene (Aswan in Egypt, where the existence of a Jewish colony is known from the Elephantine papyri). With echoes of what God did at the exodus, the prophet foretold that the new exodus would be even more marvellous.

Verse 13 is a brief hymn. Creation joins in the praise which Israel raises to God because the Lord has **comforted his people and has had pity on his own in their distress.**

### Ephesians 3. 1–6

The writer, perhaps a later editor of the apostle's works, introduces the apostle as one who prays in captivity for the Gentile Christians. He is
1 **the prisoner of Christ Jesus** in the spiritual sense that he was captured by the risen Lord on the Damascus road; he was also a prisoner in the physical sense when his arrest in Jerusalem (Acts 21.17–40) led eventually to a martyr's death in Rome. He is the one whom God has chosen to bring the gospel to the Gentiles.

3    This was the **secret that was made known to me** when Paul was
4 called by God. **The secret of Christ** was that the Church, Christ's Body, should be the means of bringing all mankind into unity. The Jews

had been the exclusive heirs of the promises of God under the covenant, of which circumcision was a sign. The Gentiles, 'separate from Christ, strangers to the community of Israel, outside God's covenants and the promise that goes with them' (2.12), had now been given access to God in Christ through his reconciling death. This divine plan was unknown in previous ages, but God has willed to disclose his eternal purpose, and by special revelation entrusted Paul with the task of proclaiming it to the Gentiles.

4    **A brief account** may refer to 1.9–10 or perhaps part of another letter,
5  Colossians. **Prophets** are probably members of the Church with charismatic gifts who shared the work of proclaiming the gospel with the apostles, or they may be OT prophets who only had an obscure and imperfect vision of the work of the Messiah.

The change in outlook involved in accepting all men as potentially members of the people of God was one which many early Christians from a Jewish family found difficult to accept, and behind the NT writings are echoes of the controversy. It was only slowly that Jewish Christians came to see that Gentiles who had repented and sought baptism need not be circumcised—i.e. become Jewish proselytes—before they were admitted into the fellowship of the Church. Paul, as the apostle to the Gentiles, insisted on this again and again in his letters, and the lesson was repeated in the early chapters of the Acts of the Apostles until the council in Jerusalem laid down conditions under which Gentiles would be admitted to communion with former Jews in the Church (Acts 15). Paul's anxiety to stress this equality of Gentile and Jew under the new covenant emerges
6  in his use of phrases like **joint heirs with the Jews, part of the same body, sharers together in the promise made in Christ Jesus.**

\*  **Matthew 2. 1–12**
See commentary on Christmas 1 Year 1.

# CHRISTMAS 2

*The Presentation in the Temple*

**1 Samuel 1. (1–19)**
The introduction to the story of Samuel's birth tells of Elkanah's annual pilgrimage with his household to Shiloh. Since the yearly offerings
4  or **shares of meat** were made according to the number of children each wife had, the occasion was bound to call attention to Hannah's barrenness

because she could only offer one share while Peninnah offered several shares, with all her sons and daughters.

11 The vow which Hannah made, **I will give the child to the Lord for his whole life, and no razor shall ever touch his head,** had a special significance. A Nazarite could be released from his vows, but Hannah's dedication of her child was lifelong. The uncut hair (like Samson's) was a sign of dedication.

### 20–28

Hannah had prayed in the temple at Shiloh (twelve miles south of Nablus) for a son and promised God that, if her request was granted, she would give her son back to the Lord and dedicate him to the Lord's service. And God intervened, as in the case of Isaac, Samson, and John the Baptist. Hannah despite her age bore a child, and he was called 20 Samuel. Although the text suggests that the name means **I asked the Lord for him,** in fact it means 'the Name of God' (*Shem-El* = Samuel). The verb used in the sentence puns with Saul, and this has led some scholars to suppose that what is recounted here is the birth of Saul.

Elkanah prayed that his wife would fulfil her vow. Eventually the time came for the child to be dedicated to the Lord's service, and this was 25 done with the offering of sacrifices. **They slaughtered** presumably refers 28 to the attendants in the sanctuary at Shiloh. Behind the phrases **I lend him to the Lord** is the idea that the child belongs to his family but that during his life he is given back to God for divine purposes. It is a curious reversal of our normal concept of vocation.

Interest in the passage also centres on the picture it gives, long before the period of the monarchy, of an annual festival attended by individuals like Elkanah as well as the twelve tribes. Pilgrimages such as this each year would nourish the people's common faith and their unity, especially when the areas settled by them were not contiguous. At the celebrations the emphasis would probably fall on recalling those traditions which all the tribes claimed as a heritage from the past: the promise to the patriarchs, the deliverance from Egypt, the covenant and the law-giving on Sinai. It may have been an early celebration of the feast of Tabernacles.

### Romans 12. 1–8

The passage is taken from that part of the letter to the Romans where Paul moves from his dogmatic exposition of justification by faith to his explanation of its consequences in the life of a Christian. Man's response is in loving obedience to God's revealed will, as a sign of that gratitude

which a redeemed and justified man must feel for what God has done for
1 him in his mighty acts (celebrated by the Church in her festivals). **My
brothers, I implore you by God's mercy to offer your very selves
to him: a living sacrifice, dedicated and fit for his acceptance, the
worship offered by mind and heart**—behind these phrases is the vocabulary of the cult (technical words are used in the Greek, 'offer', 'sacrifice',
'dedicated', 'fit for his acceptance', 'worship'). The kind of worship we
should offer is that which springs from our whole being as one created by
God with a mind and a will (as the NEB footnote brings out). The concept
of a life in obedience to God as one that is 'a living sacrifice', and 'worship
offered by mind and heart' has its roots in the OT. The psalmist realised
that what was acceptable to God was 'a troubled spirit, a broken and con-
trite heart' (Ps. 51.17). After the destruction of the temple in Jerusalem
in A.D. 70, it was said by the rabbis that although other sacrifices ceased,
the oblations of praise and thanksgiving remained.

2   Paul is able to speak about men's minds being **remade** and their
natures **transformed** because this renewal has begun in conversion and
baptism, and it is advanced in every act of obedience in a Christian's life
according to the will of God. Further, as the Christian continues in obe-
2 dience, so he is able to **discern the will of God, and to know what is
good, acceptable, and perfect.** This is an inward understanding which
has little to do with obedience to a written code or law.

The apostle then goes on to plead for humility, because all that a
Christian possesses is given by God; *charismata*, 'grace-gifts', within the
Body of Christ. The strong link he forges between the charisms and the
unity of the Church is similar to his theme in 1 Cor. 12–14. There may
have been some who possessed special or showy charisms and despised
others in Rome, as some did in Corinth. So he briefly outlines the right
6 use of these gifts. **Inspired utterance** ('prophecy' RSV JB) . . . **in proportion to a man's faith**: like OT prophecy, this was primarily a direct
communication of God's word to his people; the **proportion** of faith
means much the same as the measure of faith in verse 3, the power given
by God to men to do certain things (not 'faith' in the more usual sense
7 in this letter). **The gift of administration** (*diakonia* = 'ministry' or
'service') aligns practical tasks in the Christian community with charisms.
Teaching, exhortation, generosity, leadership, and charitable works of
mercy all follow in the list. Charisms in this passage refers to those
practical expressions of the grace (*charis*) of God under which the
Church of God stands. In this sense the whole life of the Church, and not
just its ministry, is 'charismatic'.

* Luke 2. 21–40

Lev. 12.3 lays down that a child should be circumcised; Exod. 13.2,12, that the first-born should be presented to the Lord. These laws may go back to a primitive age when the first-born were offered to the Lord in sacrifice—at least in theory: it is doubtful whether the first-born sons of Israel were ever killed for this reason. One of the lessons behind the story of Abraham's offering of Isaac (Gen. 22.1–12) seems to have been that human sacrifice is contrary to the will of God. See Tuesday before Easter Year 2. Anyway, as obedient members of the people of God, Joseph and Mary obeyed the law and brought Jesus up to Jerusalem for the presentation.

Two representatives of the old Israel came forward to witness the work of God in Christ. They were not officials of the temple but devout and 25 faithful Jews. Simeon was one who watched and waited for the restoration of Israel, and the Holy Spirit was upon him. The 'comforting of Israel' (JB—Gk *paraklesis*) was expressed in Isa. 40.1ff, 'Comfort, comfort my people, says your God', and looked forward to the fulfilment of God's promises in the messianic age. Simeon was given a prophecy concerning the Messiah and, recognizing him in the infant being presented at the temple, he utters an oracle which has passed into Christian liturgy, the *Nunc dimittis*. The hymn gathers together words and thoughts from Isaiah. The universal scope of the Messiah's deliverance is proclaimed and the special place of Israel in God's revelation is acknowledged. It is a chant of praise for the fulfilment of God's promises and for the light which he has brought into the world. As an act of devotion, it stems from the borderland of Jewish and Christian faiths and may have originated as an early Christian canticle. The old man also warns 35 the parents: the prophecy about being pierced to the heart has a double meaning—the pain that Mary would feel at the crucifixion, or the pain that Judah (personified in Mary) would feel when the sword passed through the land (Ezek. 14.17).

The second representative of the old Israel was Anna, a prophetess. The revival of prophecy in these two figures is offered by Luke as one of the signs of Christ's birth. It was believed that the Spirit would raise up prophets again in Israel as the messianic age drew near, especially among 38 those who looked for the liberation of Jerusalem (a technical name for that age). The first chapters of this Gospel are full of references to the Spirit's activity: Zechariah was told that his son John would be filled with the Holy Spirit (1.15), Mary that she would conceive a son by the Holy Spirit (1.35), Elizabeth was filled with the Holy Spirit at the news of

Mary's conception (1.41), Zechariah was filled with the Spirit when John was born (1.67). These references, including those of Simeon and Anna in this passage, culminate in the descent of the Spirit on Jesus at his baptism (3.22).

# CHRISTMAS 2

*The Visit to Jerusalem*

### Deuteronomy 16. 1–6

Deuteronomy is the English form of the Greek *Deuteronomion*, taken from the LXX version of Deut. 17.18, 'a copy of this law', 'the second law', 'this Deuteronomion'. Much of the material in the book is associated with the reforms resulting from the discovery of a law book in the temple at Jerusalem during the reign of Josiah (2 Kings 22ff), that is, about the year 622 B.C. In its final form it is post-exilic, especially in its laws relating to a single sanctuary as the focus of the people's devotion.

Alongside the loyalty to old ways and a careful preservation of what God had handed down, therefore, we must set the changes brought about over the centuries through local cultic customs. The use of the Canaanite name for 'the month of green ears', *Abib*, corresponding to March–April, indicates that it may have been after the settlement in this land that the Passover festival was linked with the feast of unleavened bread—a celebration of the nomadic era being joined to a celebration of a settled agricultural community. Originally the Passover had been celebrated in family or kin-groups (we notice this behind the regulations of Exod. 12), but the Deuteronomic reform made it one of the pilgrimage feasts which could only be celebrated within a sanctuary—together with the feasts of Weeks and Tabernacles.

We notice in this passage how some of the ritual details had been affected by this shift of focus from home to sanctuary. Originally only a lamb was to be offered; now the animal could be a kid or a calf as well, because these were sacrificial animals offered in the temple at other festivals. Originally the Passover was eaten with haste to commemorate the speedy exodus of the Jews from Egypt; now the celebrations extended for seven days. Originally unleavened bread had represented the bread of affliction, baked in memory of the bondage in Egypt; now it was eaten because leavened bread was regarded as ritually impure. Originally the Passover

victim had been slaughtered and eaten at home; now it was to be killed
6 only in the place which (the Lord your God) will choose as a dwelling for his Name. The Passover thus became one of the pilgrimage
feasts which brought Jews each year to Jerusalem, although the ritual meal
was still eaten at home or in the houses or lodgings or tents which the
pilgrims occupied when they came to the holy city.

## Romans 8. 12–17

In this part of his letter Paul has been making it clear that an individual's
conversion and baptism into the Church are not an end but a beginning,
and that the Christian must expect to be faced constantly with a series of
choices which can only be made with the guidance of the indwelling
Spirit, which gives new life to our mortal bodies.

12 **It follows, my friends, that our lower nature has no claim upon
us; we are not obliged to live on that level.** By 'lower nature' (JB
'our unspiritual selves') Paul meant that natural side of our personality
which is incapable of good in itself: 'I know that nothing good lodges in
me—in my unspiritual nature, I mean—for though the will to do good is
there, the deed is not. The good which I want to do, I fail to do; but what
I do is the wrong which is against my will: and if what I do is against my
will, clearly it is no longer I who am the agent, but sin that has its lodging
in me' (7.18–20). The unspiritual man may think of the natural way as the
way to life, but in reality it is the way to death. Augustine, looking back
on his life before his baptism, remarked wistfully, 'Such was my life—but
was *that* living?' Our lower nature is occupied by sin if it is not submitted
to the Holy Spirit.

14 **The Spirit claims us for God. For all who are moved by the Spirit
of God are sons of God.** Sonship, like marriage, is used to convey the
intimate relationship which exists between God and his faithful people;
and it is as the Christian is filled with the Spirit that he enters into that
intimate relationship. But the mastery of the Spirit is not the kind of
lordship that a slave experiences (and slavery was a common feature of the
world in which Paul lived). Rather, the Spirit liberates us into the status
of sonship with God and guarantees our future salvation. To put it
another way, the Spirit establishes our salvation in the present by anticipating what we inherit in the future. Our adoption as sons can be compared
in Pauline theology with our justification. Justification, which is a verdict
of the last judgement, is brought forward into the present through our
faith in God's manifestation of his righteousness in Christ and in us by
his Spirit.

The practice of adoption was not known in Jewish circles, where other provision was made for parentless children, but it was common in Greco-Roman society. A wealthy man might adopt a young slave, if he was childless, to inherit his possessions. Just as children of a household might look forward to receiving a portion of their father's possessions, so Christians as sons of God will one day enter into their heavenly inheritance as Christ, their Elder Brother, has already done. The Spirit of God, by bringing this inheritance forward into the present, enables us to address
15 God as Abba! Father! The Aramaic word—an intimate, family term of address—is followed in the text by the Greek translation. Though not liturgical in origin, Paul's use of it recalls contemporary practice in Christian prayer, as witnessed in the Lord's Prayer and the prayer of Christ in the garden of Gethsemane (Luke 11.2, Mark 14.35). But there is a condition attached. For Christ the path of glory involved suffering. For his fellow-heirs it is the same.

\* **Luke 2. 41–52**
It was the custom of Joseph and Mary, as devout Jews, to pilgrimage to Jerusalem to observe the Passover. The rabbis expected children to keep the Law fully from the age of thirteen. The presence of Christ at the pilgrimage at the age of twelve suggests that his parents were introducing him to the practices of their religion early in life. We are told that he was 'full of wisdom' (2.40), that he had learned the ways of God from the study of the scriptures, and so we can assume that the questions he put to the teachers in the colonnaded forecourts of the temple turned on the interpretation of certain passages in the OT. Could it be that all who
47 heard him were amazed at his intelligence and the answers he gave were listening to the uniquely fresh exposition of the scriptures which were to be a well-remembered feature of his future ministry?

The story contrasts the relationship of Jesus to his heavenly Father with his relationship to his earthly parents. Jesus recognized God as his Father long before the voice from heaven spoke at his baptism by John in the river Jordan. He was not 'adopted' at his baptism, as some have claimed all through the Christian era. Yet his obedience to Joseph and Mary is set in this context as a model of Christian family relationships.

The story has close affinities with that of Samuel, whose parents, like the parents of Jesus, used to observe the feasts year by year and who also, as he grew up, 'commended himself to the Lord and to men' (1 Sam. 1.7, 2.26).

# EPIPHANY 1
## Third Sunday after Christmas[1]

*The Baptism of Christ*

1 Samuel 16. 1–13a

Another tradition attributed the anointing of David to the men of Judah and then to the elders of Israel at Hebron (2 Sam. 2.4, 5.3). This story of his anointing serves to demonstrate the charismatic succession of leadership between Samuel and David, once God had rejected Saul.

David's family tree, that of Jesse at Bethlehem, was deeply rooted in Israel and therefore powerful support for the claim to kingship. He was a man of Judah through and through. Saul, on the other hand, came from Benjamin, and as the divisions in Israel intensified, with Judah opposed to the other tribes, Saul with Benjamin came to be regarded as apostate.

Samuel's status was somewhat ambiguous. He was fearful of Saul's power and had to adopt a subterfuge in order to travel to Bethlehem, yet he was vested with such authority that the elders of Bethlehem hurried out to find out what he wanted. The fact that Samuel said he had come to make an oblation and invited them to cleanse themselves with a ceremonial washing indicates that Bethlehem occupied a special place in the religious life of the people. It was a place of sacrifice.

The selection of the new king proceeded on romantic lines. The three brothers were inspected, but rejected by God, although Eliab was tall and handsome (as Saul was, 'a head taller than any of his fellows', 1 Sam.
7 9.2). These are not qualities that impress the Lord; **he does not see as man sees; men judge by appearances but the Lord judges by the heart.** It was the youngest, the eighth, son (eight being the number of perfection) who was chosen and anointed. Samuel was guided not to proceed with the sacrificial meal until this son had been brought forward.
13 After the anointing, **the spirit of the Lord came upon David,** as the spirit of the Lord had come on Saul at his anointing (10.6,10). Verse 14 says that the spirit had left Saul, implying that it was only upon the leaders of the people that the spirit was expected to work.

Acts 10. 34–48a

The Gentile Pentecost in the house of Cornelius, the centurion in the Italian Cohort, who lived in Caesarea and who sent for Peter from Joppa, marked the Church's decisive step out of Judaism into a world

[1] The Series 3 lectionary is one year ahead of JLG in a year which has only one Sunday between Christmas and Epiphany.

mission in the Acts of the Apostles. Luke drew up the story as a model of
the kind of response to the Gospel that evangelists should expect from the
36 Gentile world; the word of God is preached: **the good news of peace
through Jesus Christ, who is Lord of all** (words from Isa. 52.7; the
last phrase is an interesting fragment of an early Christian credal statement); the Holy Spirit comes upon all who are listening, and they are
baptized. The usual order—preaching, repentance, baptism, gift of the
Holy Spirit—was perhaps reversed on this occasion because of the need
to show Peter and the Jewish believers with him that God was moving
out into the Gentile world and that they must follow.

Peter's speech is a short gospel of its own. Like the earliest Gospel,
Mark, the apostle began with the baptism of Jesus by John. Jesus was
God's Messiah, Peter taught, quoting Isa. 61.1, for it was at his baptism
38 that the Father **anointed him with the Holy Spirit** (Messiah = 'the
anointed one'). The ministry of Jesus is summarized as beginning in
Galilee and culminating at Jerusalem on Calvary. Peter referred to the
crucifixion only briefly, for he wanted to pass on to the good news of the
41 resurrection. The risen Christ appeared, **not to the whole people, but
to witnesses whom God had chosen in advance—to us, who ate
and drank with him after he rose from the dead.** The reference to
eating and drinking (the meal at Emmaus, the supper by the lakeside) was
a proof of the reality of the apostles' fellowship with Jesus after his
resurrection. The special office of an apostle was to be a witness of the
42 resurrection and **to proclaim him to the people, and affirm that he is
the one who has been designated by God as judge of the living
43 and the dead.** Finally, with a reference to scripture, **it is to him that
all the prophets testify,** Peter declared that everyone who believed in
Jesus Christ **receives forgiveness of sins through his name.** The OT
has its indispensable place in the divine plan of salvation for Gentiles as
well as Jews.

44    Perhaps Peter had intended to say more—he was **still speaking**—
when the Holy Spirit descended on his listeners and, like the apostles
on the day of Pentecost, they spoke in tongues. Glossolalia was the sign
of receiving the Spirit in Acts 10.42 as in 2.4. It is a form of praise and
46 thanksgiving for **acclaiming the greatness of God,** and it convinced
Peter and his companions that those Gentiles should be baptized in the
name of Jesus Christ.

\* Matthew 3. 13–17
In describing the baptism of Jesus, Matthew seems to try to answer the

question, Why should the sinless one submit to the baptism of John? Jesus would more fittingly baptize John. Indeed, John had already said of him: 'I baptize you with water, for repentance; but the one who comes after me is mightier than I. I am not fit to take off his shoes. He will baptize you with the Holy Spirit and with fire' (3.11). But Jesus pressed 15 to be baptized: **We do well to conform in this way with all that God requires.** Jesus is one with the people and must join with them in those acts which express their response to God's spokesman. Divine judgement is coming, and Israel must repent and be baptized and prepare by obedience for the kingdom of God. By being baptized Christ also validated the rite for all future generations of Christians.

The descent of the Spirit of God, pictured by the evangelists as a dove —a symbol used in Jewish literature to depict both Israel herself and divine wisdom—does not mean, of course, that Jesus had not been possessed by the Spirit before. Rather, it means that the Spirit comes dynamically to those whom God chooses for his work to give them power and guidance to fulfil their vocation. The descent of the dove represents the anointing of Christ (= 'the anointed one') for the next step in his ministry, the withdrawal into the desert to do battle with the devil (see Lent 1 Years 1 and 2), and the choice of the disciples (see Epiphany 2, 17 Years 1 and 2). **Beloved** means 'chosen of God'.

Patristic commentators long recognized the baptism as a theophany of the Holy Trinity—the Father's voice from heaven, the Son's baptism, and the Spirit's descent. Jesus' stepping down into the waters of the Jordan was seen as a symbol of his crushing underfoot the power of evil (associated in Jewish mythology by water). The event looked forward to Christ's death and resurrection and the sending of the Spirit on the Church, his Passover, which he called 'a baptism to undergo' (Luke 12.50).

YEAR 2

# EPIPHANY 1
Third Sunday after Christmas

*The Baptism of Christ*

### Isaiah 42. 1–7
Part of the first of the songs of the servant of God, which form a special strand within the prophecies of the Second Isaiah. The prophet saw God 1 selecting someone and nominating him: **Here is my servant, whom I**

**uphold, my chosen one in whom I delight.** The servant's vocation
3 was to **make justice shine on the nations.** Justice in this context means
almost the same as what Paul meant by 'righteousness' when speaking of
the salvation which God accomplishes for man. As far as the Gentiles
are concerned, their gods are as nothing. Israel's Lord alone is God. This
does not mean, however, that the servant was to go and preach to other
nations. His was the way of suffering among his own people, and others
would see through his acceptance of that *via dolorosa* the salvation of God.

1    For this vocation God equipped him: **I have bestowed my spirit
upon him.** This is the spirit of God which stirred the prophets, the outpouring of which was a sign of the messianic age. When he promulgated
judgement, the servant would not follow the usual custom and announce
it in public. Instead, he would make God's justice prevail in such a way
that he avoided the harsh law of the world, which allows those who are
3 weak and defenceless—**a bruised reed, a smouldering wick**—to perish.

Verses 5–7 are another section of the song. An eulogy for God's power
and wisdom in creation and for bestowing life on the human race introduces the Lord's further call to the servant. The reason why he has been
chosen is that through him the nations will receive light and salvation
(and be drawn into the covenant, NEB footnote); the effect will be as if the
blind are given their sight and the prisoners are brought out into daylight.
These two classes of unfortunates typify the dimensions of human suffering: the first class suffer as a result of natural affliction, the second as a
result of man's cruelty. These verses were quoted by the NT writers with
reference to Jesus' work.

But who was the servant? Sometimes he is an individual bearing the
burden of Israel's sins; sometimes he is the collective representative of
Israel as a nation, called by God to suffer as a witness to all the nations
of the earth.

(–12)
God is glorified when men recognize his saving work. Verses 10–12 are
the beginning of a psalm of praise to God for what he was to accomplish
for the people in exile.

Ephesians 2. 1–10
A summary of Paul's gospel, probably written by one who was collating
his teaching in a new letter: God has brought man into the sphere of his
forgiveness and love, replacing the dark life of sinful hostility to God with
a new life within the divine will. It is all the difference between life and

death. The man who receives God's grace in Christ and the man who is
still in bondage to sin are as different as a living being and a corpse.

2 **The commander of the spiritual powers of the air** is Satan.
According to the NT outlook, the existing world has fallen at least par-
tially under his control; and just as goodness is produced by the Holy
Spirit at work in men's hearts, so evil is produced by Satan **at work**

2, 3 **among God's rebel subjects. We too were once of their number**:
perhaps the writer was aligning Paul with his fellow-Jews to distinguish
them from the Gentiles to whom he is addressing the letter. Like them,
Paul and those to whom he refers also lived in such a way that their lives

3 tended to be oriented away from God and towards their own concerns: **in
our natural condition we, like the rest, lay under the dreadful
judgement of God.**

The rest of the passage teaches what God has done. In his love and
mercy he completed his great work through Jesus Christ to bring new

5, 8 life to dead sinners. The phrase, **it is by his grace you are saved,** is
repeated twice. What God has done is in no sense deserved by us, the
writer emphasized. Then he followed the Pauline teaching of dying and
rising again with Christ, though without saying that the Christian must

6 die with his Lord (in baptism), and adding that we shall **be enthroned
. . . with him in the heavenly realms** (an idea not found in Paul).
Like John, he was concentrating entirely on the wonderful way in which
the deadness of a soul is transformed into vigorous spiritual life as a result
of fellowship with Christ. This led him, in his enthusiasm, to speak as if
the believer was already in heaven with his exalted and enthroned Lord.
There is, of course, a real sense in which this is true, in that eternal life
is something in which we begin to share here and now. Salvation is for

7 eternity—**in the ages to come.**

The last two verses of the passage compress into few words Paul's
doctrine of justification by faith in dependence on the unmerited grace
of God. It is a doctrine which expresses itself in the life of the individual
Christian through the good deeds for which God designed us. This is
what we were created for; this is what, in Jesus Christ, God makes it
possible for us to do.

* **John 1. 29–34**
The fourth Gospel handles the story of Jesus' baptism in its own distinctive way. The role of the Baptist is reduced so that he is little more than a
commentator introducing the advent of Jesus and a witness to the descent
of the Holy Spirit upon him. The actual baptism of Christ is not described.

29    **There is the Lamb of God; it is he who takes away the sin of the world.** The Baptist's announcement is rich in OT association. The lamb was the sacrificial offering of the Passover. In early Christian theology Jesus was recognized as the new paschal lamb: 'Our Passover has begun; the sacrifice is offered—Christ himself' (1 Cor. 5.7), 'Praise and honour, glory and might, to him who sits on the throne and to the Lamb for ever and ever!' (Rev. 5.14, etc.). If the Aramaic word for 'servant' has been mistranslated as 'lamb' (though this is doubtful), then the announcement would look back to the Servant of God of Isaiah who was 'Led like a sheep to the slaughter', and who 'bore the sin of many' (Isa. 53.7,12). Lambs were offered daily in the temple, not however to seek the remission of sins: that oblation was made with a goat on the Day of Atonement (Lev. 16.21f). The figure of Christ as the Lamb of God has been associated with the Christian Eucharist from earliest times, and it is not impossible that it already had this association when the fourth Gospel was being written. Above all, **Lamb of God** is a synonym for Messiah. The Baptist saw in Jesus, who was of Davidic descent, the destined

31    leader of God's people: **I myself did not know who he was; but the very reason why I came, baptizing in water, was that he might be revealed to Israel.**

33    **This is he who is to baptize in Holy Spirit.** According to Mark, only Jesus saw the Spirit in the form of a dove. In Matthew and Luke the dove was seen by the people, but in the fourth Gospel it was John who saw the sign and interpreted it. His had been a preparatory ritual of baptism in water; Jesus was the one sent from God to baptize in Holy Spirit. This Gospel distinguishes between 'the spirit' as a gift to men from 'the Spirit' as the one who gives it (the Spirit is always spoken of as 'he', indicating that he is as personal as the Word). It is the Spirit who continues the work of the Word among the faithful: 'When he comes who is the Spirit of truth, he will guide you into all truth' (16.13). To be baptized in Holy Spirit is to be immersed in his life and power by Jesus. Baptism, then, is not just a forgiveness of sins; it is a full participation in the life of God.

34    **This is God's Chosen One, the Son of God** (NEB footnote). Israel of old thought of herself as the chosen people or son of God: 'When Israel was a boy, I loved him; I called my son out of Egypt'. The Baptist testifies that the only true Chosen One or Son of God is the man Jesus of Nazareth.

# EPIPHANY 2
Fourth Sunday after Christmas

*The First Disciples*

### Jeremiah 1. 4–10
The ministries of prophets such as Amos, Hosea, Isaiah, and Ezekiel resulted from an encounter with God; the details were different in each case, but the form was the same—a command from God that was irresistible, despite excuses the one called might offer. This passage describes the call of Jeremiah. Even before he was conceived in his mother's womb, his ministry as a prophet was determined in the eternal counsels of God. God 'knew' him for his own in a knowledge that is profound and unlimited—the meaning of the Hebrew word embraces what we understand by 'to love' and 'to elect'—and had set him apart (consecrated) him to a task that would give him the power to set up or overthrow not just Judah, but nations and kingdoms. The call of Jeremiah came about 627 or 626 B.C., when the weakening powers of Assyria and the rise of Babylon made the situation around Israel dangerously fluid. Jeremiah was subsequently much involved in the political situation that led up to the exile.

6   Jeremiah protested that he was too young: **I do not know how to speak; I am only a child.** He may at the time of his call have been about twenty years old. But God's purpose is paramount. The word of the Lord is placed in the prophet's mouth, a power which God injects into human history like a fire, or like a hammer that splinters rock (Jer. 5.14, 23.29). The authority which the prophet received from the Lord foreshadowed the authority which the apostles were to receive from Jesus Christ when they were commissioned (Matt. 16.19, 18.18, John 20.23, 1 Cor. 13.10).

(–19)
The prophet was given two signs: an almond tree to denote, through a play on the Hebrew words *shaked* and *shoked*, the watchfulness of God, and a tilting cauldron to symbolize the threat to the kingdom of Judah from Assyria in the north. Then he was told to denounce the apostasy of the nation under king Josiah without fear, for God would protect Jeremiah
18  as if he were a **fortified city, a pillar of iron, a wall of bronze.**

### Acts 26. 1, 9–18
Herod Agrippa II was brought up in the court of the emperor Claudius,

was made a king of Chalcis in the Lebanon region about A.D. 50, and later took over the tetrarchies of Philip and Lysanias (cf. Luke 3.1) with certain cities in Galilee and Peraea. Paul's speech, therefore, was given to the highest representative of the Roman power in that part of the empire. In our passage the apostle's flattering form of address (verses 2–3) and his assertion that his Christian faith in the resurrection of the body is shared by the Pharisees (verses 4–8) are omitted.

The stretching out of the hand is the gesture of an orator. Some versions says that Paul spoke with boldness and with the 'advocacy' or 'encouragement' of the Holy Spirit.

This is the third account of the conversion of Paul in Acts, and his description of the way he persecuted the Church is fuller than in the previous accounts. For Paul, a devout Pharisee, hunting down Christians was his duty as a devout Jew, and his zeal for the task led him to track down Christians among the Jews of the dispersion (though only Damascus is mentioned in earlier accounts, he refers here—perhaps rhetorically—
11 to **foreign cities**). The extent of the persecution following the martyrdom of Stephen was, perhaps, greater than indicated by Luke. The theophany affected the men travelling with Paul—the light denoted the presence of God to them as it had done to the shepherds at Bethlehem. The saying
14 about **kicking against the goad** is a Greek proverb for useless resistance: the ox kicking against the goad only succeeds in hurting itself.

Paul was called directly by the risen Christ in a vision to which he could not be disobedient; he was to go to the Gentiles as God's servant and convert them to the God of Israel. The commissioning is in the terms of an
15 OT prophet. **Rise to your feet and stand upright** recalls Ezek. 2.3. The charge to be a 'servant and witness' puts Paul on a level with the Twelve, although Luke does not give him the title of 'apostle'. Verses 17 and 18 echo the mission of the servant of God who was 'to open the eyes that are blind' because God would 'turn darkness into light before them' (Isa. 42.7, 16). The conversion of the Gentiles **from the dominion**
18 **of Satan to God**, had been a prophetic expectation in OT times; under the new covenant they would enjoy, like Judaeo-Christians, the forgiveness of sins which is effected by the breaking in of the Kingdom of God.
18 They would have **a place with those whom God has made his own.**

* Mark 1. 14–20
The conclusion of John the Baptist's ministry is the signal for the beginning of Jesus' proclamation of the gospel. The manifesto, drawn from Isa. 40.9, 52.7, and 61.1, sums up the substance of Christ's preaching

and the meaning of his public ministry. The time of waiting is over, the sovereign rule of God so long expected had begun, and the moment set by God for the coming of the Messiah had arrived. Jesus did not seek recognition as the messianic figure bringing in the Kingdom of God; on the contrary, he silenced such recognition as there was among his follow- ers and took careful steps to hide his identity. He deflected his hearers' attention away from himself and challenged them about their attitude to God's rule. The call to repent shows how men must respond to the Kingdom: there must be a radical reorientation of their lives towards God, and they must believe the gospel. This was the appeal of early Christian preachers, a turning of the whole person to the message which God's prophet brings us.

John the Baptist had called on people to repent, but his baptism was a sign of a washing away of sin; the repentance of those who turn to Christ requires much more, an acceptance of the gospel. Turning to God meant unconditional obedience, even to the extent of leaving homes and occu- pations and closest ties of kinship.

This is what the first disciples did when they were called. Simon, Andrew, James, and John were the closest of the Twelve—Simon, James, and John especially. They would hardly know what it meant to be 17 fishers of men, though early Christian art saw in the image a picture of the Church gathering men into the Kingdom (as, indeed, Christ himself did in Matt. 13.47). They would be drawing men out of the waters of this world into the net of the eschatological life of the age to come.

# EPIPHANY 2
## Fourth Sunday after Christmas

### The First Disciples

### I Samuel 3. 1–10

The notable almost miraculous feature of the call of Samuel was that it involved a child in or near the sanctuary of God in Shiloh. It was not a dream, for Samuel was awake; it was not a vision, for he did not see anything. And the fact that it occurred at a time when the voice of the Lord was seldom heard in Israel enhances its importance. The call took place towards the end of a vigil, before the sanctuary lamp which was kept alight all night had gone out. Eli the priest and Samuel were in the appointed places, their 'stations'. Samuel himself was too young to have had any personal knowledge of a direct communication from God. The three-fold repetition of the summons authenticated the experience and stressed its importance. When the old priest realised what had happened to Samuel, he ordered him to go back to his station and reply to the voice. This Samuel did: the servant of God had begun to respond to the divine call.

3    Tradition associated the **Ark of God** with the chest which had accompanied the Israelites in the wilderness. It was the symbol of the divine presence and the throne on which God rested. It contained the tablets of stone on which the commandments were written when Moses confronted God on mount Sinai, and as a visible memorial of the promise made by God to his people it was known as 'the Ark of the Covenant'. Measuring about $3\frac{3}{4}' \times 2\frac{1}{4}' \times 2\frac{1}{4}'$, it was a casket made of acacia wood overlaid with gold and carried by gold poles through gold rings. A movable shrine, it demonstrated that God is not limited to one sacred place but goes where his people go. When it was finally placed in the temple at Jerusalem, it rested in the holy of holies. Its cover, a slab of pure gold known as 'the mercy seat', was sprinkled with blood on the Day of Atonement for the sins of the people.

(–20)
The Lord told Samuel that the priestly family of Eli was to be set aside as unworthy because Eli had not rebuked his sons' blasphemous behaviour.
18  Eli accepted the news with touching resignation, **The Lord must do what is good in his eyes.** Samuel grew up to establish the all-important prophetic movement in Israel.

### Galatians 1. 11–24
One of Paul's objectives in writing this letter was to justify his claim to apostolic authority. To do this he recounted the circumstances of his conversion and the way in which the gospel was given to him by the Lord. It is problematical precisely what Paul intended to convey by **I did**
12  **not take it over from any man; no man taught it me; I received it through a revelation of Jesus Christ.** He wanted to stress that he received the gospel from the same source as the Twelve and that, like them, he had encountered the risen Christ. He could have meant that all, or most, of what he knew about the Christian faith came to him as a gift

of knowledge on the Damascus road. In that case he was claiming that God, who had set him apart from before his birth, had revealed his Son to him in such a way that Paul needed no further instruction. But he could also have meant that, as a result of his conversion, he needed no further persuasion from any Christian evangelist but, knowing the basis of the gospel, spent years afterwards meditating on it and working out its 14 implications. This he was well fitted to do for, as one who was **outstripping many of my Jewish contemporaries in my boundless devotion to the tradition of my ancestors,** he had been trained as a rabbi. The period in Arabia may have provided the opportunity for adjusting his ideas when he worked out his distinctive doctrine of salvation through faith and not through the Law. He also came to see that Christ was the Lord of all men, not just of the Jews, pointing Paul to his mission to the Gentiles.

We have here, then, a piece of autobiography. The details of the conversion are not given as fully as in Acts. Presumably they were well known to the Galatian Church. The way Paul said that he spent the seventeen years after his conversion (1.18 and 2.1) do not exactly fit in with the account of his life in Acts, but the difference can be explained if we take into account the possibility that Luke may have been selective in the sources he used.

\* **John 1. 35–51**
John the Baptist witnessed to Jesus as the paschal Lamb sent by God for the redemption of the world and, hearing this, two of the Baptist's disciples let John follow Christ. The process by which Jesus would draw all men to himself had begun. John was content to become less while Christ grew greater (3.30). The disciples asked where Jesus was staying; they assumed that, as a teacher, he must have a school somewhere. Jesus 39 replied by inviting them to **Come and see.** They accepted his invitation and spent the rest of the day with him, but that 'day' was to be the whole of their lives and the entrance to eternity. The place where Jesus 'stays' is the Christian community, where his disciples dwell in him and he in them (15.4ff).

One of the two was Andrew; the other may have been John the son of Zebedee. Andrew became the first home missionary, for his first action (next morning?—NEB footnote) was to find his brother Simon and tell 41 him that the greatest of all possible discoveries had been made, **We have found the Messiah.** Christ gave Simon the name of 'Rock Man', *Cephas*; *Petra* is the Greek equivalent of the Aramaic name. In the

Gospels Peter is more of a waverer than a rock, but Jesus was prophesying through that new name what Peter would one day become, after he had witnessed the resurrection and received the Holy Spirit.

Bethsaida, 'Fishertown', was also the home of Philip and Nathanael, who is usually identified with Bartholomew: the name means 'gift of

45 God'. Philip told him, **We have met the man spoken of by Moses in the Law, and by the prophets: it is Jesus son of Joseph, from Nazareth.** He believed Jesus was the person to whom so many passages in the OT pointed, the Messiah, the Christ. Nathanael was dubious. The Messiah was supposed to be *incognito*. Besides, Nazareth was not even mentioned in the OT as the Christ's place of origin. Again the invitation was repeated, **Come and see:** the best way of presenting the gospel is to see it in action in men's lives. And when Nathanael came, Jesus recognized him as one who had nothing false in him (the RSV phrase, 'without guile', hints at Gen. 32.28: Jacob's new name was 'Israel', but he remained

47 a man of guile; Nathanael, without guile, is **an Israelite worthy of the name**). Christ, the good shepherd, had recognized one of his own sheep

48 (10.3). To a Jew the words **under the fig-tree** would suggest the domestic bliss of a place for studying the Law, for the rabbis recommended men to meditate on the law 'under their own vine and fig-tree'. Nathanael

49 pronounced Jesus as **Son of God . . ., king of Israel.** He had not yet understood that Jesus is the Saviour of all men and his Kingdom is not of this world.

The passage closes with the promise to Nathanael and the others,

51 **I tell you all, you shall see heaven wide open, and God's angels ascending and descending upon the Son of Man.** The allusion to Gen. 28.12 is unmistakable: 'Jacob dreamt that he saw a ladder, which rested on the ground with its top reaching to heaven, and angels of God were going up and down upon it.' The vision reveals the office of the one who bears the mysterious title 'Son of Man': he was to be the link between heaven and earth, and his destiny was to be played out in both.

# EPIPHANY 3
Fifth Sunday after Christmas

## *The First Sign: The Wedding at Cana*

### Exodus 33.(7–11)

Moses was at mount Sinai with the people of Israel. They had arrived there on their way to the promised land. They had a mobile Tent of the Presence outside their encampment for divine guidance, and they had the Ark for the two tablets of the Tokens. Moses acted as intermediary between God and the people; only he and his young assistant Joshua went into the tent to speak to the Lord.

### 12–23

The leader was anxious because he had to take the people into strange territory. He asked God who would be sent to go with him. In doing so, Moses invoked the relationship which God had established with him when he had revealed to Moses the divine Name and told him that he had found favour with God. **Teach me to know thy way, so that I can know thee and continue in favour with thee, for this nation is thy own people,** Moses said. The Lord promised that he himself would go with Moses and the people in person and that he would set their mind at rest (in Num. 10.33 the Ark of the Covenant of the Lord set out a day's journey ahead of the company to find a site in Canaan). The request and the reply are repeated in verses 15–17, with the added indication that it was the presence of God in Israel that made the nation distinct from all the other peoples on earth.

Then Moses, emboldened by the response to his first request, made another. He asked the Lord to grant him a full manifestation of the divine glory. This was daring indeed, for it was believed that God is so holy that he cannot be seen by the eyes of sinful men. Man must perish if he looks on God (Exod. 20.19). Moses (Exod. 3.6) and Elijah (1 Kings 19.13) and even the seraphim covered their faces in his presence (Isa. 6.2). The Lord did not grant all that Moses requested, but he pronounced his name in the hearing of Moses, an act indicative of an intimacy with God of a very profound kind, and he permitted Moses to see his back, not his face. In Exod. 24.9–11 the vision of God is presumably at some distance; here God passed by a cleft in the rock on which Moses stood.

Elijah was granted a similar favour (1 Kings 19. 11f). Moses and Elijah, then, were the only two in the OT who looked on God in an intimate way,

93

and it is they who shared the glory of God in the transfiguration of Christ
on the mountain (Matt. 17.3, etc.).

### 1 John 1. 1–4

The theme of 1 John is communion with God: eternal life, which depends
on the incarnation of Jesus Christ, and on brotherly love within the
apostolic community of those who believe in him. This passage is the
prologue to that epistle, introducing this theme.

1    As in the Gospel, Jesus Christ is the divine Logos, **the word of life.**
The pre-existence of the divine Logos is acknowledged in the first few
words of the passage, and then the author, speaking on behalf of the
apostolic witnesses, declared that the Logos made eternal life known in the
historical Jesus. A succession of verbs, used to emphasise the encounter
with the historical Jesus—**heard it, seen it, looked upon it**—sum up
all that is contained in the word 'epiphany'. It was the act of God in
Christ Jesus to manifest himself in human terms.

The manifestation of God in Christ was not made to the apostles for
their own benefit, however; it was made so that they, as witnesses to what
God has done and is doing, might declare it to others and with them
share in the common life which joins them to God the Father and his
4    Son Jesus Christ. **And we write this in order that the joy of us all
may be complete.** It is only as others share in that life that Christians
themselves find fulfilment.

### * John 2. 1–11

The fourth evangelist's word for 'miracle' is 'sign', an act of Jesus Christ
which is not simply a wonderful demonstration of power but one which
shows forth or manifests the meaning of his life, his ministry, his death,
11   and resurrection. It was through these signs that **Jesus revealed his
glory and led his disciples to believe in him.**

The first sign, the changing of water into wine at the wedding at Cana-
in-Galilee, has long been associated with the feast of the Ephipany
because of its significance as a manifestation. The circumstances were
straightforward; Mary's remark was hardly a request for a miraculous
5    intervention by Jesus, yet he seemed to take it so: **My hour has not
yet come.** It was not the time to show forth his glory, which in the
fourth Gospel reaches its culmination in the *hour*, the death in the cross.
We note in passing that Mary was present when Jesus manifested his
glory the first time in this sign; she was also present when he manifested
his glory on the cross (19.25–27). This was the hour when he showed his

glory: it was when he was crucified and returned to the Father's right hand. Elsewhere in the Gospel Christ said the hour was determined by the Father and cannot be anticipated. But the miracle worked through Mary's comment is a prophetic sign of the hour. The reluctance of Christ to respond to the invitation from his mother is understandable if we remember that he had set aside the temptation to use his authority for his own purposes (Matt. 4.3f, Luke 4.2–4). He performed the miracle for the simple reason that he wished to save his host embarrassment.

It was an appropriate occasion for the first manifestation of the glory of God in Christ, for a wedding feast was a parable of the messianic kingdom. Jesus sanctified marriage by his presence at Cana, and made marriage a symbol of his own relationship with his Church. The substance of the miracle has been variously interpreted: the purifying waters of the old covenant now give place to the superabundant wine of the new covenant; the new life that is Christ's gift replaces the old. Large quantities of liquid were involved, between 120 and 180 gallons! Christ's wine is the best. The secret of its quality was known, not to the guests or even to the steward, but to the ordinary servants who had drawn the water.

# EPIPHANY 3
## Fifth Sunday after Christmas

*The First Sign: The New Temple*

1 Kings 8. 22–30

Solomon offered his prayer for the dedication of the new temple in Jeru-
22 salem **standing in front of the altar . . . spread out his hands;** that was the normal attitude for prayer in the ancient Near East. To stand is the attitude of an inferior before a deity, who is normally represented sitting. That it was Solomon who offered the prayer and not a priest reflects the sacerdotal status of the king in pre-exilic times. The monarch was not only the divinely appointed sovereign over the people; he was also the mediator between God and the community.

The prayer, which shows signs of later editing, opens with an ascription to the Lord reminding him of the covenant he had made with the people at Sinai, conditional upon their faithfulness, and recalls also the new covenant which the Lord made with David and his house. A new element in the religion of Israel, this is elaborated: **Thou hast kept thy promise** 24–25 **to thy servant David my father; by thy deeds this day thou hast fulfilled what thou didst say to him in words.** Now therefore, O Lord God of Israel, keep this promise of thine to thy servant David my father: 'You shall never want for a man appointed by me to sit on the throne of Israel, if only your sons look to their ways and walk before me as you have walked before me.' The introduction of the promises to David into the covenant prepared the way for the conception of the Messiah as a descendant of this monarch, as one of the house of Jesse.

Solomon's prayer goes on to acknowledge that the Lord cannot be limited to a building. The temple is only a place where, or towards which, men can address their petitions to God. He is present only in the sense that his Name is there. God's true presence, where he ultimately receives ('hears') all intercession, is his transcendent dwelling in heaven.

### 1 Corinthians 3. 10–17

The reading comes from that part of the Corinthian correspondence where the apostle introduced the concept of the Church as a building—a concept common in other NT writings. Where the reading opens, he developed the metaphor, seeing himself as a **skilled** ('wise' with God's 10 wisdom) **master-builder,** one who supervises the work of others. As the first evangelist at Corinth, he had laid the foundations of the local church there, leaving it to others to continue the superstructure. Perhaps he had in mind Apollos and Peter, who seem to have visited Corinth as well. By **the foundation,** however, Paul means, not the first converts in themselves, but their faith in Jesus Christ who is himself the only true foundation of the Church. There can be no other foundation, such as a party loyalty to a particular apostle (there were groups in the Corinthian congregation who claimed a special allegiance to Apollos or to Peter, 1.12–13).

If it is an error to attempt to build on the wrong foundations, it is another error to use the wrong materials. Paul listed the various kinds of materials, some worthy, some unworthy, and pointed out that when they are tested the unworthy materials will be burnt away. The day of judgement will reveal the true value of what each has contributed to the building up 13 of the Church. **For that day dawns in fire, and the fire will test the worth of each man's work.**

God's approval of work done is expressed in terms of a reward; God's disapproval, however, the apostle sees in terms of destruction by fire. The day of judgement will be a day of conflagration, and the workman who is caught in his own badly-constructed house will run the risk of being engulfed by flames unless he escapes by a quick dash through them.

Paul then develops the metaphor a stage further by describing the 16 Church as **God's temple**. The building erected on the foundation of Jesus Christ is the meeting place for God and man, where man offers God the worship and obedience due to him. The presence of God in this living temple of the baptized is effective through the Holy Spirit. The apostle warns that those who destroy the Church will themselves be destroyed. How this destruction of the Church might be brought about the apostle does not specify. He was, of course, thinking of the Church as a local congregation; and perhaps he had in mind those who tried to import elements into it—excessive legalism, for example, from Judaism—to destroy its nature as a family living under the grace of God. Congregations have been destroyed in Christian history through heresies as well as through persecutions.

\* **John 2. 13–22**
In the synoptic gospels the cleansing of the temple occurs before the passover when Jesus was crucified. In John it is the opening act of Jesus' public ministry. It therefore assumes the character of a prophetic demonstration of the Messiah's advent: 'Suddenly the Lord whom you seek will come to his temple. . . . Who can endure the day of his coming? Who can stand firm when he appears?' (Mal. 3.1–2); 'When that time comes, no trader shall again be seen in the house of the Lord of Hosts' (Zech. 14.21).

The cattle, sheep, and pigeons were sold in the temple precincts for the purposes of the sacrificial cult—their suitability as oblations was guaranteed by the temple authorities—and the money-changers exchanged coins bearing effigies forbidden in the temple for the shekel and half-shekels required for paying religious dues and offerings. Even though the traders made a profit out of their business—Jesus said they were making the temple 'a robber's cave' (Mark 11.17)—their stalls must have been convenient for pilgrims and worshippers. According to this evangelist, however, it was not the dishonesty of the traders that Jesus attacked but 16 the pursuit of commerce within the holy place. **Take them out; you must not turn my Father's house into a market.** The personal pronoun stresses the unique sonship of Jesus. It is *his* Father's house that they are desecrating. Judgement begins at the house of God, and Jesus the Messiah began his ministry by acting judgementally in the temple 17 to expose the Jews' impiety. **Zeal for thy house will destroy me** (Ps. 69.9) asks God to vindicate the righteous man who has been oppressed because of his eagerness for the things of God. Here the verse becomes a prophecy that the zeal which Jesus showed would lead to his own destruction.

Jesus' answer to the Jews' request for a sign appears evasive. In the fourth Gospel signs are used to confirm faith, not to convince sceptics. So Jesus refused to give them a sign and uttered a warning instead. The unbelief of the Jews will lead to the destruction of the temple, but Jesus will raise a new temple in three days—a saying which was quoted in a garbled version against him at his trial (Mark 14.58). Typically the Jews missed the point. Herod began his rebuilding of the temple about 20 B.C. so it must have been completed—or the major part of it completed (Josephus records that it was not entirely finished until A.D. 63) by about 20 A.D. 26, a year or two before this incident. **Are you going to raise it again in three days?** they asked him.

21     But Jesus **was speaking of his body.** His resurrected physical body is the new temple, but, although John does not say so here, we may understand that the new temple is also his Body in the Pauline sense, the Christian Church. Thus the cleansing of the temple at Jerusalem takes on a more profound meaning. It was not only a demonstration against an improper use of the Lord's house; it was also a sign that the sacrificial worship associated with that house was coming to an end, because of the one perfect and sufficient sacrifice which the paschal Lamb of God was to offer in Jerusalem in two years' time (the cleansing of the temple took place during the first of three Passovers mentioned by John, 6.4 and 13.1, the last one being the occasion of the crucifixion). As the gospel replaced the Law, so Jesus replaced the temple where God dwelt and where men worship him. The new temple, the community of which Christ is the living Head, fulfils the prophecy of Isaiah, quoted in Mark 11.17, that God's house 'shall be called a house of prayer for all nations'.

# EPIPHANY 4
## Sixth Sunday after Christmas

*The Friend of Sinners*

### Hosea 14. 1–7

The book of the prophet Hosea, which teaches the faithfulness and for-giveness of God in terms of a husband-wife image, ends with a form of confession and absolution that might be called a rite for a liturgy of penance. Although no actual service is proposed, it contains the necessary elements: verses 1–2a, an exhortation to repentance; 2b–3, a form of confession said by the people; and 4–7, a promise of forgiveness spoken by the Lord.

2    The people were to approach God: **Come with your words ready.** Theirs was not an approach through the sacrificial cult. The phrase **with cattle from our pens** is better rendered **with fruit from our lips** (NEB footnote and most commentators). What they renounced was a
3 military alliance with Assyria (**horses to ride** means additional cavalry and chariotry) and idolatry, which the prophet has often denounced in his book.

   God's forgiveness is expressed in terms of healing, of loving them
4 freely, **of my own bounty**, of turning away anger, and of fertility—the opposite of those disasters which had been brought on Israel by her sin-fulness. The effect of God's love is described by a comparison with plant life. He is like the dews necessary to bring fruitfulness to vegetation during the dry summers; his permanence is like the deep roots of the giant trees of Lebanon; his beauty is like the olive tree, and his scent like the slopes of Lebanon, where the moist atmosphere rises among flowers and shrubs. The picture is changed in verse 7 for one of a forgiven Israel living in God's love like a man dwelling securely under a fig or vine-tree, enjoying the abundance of the harvest, especially the bread and the wine, the corn and the vine.

### Philemon 1–16

The punishment due to a runaway slave in the ancient world was severe. He could be executed. The situation in which Paul intervened in this letter, therefore, was an extremely delicate one. Philemon was the head of a household, perhaps in Colossae, who had been converted by Paul (19) and whose dwelling was used as a meeting-place for a Christian congregation consisting of his own relatives (Apphia, his wife?, and

Archippus) and his servants and perhaps also people from the neighbourhood. It was a typical arrangement for a local church in the early centuries.
One of his slaves, Onesimus ('useful' or 'profitable'), had run away, probably with stolen goods, had met Paul in prison, and had been converted
or brought to repentance by the apostle. Paul was now sending him back
to his master with a promise to repay any debts outstanding.

 8 The apostle might have reminded Philemon that it was his Christian
duty to forgive the slave and accept him back, **I might make bold to
point out your duty.** But instead he appealed to him as a Christian
brother to restore him as one who is more than a slave. There is a gentle
 11 pun on Onesimus' name in the phrases **once so little use to you, but
now useful indeed.**

Against the background of slavery as an institution in the society
within which the Church had to work, there is much in this passage which
demonstrates how the relationship between Christians transcends social
barriers and institutions. The case of Philemon gave Paul the opportunity
to call for a practical demonstration of love between members of the
Christian community with profound theological meaning. The act of
forgiveness of a master for a slave is a reflection of the forgiveness of God,
who saves men from the slavery of sin and accepts them as children, as
brothers of his Son, Jesus Christ.

In a letter to the church at Ephesus, written about A.D. 100, Ignatius
refers to a bishop at Ephesus called Onesimus, 'a man whose love is
beyond words' (Eph. 1.3). If he was once Philemon's slave, then Paul's
letter of recommendation and Philemon's act of clemency brought a great
blessing on the Church.

\* **Mark 2. 13–17**
The passage links two incidents demonstrating Jesus Christ's friendly
relationships with the moral and religious outcasts. The Jewish principle
of separation from what was unclean was carried to an extreme degree by
the Pharisees, whose name meant 'those who are separated'. Although
they are frequently depicted as Christ's enemies, many of them were men
of high principle and integrity; Psalm 119 represents the ideal of their
party.

The call of Levi was similar to the call of the other disciples in this
Gospel; it took place in the same vicinity, by the lake-side, and the man
called was busy with his profession. But the power of Christ was such that
immediately the man left what he was doing, followed Jesus, and entertained him at his house. It was this that caused the criticism. Table-

fellowship was a sign and pledge of intimacy in the ancient world, and it was inconceivable to a Jew that a man of God should take a meal with one who not only was a swindler but also served a foreign authority. Public taxes in the Roman empire were farmed out to contractors who were allowed to make their own profits before they paid the revenue into the state treasury. It was explicitly required that one must avoid such company.

But Jesus' conduct was not determined by the law. He acted because of his unique status as Messiah, as the one sent by God to bring forgiveness to sinners who repent. He did not need to fear the contagion of human 17 sinfulness, and he said as much in his use of the doctor-patient parallel. **It is not the healthy that need a doctor, but the sick; I did not come to invite virtuous people but sinners.** The 'virtuous' are not those who are saved (healthy) but those who think they are so free of sin that they have no need of a saviour. The danger of the Pharisaic ideal was that it blinded its followers to their need for salvation so that they were unable to recognize the Messiah in their midst. Christ's use of the word 'invite' suggests that in his mind was the heavenly banquet which, in traditional Jewish imagery, was the destined reward of the righteous.

Matt. 9.9 identifies Levi with one of the Twelve, Matthew, probably because he too was a tax-gatherer. Capernaum, on the northern shore of the Sea of Galilee, was an important station on the route which carried trade from the cities of the Decapolis to the Mediterranean ports. On the frontier between the territories of Herod Antipas and Philip and a centre of the fishing industry on the lake, it was an obvious place for a profitable customs-house.

# EPIPHANY 4
## Sixth Sunday after Christmas

*Life for the World*

### 1 Kings 10. 1–13

The Queen of Sheba was one of the most notable of Solomon's visitors. She made the 1,200-mile journey from Arabia by caravan, posed riddles in true oriental fashion to test his wisdom, and was then entertained by him on a lavish scale. She was queen of Sabaeans (of Saba), a Semitic people who lived in what is now the Yemen. As merchant traders, they were surpassed only by the Phoenicians and gained enormous wealth through transshipping luxury goods from India to the north-east—gold, perfume, incense, spices, precious stones—which stocked the bazaars of towns like Tyre. The degree of their wealth was reflected in the gift the queen bought to the king.

The real significance of the visit was probably to mark out trading agreements with Solomon who, with king Hiram of Tyre, was sending a merchant fleet to corner a market in this luxury trade from India. Tradition has elaborated the significance of the visit: it said that she became a wife of Solomon and bore him a son, Menelik, who later migrated to Abyssinia. The present royal house of Ethiopia, who are Christians, claim descent from Solomon and the Queen of Sheba. For early Christian teachers the abundance of wealth attributed to Solomon was as nothing compared with the 'unfathomable riches' (Eph. 3.8) offered by the one who is 'greater than Solomon' (Matt. 12.42).

### Ephesians 3. 8–19

The Pauline writer opens this passage with an expression of thanksgiving for the apostle's mission to the Gentiles and, in so doing, speaks of the
8 gospel as a **hidden purpose**. (RSV, JB 'mystery' in the contemporary sense of that word. See p. 50) of incalculable richness. It is the treasure hid in the field which the apostle now has the privilege of revealing and explaining to the world.

The Greek original of verse 9 is difficult. A literal translation would be something like this: 'To me . . . was this grace, to preach to the nations the unsearchable riches of Christ, and to bring to light what (is) the stewardship (*oikonomia*—a household term) of the mystery hidden in the ages from God'. JB translates it: 'I . . . have been entrusted with this special grace, not only of proclaiming to the pagans the infinite treasure of Christ, but also of explaining (showing clearly to all, *Vulg.*) how the mystery is to be dispensed'. Earlier the letter had spoken of the unity of Jews and Gentiles in the Body of Christ; here the writer is asserting that the God, who brings about that unity through the redeeming work of Christ, is also the God who creates and rules all things. So the unity achieved in the Church is a permanent revelation of the very essence of God's nature. He is the one whose nature is love, and love unites men to him and to one another.

The mystery now revealed is 'that through the Gospel the Gentiles are joint heirs with the Jews, part of the same body, sharers together in

10 the promises made in Christ Jesus' (verse 6). The reference to **rulers and authorities in the realms of heaven** can mean that the Church declares the purpose of God to all the universe, but it is more likely to imply that the existence of the Church is a sign to the cosmic powers of evil that they have been defeated in the victorious purpose of God. The priestly office of Christ, taught in other NT writings (e.g. Rom. 5.2, 1 Pet.

12 3.18, Rev. 1.5f), is brought forward: **In him we have access to God with freedom, in the confidence born of trust in him.** Paul's sufferings, incurred in the course of his efforts to bring the gospel to the Gentiles, should not be interpreted as evidence of divine displeasure.

13 **Indeed, they are your glory**; they spring from God's work of salvation among the Gentiles.

The idea of glory is taken up in a prayer of intercession to the Father on behalf of Paul's readers, outlined in verses 14ff. There is a play on the words *pater*, Father, and *patria*, family. One meaning can be that every family, Christian or not, derives its paternity from God's overall Fatherhood (*patria* = a group of people descended from a common ancestor). Another meaning, taking the NEB footnote, could be that God's whole family, the Church militant and triumphant, Christians together with angels in heaven, is united under his Fatherhood. Paul prayed that his

17 readers might be granted **strength and power through his Spirit in your inner being, that through faith Christ may dwell in your hearts in love:** that the innermost part of their personalities, that part which is laid hold of and transformed by the Holy Spirit, might be so inspired that they might accept all the love that Christ has for them. The vastness of that love can only be hinted at in spatial terms of breadth and

19 length and height and depth. **So that you may attain to the fullness of being, the fullness which God requires** (NEB footnote): in this way a Christian enters into that new creation in Christ for which he is destined by God.

\* **John 4. 7–14**
Jesus' request for a drink startled the woman, not only because the relationships between Jews and Samaritans were such that the common use of vessels was regarded as undesirable, but also because the rabbis taught that a man should not speak to a woman in a public place, even if she was his wife. But Jesus discerned the woman's need and took the initiative —as, indeed, God always does in dealing with men and women. If she

10 knew the gift of God and the identity of the speaker, she could have **living water.** The phrase is ambiguous. Christ meant 'the water that gives life'.

The Samaritan woman thought he meant the flowing fresh water of a stream as distinct from the static water in the well. The well was there because it had been discovered by Jacob. Samaritans were proud of their descent from the patriarchs. Is Jesus greater than Jacob, asked the woman, in that he can provide a stream where the patriarch could only dig a well? Jesus then explained that the water he offered was a new kind, for 14 whoever drinks the water that I shall give him will never suffer thirst any more. He used similar terms later in this Gospel: 'I am the bread of life. Whoever comes to me shall never be hungry, and whoever believes in me shall never be thirsty' (6.35). The water, like the bread, remains in a man and nourishes him for eternal life.

The grace which God brings to the believer is often spoken of in the OT in terms of quenching thirst: 'Like as the hart desireth the water-brooks: so longeth my soul after thee O God. My soul is athirst for God, yea even for the living God: when shall I come to appear before the presence of God?' (Ps. 42.1–2); 'Come, all who are thirsty, come, fetch water; come, you who have no food, buy corn and eat.' (Isa. 55.1). The living water is the presence of God in the spirit of man, the activity of the Holy Spirit whom Christ sends to the Christian who seeks him. In the fourth Gospel the saying also had a baptismal connotation. Just before this passage is the account of how Jesus' disciples were baptizing in Judaea, and the conversation with the woman is reminiscent of a baptismal catechesis. To be baptized is to accept God's gift of 'living water', the name of Jesus Christ and the indwelling of the Holy Spirit.

## EPIPHANY 5
Seventh Sunday after Christmas

*Christ Today*

Joel 2. 15–19, 21–22
Sometime about the fourth century B.C. a locust plague in Judah prompted the prophet Joel to warn the people that the day of the Lord would be a similar but even more terrible experience. An act of penitence was to be proclaimed for the whole nation, with fasting and prayer, in which all would be invited to participate—elders, children, babes-in-arms, the

newly-wed, and the priests. The blowing of a trumpet was the normal
call to worship. The penitential procession was led by the priests into the
temple. The prayer offered asked the Lord for mercy. Surely in the face
of such a disaster other nations will ask if Israel's God has deserted them?

From verse 18 the prophet tells of God's response to the people's
penitence. His love and his compassion were rekindled for them. They
would be saved from the locusts, and food—bread, wine, oil—would be
provided in abundance again. Other nations would no longer reproach
them. Fear would be removed from the earth.

The distinction between a 'fast' and an 'abstinence' belongs to the later
history of the Church.

## 2 Corinthians 3. 4–11

Having explained why he has not visited them, Paul at this point in his
letter reminded the Church in Corinth that he had no need to make such
explanations, because his relationship with them and their relationship
with God in Jesus Christ were such that they could accept him as the
divinely appointed minister of the new covenant. He then went on to
explain how this new light reached Christian converts through an apostle,
using two illustrations from the Old Testament.

The first of these is that of the law, 'written not with ink but with the
Spirit of the living God, written not on stone tablets but on the pages of
the human heart' (verse 3 comes just before our passage, but it is taken
up again in verse 6). Behind this sentence are the words of Jeremiah about
God writing his law in the inward parts of his people (Jer. 31.33) and
those of Ezekiel about God giving his people hearts of flesh instead of
hearts of stone (Ezek. 11.19). These concepts are contrasted with the law
of Moses inscribed on tablets of stone (Exod. 31.18). The apostle could
write with complete confidence because his 'qualification' was found not
6 in himself but in God: **it is he who has qualified us to dispense his
new covenant—a covenant expressed not in a written document,
but in a spiritual bond.** This was what made Paul a minister of the
new covenant which, being in the Spirit and not in a document, gives life
instead of death.

For his second illustration Paul turned to the story in Exod. 34.29–35,
which described how Moses had to put a veil over his face after he had
been communing with God because, when he came near to the people of
Israel, the divine glory was reflected in it. Moses was a foreshadowing, or a
type, of Christ. Just as the Israelites saw the glory of God reflected in
Moses' face, so Christians possessing the Holy Spirit see the divine glory

reflected in Jesus Christ. But how much greater is the glory of the new covenant, since it works for the salvation of man instead of his condemna-
11 tion, as the old dispensation did. **For if that which was soon to fade had its moment of splendour, how much greater is the splendour of that which endures!**

The letter continues by teaching that the divine glory manifested in Christ is reflected in the lives of Christians through the Spirit (see Lent 4 Year 1).

* ## Mark 2. 18–22

Jesus' coming, and the good news which he brought of the Kingdom of God, were above all occasions for rejoicing. Fasting may have been an appropriate way of preparing for the Kingdom, but now the Kingdom was among them, Jesus told his disciples, fasting and mourning were as out of place as they would be at a marriage. The teaching arose out of the question put to Jesus about fasting. Some people asked why his disciples did not keep a fast as the disciples of John and the Pharisees' followers were doing. The only obligatory fast for the Jew was *Yom Kippur*, the Day of Atonement. Special fasts were declared in times of emergency, and some individuals kept a fast on Mondays and Thursdays (*Didache* 8.1). And Jesus himself at one point in his ministry laid down conditions for keeping a fast (Matt. 6.16–18).

In the ancient east the bridegroom rather than the bride was the focus of the nuptial festivities, and the party ended when the bridegroom took his bride to his home. Behind Jesus' reply there may have been the idea of himself as the heavenly bridegroom who had come to claim his bride the Church. But the idea was not developed, and verse 20 departs from it: **the time will come when the bridegroom will be taken away**
20 **from them, and on that day they will fast** (the crucifixion). Some commentators believe that this verse was a later addition, perhaps pre-Marcan, included to justify the Church's practice of fasting after the resurrection, the ascension, and the gift of the Holy Spirit. A similar thought lies behind John 16.19–20, 'A little while, and you will not see me. . . . But though you will be plunged into grief, your grief will be turned into joy'.

For the new age of the Kingdom of God a new spirit is necessary in religious practices. God's new order requires a new kind of spirituality. Jesus introduced two similes to help his hearers understand what he meant: old material will not take the strain of a new patch that pulls on it when it begins to shrink; and new wine (which was poured off from the vats into jars or skins before it had finished fermentation) needed new and supple wineskins, not old and brittle ones which would burst under the pressure. The deeper meaning of what Christ said rests on his office as Messiah and the eschatological nature of his advent. But this is entirely lost on his readers. To the evangelist and his Christian readers, however, the signs are there.

## EPIPHANY 5
Seventh Sunday after Christmas

*Christ Today*

### Lamentations 3. 19-26

The passage is taken from the five liturgical poems which arose out of the disasters of the Babylonian invasions; they were probably composed by a group who escaped the capture, looting, and destruction of Jerusalem in 597 and 586 B.C., and who saw God at work even in the midst of the disasters. Sorrow for what had happened led to repentance for the sins of the people, and out of this repentance was born the hope that God would at length be victorious.

The use of the first person plural is a feature of that part of the third poem from which this extract is taken; as in some of the Psalms, the individual spoke for the whole community. The poet's conviction that God would yet again deliver his people was based on the knowledge
23 that God's love and compassion never fail; they are new every morning. Patience is what is required of his people, and expectancy, for in the Lord they have all that they need.

### 1 Thessalonians 5. 12-24

The apostle had been asked, What about the Christians who die before the return of the Lord? They will be at no disadvantage, he had said; but Christians who are alive now are living in the messianic age, and the chief characteristic of this age is joy. In his final admonitions in this letter, therefore, he described the kind of living that should have prevailed in the Thessalonian congregation if it was infused by joy. Interlocking love and support are features of the true Christian community, giving respect to
15 those who lead and encouragement to others. Always aim at doing

the best you can for each other and for all men. The life of love and peace should overspill the bounds of Church membership into society at large.

Out of the joy which God gives his people through the Spirit springs continuous prayer, especially praise and thanksgiving. To give thanks 18 whatever happens; for this is what God in Christ wills for you, is to express a faith in God which knows that, even if the worst happens to us, the circumstances have within them or around them a victory for God in our lives. That victory can be appropriated by thanking God in faith in the midst of what appears at the time to be disastrous.

19 Do not stifle inspiration, and so not despise prophetic utter-
20 ances. Put everything to the test (NEB footnote). Christians must respect the charismatic gifts which accompany the outpouring of the Holy Spirit on the Church. The Thessalonians knew this, for they had 'rejoiced in the Holy Spirit' when they responded to the gospel, even though it had meant 'grave suffering' for them (1.6). But the charisms must be tested for the good of everyone. Counterfeit manifestations must be avoided. Finally, Paul wrote a short prayer, invoking the power of God upon his readers that in every one of them the entire personality—
23 spirit, soul, and body—would be preserved and kept holy until the
24 Second Coming. They must depend utterly upon God for this: He who calls you is to be trusted; he will do it. Behind Paul's prayer there may be a liturgical formula in use at the time.

* Matthew 20. 1–15
The parable of the vineyard owner comes at the end of a series of Christ's sayings on the Kingdom of heaven. Jesus was on his way to Jerusalem for the final act of his ministry, and the evangelist collected in this part of his book Christ's teaching on the nature of this Kingdom, the kind of life his disciples were to follow, and the position that the Kingdom would have in relation to the old Israel. Peter had asked, 'What will there be for us?' Christ had replied with the promise of twelve thrones and the warning, 'Many who are first will be last, and the last first' (19.30).

The setting of the parable is vintage-time in Palestine, the period of the year when extra labour was required. Normally the landowner would hire all the men he needed early in the morning, but this particular landowner in the parable had miscalculated his labour requirements and took the unusual step of hiring additional men at different times through 6 the day, right up to an hour before sunset. He was bound by law (Lev. 19.13) to pay the stipulated wage to those who had done a day's work; but, with regard to the rest, he could either wait until they came again next day and made up the full time or, if the work was finished, pay a fair wage for the number of hours worked. On this occasion he instructed 8 his steward to pay everyone a full day's wage, beginning with those who came last.

The parable has had various applications. It could refer to those who respond to the gospel later in life as contrasted with those who have been Christians since childhood. Or it could refer to the contrast between the people of Israel who have been covenanted to God and served him through centuries of success and failure, and the Gentiles who have been invited into God's vineyard only recently (in Matthew's day). The lesson is the same for each application. God has fulfilled his covenant generously. The Kingdom is his gift. His wisdom will not disappoint anyone but should lead them to praise him more and more for his goodness. Peter's question had been irrelevant. Positions and rewards in the Kingdom of heaven cannot be assessed on the world's ideas of what is fair and just.

The image of a vineyard is used in the OT extensively with reference to Israel, and it appears as a symbol for the nation on the coins of the Maccabean period. 'The vineyard of the Lord of Hosts is Israel, and the men of Judah are the plant he cherished' (Isa. 5.7); 'Thou didst bring a vine out of Egypt' (Ps. 80.7).

# EPIPHANY 6
Eighth Sunday after Christmas

*Christ and Complacency*

### Isaiah 1. 10–17
Isaiah castigated the ritual of the temple because it was divorced from righteous conduct—a common theme among the pre-exilic prophets. Addressing them in the names of the two cities who were symbols of unfaithfulness and wickedness, he declared that their sumptuous sacrificial oblations were worthless in the eyes of God.

Although we cannot recover the precise circumstances under which

this oracle was pronounced, we can guess that it was before 735 B.C., when Judah came under the power of Assyria. Perhaps it was spoken in the temple on a festival, calling on the rulers and the people in Jerusalem to
10 listen to the word (the instruction) of God, given authoritatively by the prophet and later written down. Their wickedness included blood on
15 your hands—perhaps more than the worthless sacrifices: unjust executions or murders?—and a neglect of those in need, the oppressed, the widows, and the orphans.

The attack on the cult does not necessarily mean that the prophet wished these religious observances to be abolished. Rather, Isaiah was insisting that faithfulness to the Lord and obedience to his covenant law was the essence of true religion; without these the worship of the temple was a mockery and offensive to God.

The prophecy gives us a vivid picture of worship in Isaiah's day: the succession of sacrifices, rams, bulls, sheep, and goats being driven into the temple for slaughter; the processions of worshippers entering the gates of the courts; the days and seasons calculated by observations of the moon interspersed with the regular assemblies on the sabbath; the long
16 and numerous prayers offered with hands outstretched. Wash yourselves and be clean, he told the worshippers, an injunction which applies to every Christian congregation.

## 1 Corinthians 3. 18–23

The apostle continued his discussion about wisdom and folly, which arose out of his opposition to party conflicts in Corinth, by showing how false were the premises on which both the Corinthians' arguments and partisanship rested. Those who think themselves wise fall into the error of self-deception, for no one can advance in divine wisdom through human wisdom. On the contrary, if a man is to advance in divine wisdom, he
19 must be prepared to negate the wisdom of the world. The wisdom of this world is folly in God's sight because—and here the apostle quotes scripture, Job. 5.13 and Ps. 94.11, to give authority to his conclusions— even those who expound wordly wisdom are, in any case, no more than instruments in the hand of God. Since all men are only God's instruments, it is equally ridiculous to set one's ambitions and hopes in any man. You may think of yourselves as belonging to Paul, Apollos, and Cephas, he told them, but in fact you are not these men's, but Christ's.
22 The addition of the world, life, and death, the present and the future to the apostles' names seems puzzling at first sight. Obviously the world does not belong to the Church in the same way that Paul did.

But Paul's thought had moved on as he wrote the names of his apostolic colleagues to the truth that, as Christ is sovereign Lord over the apostles, the Corinthians, and the Church, so he is also Lord of these other things—he has overcome the world, he has conquered life and death through his crucifixion and resurrection, and he is Lord of the future as well as the present because all things belong to him. These things, then, could be 23 said to belong to the Christian Corinthians because they belonged to him. And Paul rounded off this extension of his argument by reminding the Corinthians that Jesus is the willing agent of the Father, and that through him they owed obedience to God. In a later passage Paul was to amplify the meaning of this: 'When all things are thus subject to him, then the Son himself will also be made subordinate to God who made all things subject to him, and thus God will be all in all' (15.28). The Son, being of one substance with the Father, is differentiated from the Father precisely in this, that he renders the obedience of perfect love to the perfectly loving will of the Father.

**\* Mark 2. 23–3. 6**
Early in Mark the evangelist introduced the conflict which arose between Jesus Christ and the religious leaders of Israel, especially the Pharisees; and the particular point at issue was the observance of the sabbath.

The origin of the sabbath (Heb. *shabbath* from the verb *shabath*, 'to desist' or 'to break off') is unknown. 'A day of sacred rest, a sabbath holy to the Lord' (Exod. 16.23) is the first reference to it, and in the Priestly tradition it was symbolic of the conclusion of God's creative activity: 'It is a sign for ever between me and the Israelites, for in six days the Lord made the heavens and the earth, but on the seventh day he ceased his work and refreshed himself' (Exod. 31.17). The Book of the Covenant also gives the establishment of the sabbath (Exod. 23.12), adding the humane provision that servants, farm animals, and strangers are to be included in the rest. Deut. 5.12–15 teaches that the sabbath is to be a reminder that God brought Israel out of Egypt.

The Hebrew sabbath began at sundown on Friday and lasted until sundown on Saturday. It was characterized by a complete cessation from labour, even from buying food. It was a day of rest and gladness, but not of a mournful kind: rather, it was a pleasant day for meditating on the things of God. People were expected to assemble for the reading of the law, for prayer and praise, in the temple, and after the exile in the synagogue. But everyone had to observe the sabbath in their own homes. At the blast of a ram's horn the mother lit a candle, best clothes were worn, and the best meal of the week was served, the father of the house-hold saying a special blessing (*kiddush*) over bread and wine.

Jesus did not attack the sabbath observance as such, but liberated the people from a hidebound attitude towards it. The rigid application of the Law concerning the sabbath by the Pharisees robbed it of its spiritual value. Normally a traveller was allowed to help himself to corn by plucking it with his hands (Deut 23.25), but to do this on the sabbath was equivalent to harvesting in the eyes of the Pharisees (harvesting was forbidden on the sabbath, Exod. 34.21). Jesus' reply to the Pharisees' accusation by
25 use of the OT, **Have you never read?** was in the style of a rabbinic dis-cussion; he pointed out that since the greatest king of all, David, had trans-gressed the law of the sabbath according to the scriptures, this must mean that the Law was subordinate to human needs. (The Midrash on 1 Samuel 21 adds that David's action was performed on the sabbath.) The con-secrated loaves which Christ referred to were baked on the Friday and laid on the holy table on the sabbath. The incident took place when
26 Ahimelech was High Priest, not **Abiathar** (the reference to Abiathar is omitted in some MSS. and may be a gloss).

27    **The Sabbath was made for the sake of man and not man for the Sabbath,** has a rabbinic ring about it; a Jewish saying is attributed to R. Simeon (*c.* A.D. 180), 'The sabbath is given over to you, and you are not given over to the sabbath'. Jesus claimed his authority over the sabbath as the eschatological Son of Man, now present on earth not only to forgive sins (Mark 2.10) but also to interpret and, if necessary, to modify the Law.

The same authority was demonstrated in the incident of the man with the withered arm. For Jesus the primary consideration was that healing is part of the gospel; 'to save' includes physical as well as mental and spiritual wellbeing. The sabbath law had been hopelessly misinterpreted if it was used to thwart God's saving grace. The gospel had ushered in the new age of the Kingdom of God, and in the light of that gospel, the old Law must now be assessed.

# EPIPHANY 6
Eighth Sunday after Christmas

*Christ and Complacency*

### Exodus 19. 16–24

The introduction of the narrative which tells how God inaugurated the covenant with his people (Exod. 19—24, the 'Book of the Covenant'). The people prepared themselves with three days' purification, and then they were brought to the foot of mount Sinai by Moses. This was significant. A priest stands nearer to the altar than the worshippers; Israel, standing nearer to the mount of God than any other nation, had a priestly office among the nations of the world. And, like priests, they had to be distinguished by their obedience to the religious and moral law of God. Among them, only Moses and Aaron were allowed to ascend the mountain into the presence of God.

Sinai was not the dwelling place of God but the locus of his manifestation to the people. His epiphany is described in terms of a volcano with smoking and quaking: fire, cloud, and storm heralded an uncanny trumpet blast and an unearthly voice. So awesome was the mountain that it was death to touch it, and the people besought Moses to speak to God on their behalf.

The passage is a mixture of Jahwist and Elohist sources. It raises questions of detail which are not easy to answer. How did Moses get the people to stand at the foot of the mountain during what seemed like a volcanic eruption? Who were **the priests who have access to the Lord**? Priests were not officially appointed as an order until Exod. 32.29. But there is a tremendous sense of the presence and power of God in the passage, and of his holiness and otherness that divides him from his people—a divide which Moses and Aaron cannot begin to bridge.

Various mountains in the Sinai peninsula have been suggested as the peak where this theophany took place. A granite ridge some two miles long among the mountains at the apex of the peninsular, rising from nearly 7,000 feet as mount Ras-es-safsafseh above the plain of Er Raha to 7,400 feet as Jebel Musa, is the traditional spot. Volcanic mountains, however, have to be sought in the area east and south of the Gulf of Akaba.

### Hebrews 12. 18–29

The passage contrasts Judaism and Christianity in their ability to bring men face to face with God. Moses, who was the mediator of the old covenant, stood trembling at the foot of mount Sinai where God manifested himself in a terrifying theophany. The author deliberately stressed the awe-fulness of that occasion by recalling the details of the event—the fire, the darkness, the wind, the trumpet, the voice of God. Coupled with this was the knowledge that the holiness of the mountain meant death to anyone who trod upon it. But Jesus, who is mediator of the new covenant, brings the Christian to the foot of another mountain, Zion, the heavenly reality of which the earthly mountain is but a shadow.

Mount Zion was traditionally the hill of Moriah on which Abraham sacrificed Isaac and where the Jebusites later built a fortress which was captured by David. Solomon's temple was built there, also the second temple, and the temple of Herod. It was there that God was to be worshipped with joy and gladness (Ps. 65.1) and it was there that the Messiah would be manifested (Ps. 2.6). In the New Testament Zion was seen as the foreshadowing of the heavenly Jerusalem (Gal. 4.26, Rev. 3.12, 21.2), an idea also current in contemporary Judaism. The earthly sanctuary was but a copy of the heavenly.

**Myriads of angels**, the messengers and ministers of God according to the religious ideas of the time, are described as gathered in festal 23 array. With them were **the full concourse and assembly of the first-born citizens of heaven** (there is disagreement as to who these might have been: some scholars say they were the first-born of new Israel, the Church triumphant, others that they were the angels themselves who were 'first-born' because they were created before man). God was seen in heaven in his office as Judge—justice is closely connected with the 23 concept of God in this letter. With him were the saints, **the spirits of good men made perfect**, those who in virtue of their faithful lives have passed the scrutiny of the Judge and have been rewarded with eternal life. The order in which they appeared may mean that they were the saints of the Old Testament, though the author would not have seen them as having been saved apart from the sacrifice of Christ.

In the midst of the heavenly Jerusalem was Jesus, the name being used to emphasise that Christ's status is as a man as well as Son of God. He it was who sacrificed himself and who through the cross inaugurated 24 the new covenant. The phrase **sprinkled blood** recalls the inauguration of the old covenant, when Moses sprinkled the blood of the sacrifice over the altar and the people (Exod. 24.6–8, Heb. 9.19). The blood of Jesus is so much more effective than other blood that had been spilt. The blood of Abel, regarded by the Jews as the proto-martyr, only demanded vengeance (Gen. 4.10); the blood of Christ proclaims forgiveness.

But the fear which the inauguration of the old covenant inspired has its lessons for Christians. Those who refused to hear the voice of God spoken through Moses ('Moses received the living utterances of God, to pass on to us' Acts 7.38) did not see the Promised Land, but died in the desert; similarly, those who do not listen to the voice of God spoken by Jesus, who came from heaven, will never enter the promised land of eternal life with God. If the circumstances under which the old covenant was promulgated were frightening enough, that is nothing compared with

25 the results of apostasy from the new covenant. **Those who refused to hear the oracle speaking on earth found no escape; still less shall we escape if we refuse to hear the One who speaks from heaven.**

The author quoted Hag. 2.6 in support of his contention. The shaking of mount Sinai would be followed by a second shaking at the end of time,—the earthquake was a signal of the end of all things, an apocalyptic sign of consummation. Heaven and earth would pass away (Mark 13.31) and only what was endurable would remain—the Kingdom of God which Christians are being given. The present tense denotes a continuous process, not a completed one. The Christian, then, stands before God to give thanks to him in reverence and awe, knowing that he worships a

29 God whose holiness is as **a devouring fire.**

\* John 4. 19–26

The question as to whether mount Zion or mount Gerizim was the place of worship was an ancient contention between Jews and Samaritans. After the return from the exile, the Jews had debarred the Samaritans from access to the temple in Jerusalem, and the Samaritans had set up a rival shrine on mount Gerizim, which with mount Ebal encloses the valley, at the mouth of which Canaanite Shechem once lay. The two summits control the important approach from the north to Jerusalem and most of Palestine is visible from the top. From the slopes of mount Gerizim Joshua and other religious leaders pronounced the blessings which come to those who keep the law (Deut. 11.29, 27.12f; Josh. 8.33–35); hence its name, 'mount of blessings'. The temple was destroyed by John Hyrcanus about 128 B.C. and was never rebuilt, but for centuries afterwards it was regarded as a holy place by the Samaritans.

After recognizing that Jesus had unexpected insight into her immoral life, the woman at the well of Samaria put to Jesus a question about this ancient dispute on the two sanctuaries (Gerizim is visible from Jacob's well). Jesus' reply informed her that the relevance of the dispute was passing away; a new era was beginning in which local religious rivalries

21 would yield to a true and universal worship. The phrase **Believe me** introduces his prophecy.

Nevertheless, Jesus did not entirely ignore the Samaritan heresy. As a Jew, he confronted the woman with the truth about her religion as it had 22 been up to that point. **You Samaritans worship without knowing what you worship, while we worship what we know.** Samaritans denied any revelation of God through the prophets and the psalmists; their scriptures consisted only of the Pentateuch. They virtually worshipped an Unknown God. The Jews, on the other hand, worshipped the God who had been revealed to them, and this was why Jesus could say **it is** 22 **from the Jews that salvation comes.** 'The commonwealth of Israel was the school of the knowledge of God for all nations' (Athanasius).

But the ancient grievance must be forgotten. With the breaking in of the new order, symbolized by the living water which had featured earlier in the conversation (see verses 7–15), the worship of God the Father had been lifted to another dimension. The Spirit, who comes through Christ into the people of God, inspires a new principle of worship. **God is** 24 **spirit**—what is stressed is God's essential being—and because he is spirit it is in a spiritual dimension that worship must be offered. God's mode of operation is in the realm of life-giving power, and it is only those who receive this power through Jesus Christ who can offer to God real worship. To worship 'in truth' is to worship in such a way that one's worship is utterly real, the only kind of worship that meets the conditions revealed by God through Jesus Christ. The truth in which God is to be worshipped points away from both mount Gerizim and mount Zion to God's faithfulness in fulfilling in Christ that to which both Gerizim and Zion, in their varying ways, pointed. It is, perhaps, worth adding that 'spiritual worship' does not mean worship without rites and ceremonies; the Christian sacraments derive their validity through the union of the spirit and the flesh in the divine Logos to which all the baptized are united. Yet there is a lesson to be learned from Isaiah's condemnation of a cult unrelated to moral and spiritual values, nevertheless.

Like the Jews, the Samaritans also looked for the Messiah. They called him 'the Restorer'—*Ta'eb*. 'The Lord will raise up a prophet from among you like myself, and you will listen to him', Moses said in Deut. 18.15. And the woman acknowledged this. Her confession led to Jesus' remark- 26 able disclosure. The **I am he** echoes the act of divine revelation when God answered Moses with his name (Exod. 3.14); and the Deuteronomic prophecy, 'You will listen to him', seems to be reflected in the words of Christ: **I who am speaking to you now.**

# SEPTUAGESIMA
Ninth Sunday before Easter

*Christ the Teacher*

### Isaiah 30. (8–17)

Isaiah's protest against Judah's policy between 705 and 701 B.C. had been rejected, so he was to write down the Lord's words that they might be
8 there in future days, **a testimony for all time**, against the ones who had ignored them. Instead, they had demanded comforting words from the prophets.

Two oracles follow this declaration, prophesying doom and destruction. The people's sins would crash down on them like a bulging, cracking
14 **high wall, as an earthen jar is broken . . . , mercilessly shattered**. And the faith they had in military alliances would prove to be useless; they
17 would be as exposed as **a pole on a mountain-top, a signal post on a**
15 **hill**. They had not listened to the Lord's advice, **In stillness and in staying quiet, there lies your strength**.

### 18–21

However, the Lord promised that he would act on behalf of his people, and this was followed by an acclamation in the form of a beatitude:
18 **Happy are all who wait for him!** This is expanded in verses 19–21. At the right moment the Lord will show his favour and mercy, so there need be no more weeping. In spite of suffering, linked in the prophet's
20 thought with the **bread of adversity and water of affliction** of the exodus, God would lead his people by teaching them his law. Furthermore, he would guide them in the right way by revealing himself: **with your own eyes you shall see him always**.

### 1 Corinthians 4. 8–13

The dominant thought at the beginning of this passage is that no man should boast of his gifts or his status, because all things come from God. The Corinthians were behaving as if they were so far in advance of their teachers that they considered the various gifts they manifested as entirely due to their own efforts. Paul therefore resorted to irony to bring their spiritual pride out into the open. They were acting as if the age to come had already been consummated, as if they now had their heavenly reward and possessed the Kingdom of God. Paul went on with sad sarcasm to remark that he wished it was already true, for then they could share it with apostles like himself!

Then he turned to contrast their attitude and mode of living with that
of the apostles. These leaders of the Church had no feeling of superiority
and self-satisfaction, such as the Corinthians had, for theirs was a life of
constant shame, suffering, and slander. Those who are greatest in God's
plans certainly come low in human estimation. The apostles were like
the wretches brought in at the close of a display in the arena, men condemned to death at the hands of gladiators or in the paws of wild animals.
Their fate provides entertainment for the whole of the created universe
(a prophecy of what the Church was to suffer in the next two and a half
centuries). The contrast sharpens: **We are fools for Christ's sake, while**
10 **you are such sensible Christians. We are weak; you are so power-**
11 **ful. We are in disgrace; you are honoured.**

The journeyings and difficulties of the apostles are then pictured in
terms designed to move the self-satisfied Corinthians. For a teacher to
have to work with his hands was scandalous to the Greeks: the educated
13 ought never to engage in manual labour. **They curse us, and we bless;**
**they persecute us, and we submit to it; they slander us, and we**
**humbly make our appeal** echoes parts of the Sermon on the Mount—
indeed, the picture we are given is a working out of the principles of the
Beatitudes in apostolic life. In the final half of verse 13, the words for
**scum** and **dregs of humanity** may have a special sense of victims
chosen for pagan sacrifice in times of disease, disaster, or famine, to avert
the anger of the gods.

## * Matthew 5. 1–12

Matthew, particularly sensitive to the Old Testament setting of the new
covenant, introduced events on mountains in his narrative at key points—
the temptations (4.8), the sermon (5.1), the transfiguration (17.1) and the
resurrection (28.16). The mountain was the meeting-place of God and
man in the old covenant, and in the new dispensation inaugurated in
Jesus Christ, mountains still figure in the background as symbols of
divine presence. The old law was given on mount Sinai; now, on another
mountain, the new law is promulgated by God through Jesus Christ.
Earlier in the Gospel he had called on the people, 'Repent; for the
Kingdom of heaven is upon you' (4.17). Now Christ listed the characteristics of those who are being called into that Kingdom.

The new law is not a series of commandments restraining conduct,
obedience to which earns divine favour. Rather, the new law is expressed
in terms of the spirit which prompts human conduct, those signs in a
man's attitudes which denote the indwelling and overflowing of the

Holy Spirit, who is given to those who repent and believe the gospel. It is by an inner quality of life known to God that spiritual progress is assessed, not by external acts; though these, of course, may be expressions of that inner quality.

The rabbis sat to teach. Christ taught as a rabbi, sitting and speaking to his disciples, though we understand that there were crowds present.

The beatitudes are in three groups:

verses 3–5, three contrasts with the standards of the world;
verses 6–9, four characteristics of the Christian life; and
verses 10–12, the world's reaction to them.

To be 'blest' means to be happy in the sense of a deep quality of contentment and security, the joy that passes understanding for those whom God loves and who know that he loves them. The JB translates 'How happy are....'

3    How blest are those who know their need of God, the kingdom of Heaven is theirs. The NEB brings out the meaning of 'poor in spirit' (RSV, JB). In the OT 'poor' is sometimes synonymous with 'saintly' and 'God-fearing', though such are often neglected and downtrodden (Ps. 9.19, Isa. 66.2). Although the beatitude applies to those who are materially rich as well as materially poor, Jesus usually has in mind actual poverty, and set himself the example of the poor and the humble. Spiritual poverty among the rich is only maintained by strict stewardship. Matthew may have modified Luke's version of this beatitude.

4  How blest are the sorrowful; they shall find consolation. (RSV 'Those who mourn . . . be comforted.') Christ did not mean those who mourn for the loss of a loved one, or who are weighed down by life's sorrows, but those who have a capacity to enter into spiritual sorrow for the sins of the world. This is not found in a mournful morbidity, but in a recognition that it is difficult to 'sing the Lord's song in the land of our captivity' (Ps. 137.4). The consolation they shall receive was promised to all those who waited for deliverance, like Simeon (Luke 2.25).

5  How blest are those of a gentle spirit; they shall have the earth for their possession. The word is taken from the Greek version of Ps. 37.11, 'The meek-spirited shall possess the land: and shall delight in abundance of peace'.

6  How blest are those who hunger and thirst to see right prevail; they shall be satisfied. (RSV 'righteousness') These are they to whom the fulfilment of God's purposes is the fundamental need in this life.

7    How blest are those who show mercy, mercy shall be shown to

them. The beatitude is found in the Lord's Prayer. Luke 6.36 comments on this, 'Be compassionate as your Father is compassionate'.

8    How blest are those whose hearts are pure; they shall see God. Purity has the connotation of chastity, but it means (and includes) more than this: it is a single-minded application of the gospel to one's life, putting one's hand to the plough without looking back. Such will 'see God'—and 'to see God' meant to appear before God, both in worship and at the end of time.

9    How blest are the peacemakers, God shall call them his sons. The Christian is called to be one who reconciles and builds right relationships, not only of man with man but also of man with God (2 Cor. 5.18ff). This was the office of the Son of God; sharing in this work, the Christian shares in the divine sonship.

10   How blest are those who have suffered persecution for the cause of right; the kingdom of Heaven is theirs. Christ had in mind the prophets, who suffered for proclaiming God's word, and also those who would suffer for the gospel—as verses 11 and 12 indicate.

The beatitudes have affinities with Isa. 61, the first verses of which Christ chose to introduce his ministry to the congregation of the synagogue at Nazareth (Luke 4.16). Modelled on the way the Wisdom writers described the wise and favoured ones of God, they also give us a picture of Christ's own human personality.

## SEPTUAGESIMA
Ninth Sunday before Easter

*Christ the Teacher*

### Proverbs 3. 1–8
The Book of Proverbs is the best representative of the Wisdom literature of Israel. Some of its sources can be traced back into the ancient history of Egypt and Assyria, where aphorisms or sayings of a moral and ethical nature developed in folk or government circles for the guidance of the young. The sayings were usually divided into 'instructions', which command or exhort giving reasons for the action or the attitude taken, and 'proverbs', observations of a more impersonal nature which were not

ordered or explained but allowed to stand by the authority of their own inherent wisdom. When adopted and developed by the wise men of Israel, these sayings were moulded into the religious piety which regarded the God of Israel as the one who punished evil and rewarded virtue. In its later development, the sayings of the sages came to be attributed to a personified Wisdom, (though the strong monotheism of the Jews prevented any idea of ascribing divine nature to her). Christian theologians developed this by seeing in the figure of Wisdom the Word of God.

Chapters 1 to 9 are an introduction to the Book and in their present form are ascribed to the post-exilic period, perhaps the fifth century B.C.

The earliest sections of the book, chapters 10—22 and 25—29, are attributed to Solomon who, according to 1 Kings 4.32 was the author of three thousand proverbs. They may well have been current at his time.

The master addressed his pupil as 'my son'. **Years in plenty** translates
2 the Hebrew *shalom*, 'peace', of which a long life is an adjunct. The teachings of the sage should be inscribed on a tablet worn round the neck as a sign that they are indelibly moulded into the young man's character.
5 Total reliance on God is the keynote: **Put all your trust in the Lord and do not rely on your own understanding.** The one who follows God's ways faithfully will be kept in good health.


(–18)
The payment of tithes was a primary duty and brought its own rewards. But in verse 11 comes advice to accept suffering as within the purposes of God—unlike the prophets such as Isaiah and Jeremiah, the sage did not see that obedience to God in itself involved suffering. Verses 13—18 sing the praises of Wisdom in terms of a beatitude. Wisdom brings prosperity, longevity, and security. She is a staff of life to all who grasp her, and those who hold her fast are always safe.


### 1 Corinthians 2. 1–10

Paul was not, according to references in 2 Cor. 10. 1 and 10, an eloquent speaker, 'so feeble' and 'beneath contempt'. His writing is graceful, and, in spite of its semitisms and Jewish influence, represents notable examples of fine Greek prose (Rom. 8 and 1 Cor. 13). His lack of eloquence, however, strengthened rather than weakened the authority of what he said. The Corinthians, so concerned about their wisdom, had to be told that
1 mere cleverness was not the vehicle of **the attested truth of God**. The

NEB marg. reflects some doubt as to whether the original Greek word was 'attested truth' in the sense of 'the gospel' or 'secret purpose' in the sense of 'divine mystery'.

The apostle was not, of course, rejecting human wisdom in its entirety. The skilful marshalling of facts and the sensitive engagement in dialogue have their proper place. But what Paul was suspicious of was the use of human wisdom for personal ambition, to sway people and to gain power, when it so easily became subject to those evil powers which Paul, like his contemporaries, believed ruled the destinies of men if they did not commit themselves to the greater power of God.

This power of God was demonstrated through the cross of Jesus Christ 'to those of us on the way to salvation' (1.18). It was this that Paul

3 preached **nervous and shaking with fear** (a Biblical cliché for men acting under the authority of God). What brought the Corinthians to faith in God was not the persuasiveness of Paul's speeches but the influence of the Holy Spirit in their minds and hearts as they listened to the gospel: 'In my speeches and the sermons that I gave, there were none of the arguments that belong to philosophy; only a demonstration of the power of the Spirit' (JB verses 4–5).

Not all are ready or able to be moved by the Holy Spirit in this way, said the apostle; words of wisdom can be appreciated only by those who are mature in the Christian faith, 'people who have the Spirit' (3.1).

6 Those who belong to **this passing age**—and here Paul adopted the terminology of Jewish apocalyptic thought which saw the present order as giving way to the messianic age and the establishment of God's Kingdom—had only the wisdom of this age and would not appreciate

6 the word Paul spoke; the **governing powers**—the evil influences which were believed to influence the course of men's lives—could not recognise it. What Paul declared (the word 'speak' has an authoritative

7 connotation) was God's **hidden wisdom, his secret purpose** in redeeming mankind through his Word, who was active from the beginning of all things. The saving work of Jesus fulfils the concept of the Wisdom of God personified in the OT: 'Hear how Wisdom lifts her voice . . . "Men, it is to you I call . . . Understanding and power are mine . . . The Lord created me the beginning of his works, before all else that he made, long ago. . . . Happy is the man who keeps my ways. . . .' (Prov. 8.1ff).

Paul himself summarized this secret purpose later in the letter: 'There is one God, the Father, from whom all being comes, towards whom we move; and there is one Lord Jesus Christ, through whom all things came to be, and we through him' (8.6). This was unknown to the authorities

who crucified Jesus, acting as they were under the influence of evil
spirits who were also ignorant of God's plan. But through them the
8 Lord of glory—Paul did not hesitate to attribute to Christ the glory
of the Godhead—was crucified, and as a result it is in that glory that we are
called to share.

Men come to know these things only because they are revealed by
God and because their minds are enlightened by the Holy Spirit to recognize and to rejoice in their relevance and importance. The Spirit is the
agent of the messianic age into which Christians have been brought, and
it is a sign of their maturity that they can grasp the divine purpose.

The quotation from Isa. 64 in verse 9 is not word for word; the apostle
was apparently quoting from memory.

\* Luke 8. 4-15
The parable of the sower might be called more aptly 'the parable of the
soils'. The message it conveys applies the quality of different soils to the
kinds of minds and hearts of those to whom the gospel is proclaimed. It
was addressed to the people who had gathered in large numbers, but the
exposition was given only to the disciples. Associated with it is a saying
10 from Isa. 6.9, they may look but see nothing, hear but understand
nothing. To grasp the meaning of this puzzling remark we have to go
back to the context of the quotation in the book of Isaiah. It comes within
the call of the prophet and tells him not to be dismayed by the apparent
failure of his message. The verse did not mean that the people's obstinacy
had been directly willed by God, but that he had foreseen it and taken it
into account in his plan. 'They did not open their minds to love of the
truth, so as to find salvation' (2 Thess. 2.10). The parable set a truth
before its hearers. Those without discernment would fail to perceive its
teaching and importance, but those who were enlightened would recognize that it contained the word of life.

10    The secrets of the kingdom of God are those inner mysteries which
reveal God's intentions for the establishment and nature of his Kingdom.
In the gospels they are taught both directly and in parable form; they tell
of God's plan in time, the word and destiny of the Messiah, and the way
people will enter the Kingdom and belong to it.

The parable was particularly applicable to the Church's preaching
13 after Pentecost. Phrases like receive the word with joy when they
hear it, and bring a good and honest heart to the hearing of the
15 word, hold it fast, and by their perseverance yield a harvest,
indicate the manner in which converts embraced the faith. In early

12 Christianity **to believe and be saved** was almost synonymous with 'to
13 become a Christian' and to **desert** was to apostatize.

The failure of the seed which fell on stony ground was explained more
fully in Mark 4.5, 'on rocky ground, where it had little soil'. The fate of
the seed which fell into the first three kinds of soil might well typify the
14 effects of the world, the flesh, and the devil: **choked by cares and
13 wealth and the pleasures of life** (the world), **have no root** (the flesh),
12 **and the devil comes and carries off the word from their hearts.**

## SEXAGESIMA
Eighth Sunday before Easter

*Christ the Healer*

### Zephaniah 3. 14–20
Zephaniah was an aristocrat, a great-great-grandson of King Hezekiah;
apart from this we know little about him, except that he lived in the reign
of King Josiah or King Jehoiakim (if the reference in 1.1 is a later and
mistaken addition). Like Jeremiah, he re-echoed the teaching of the
eighth-century prophets, continuing Amos', Hosea's, and Isaiah's
denunciations of foreign superstitions, social wrongs, and false prophets
and priests. National misfortune is God's punishment for sin, and he
warned of a Day of Wrath in a passage which later inspired the *Dies
Irae* (1.14–16).

These last verses of his book, however, exult in messianic joy at the
protection which the Lord will give to Israel, when God will stand
among them as a king and warrior. The faith and hope that is so often
found towards the end of the prophetic books expresses the inspired
authors' (or their editors') confidence in a God of mercy and forgiveness,
who will provide Israel with all her needs. The joyful shout of these
verses is in the spirit of the Second Isaiah.

Verses 14–15 and 16–18 are psalms of joy, the former echoing Ps. 48.9–
14, one of those set for today. The last section of the passage, verses
18b–20, may be of a later date, echoing the promises made to the Jews
exiled in Babylon. The time of their vindication is near. The day will be
one in which all their foes are overthrown, their scattered members will be
gathered together, and they will be brought back to Jerusalem amidst the

20 wonder of all other nations. When the time comes for me to gather
you, I will bring you home. I will win you renown and praise
among all the peoples of the earth, when I bring back your prosperity; and you shall see it. The final words give the prophecy the
stamp of authority: It is the Lord who speaks.

## James 5. 13–16

We are given here a tiny picture of the early Christian congregation to
which the epistle was addressed, in its care for the troubled, the sick,
and the sinful.

Prayer is not just a remedy for those in trouble, says the writer. We
should pray when things go well, too, but then our prayers will take the
form of praises. In illness the elders of the congregation are to pray over
14 the sick man and anoint him with olive oil in the name of the Lord.
Oil had a medicinal purpose (Isa. 1.6, Luke 10.34) for soothing bruises
and wounds; it was used among Christians not only for its natural
qualities but also because it was regarded, like touching and the laying
on of hands, as a vehicle of miraculous healing power. The twelve healed
the sick by anointing them during their first mission (Mark 6.13). That it
was done 'in the name of the Lord' gave it a sacramental significance—
it has continued in the use of unction in the Church down to the present
day (though as 'extreme unction' it was, for centuries, regarded more as a
preparation for death).

We are not able to deduce much about the organization of the New
Testament Church from this passage, except that apparently in this local
congregation the Christian elders had the same status as the elders of the
synagogue in the Jewish community. This was the pattern in many local
churches in this period.

Forgiveness was also offered to those who were sick. People in the ancient world often concluded that there was a correlation between sickness
and sin. The disciples believed that a man blind from his birth was suffering the consequences of his own sin or that of his parents (John 9.2).
15 The Lord will raise him from his bed recalls the miraculous healing
that Jesus effected; the Church's ministry of healing is a continuation of
Christ's work.

Reference to confession of sin led the author to recommend the practice
generally among all Christians. It was assumed that they would confess
their sins to one who was close to God and whose prayers would be heard.
There is no suggestion of confessions being made only to the elders. In
fact, confession of sins to holy men (that is, laymen) was customary in the

Church, especially among the Orthodox who confessed to holy monks, down to the middle ages.

\* **Mark 2. 1–12**

The incident took place in one of the common dwelling-places of the time, with an outside staircase and a roof of wood and clay that could be easily opened up and repaired. Jesus was addressing a large crowd in the space in front of the door when four men brought the paralysed man to him on a stretcher. Unable to get close to Jesus, they took the patient round the back of the house and on to the roof, lowering him into the room beside Christ.

The real point of the story is that Jesus is the bringer of forgiveness, and to demonstrate this authority the remission of a man's sins is made outwardly visible by the healing of his paralysis. The ancient world was well aware of the link between sin and suffering (in ways that modern psychosomatic research has sometimes vindicated) and the particular disease from which the man was healed can also be taken as a sign of the paralysing effect of sin. The story has been used as an illustration of the Church's liturgy of penance from early times, the four men being seen as those who intercede in faith for the forgiveness of the penitent (an important feature of the early discipline, where the public acts of penance were supported by the prayers of the clergy and the congregation).

From the viewpoint of Mark and his readers, it is not surprising that Jesus began his ministry to the paralysed man by declaring that he had been absolved from his sins. We expect Christ, as God's Messiah, to exercise divine authority. But the Jewish men of the law neither recognized Christ's authority, nor indeed did they expect the Messiah to forgive sins when he came. That was the prerogative of God alone. The most a man could do in this life was to plead to God for forgiveness, adopt the signs of penitence—ashes, sackcloth, fasting—and offer the appropriate sacrifices for ritual cleansing, joining in the ceremonies of the Day of Atonement. Divine forgiveness would then be demonstrated in the blessings which God gave him.

5   But Jesus having announced, **my son, your sins are forgiven**, went on boldly to perform a miraculous sign of his authority in healing the
10  man and, in so doing, claimed for himself the title of **Son of Man**. So far in this Gospel he had been called only 'the son of God', 'my Son, my Beloved', 'the Holy One of God'; now he assumed the messianic title in an act which demonstrated more than his other healings the inner meaning of his mission. The result is that the onlookers were astonished

and praised God—the reaction of awe and wonder at the mighty work of
God.

Most commentators believe that the story was formed by the bringing
together (probably before Mark received it) of two incidents, a straightforward healing (verses 1–5a, 11–12) and a dialogue with the lawyers about
the forgiveness of sins (5b–10), the phrase **he turned to the paralysed**
10 **man** forming a bridge between the two narratives. The authority of
Christ was linked with the Church's ministry of reconciliation in the
Matthean version of this passage, which ends, 'The people . . . praised
God for granting such authority to men' (9.8).

# SEXAGESIMA
Eighth Sunday before Easter

*Christ the Healer*

### 2 Kings 5. 1–14

One of the stories of the Elisha saga which gives us a vivid impression of
1 the personalities involved. The name **Naaman** is attested from non-
biblical sources as a common Arab name in pre-Islamic times. We notice
in passing that his success as a warrior was accredited to the Lord's
doing—an instance of how the God of Israel was recognised at work
outside his chosen people. The leprosy was not of a kind that debarred
Naaman from society; it was more of an embarrassment than an affliction.
The maid, who plays a role in the story not unlike that of her kind in a
Mozart opera, was presumably a victim of the kidnapping raids by
Aramean gangs along the borders of Syria and Israel, who had been sold
in the market at Damascus. Elisha was brought into the story by the
3 maid, not as 'the man of God', his usual title, but as **the prophet**; he is
not associated here with any school or community as in other stories but
is shown to have his own house in Samaria, where he had the opportunity
of keeping an eye on the affairs of state and interpreting the word of God
6 in the court as required. **This letter is to inform you.** . . . Letters
between kings asking for favours are known from other non-biblical
sources. The letter itself was shortened in the report; the preliminary
greetings were omitted. The request was sent direct to the king, not to the
prophet; evidently the king of Aram regarded Elisha as a servant through

whom the royal virtue of healing was exercised. The king, suspecting that the king of Aram was picking a quarrel, rent his clothes in anguish. Elisha intervened, and eventually Naaman came to the prophet's house, in great pomp and carrying an enormous gift.

But he was humiliated. Elisha did not go out to greet him personally, and his advice was beneath the general's dignity. Naaman was expecting a ritual healing, but Elisha put his pride to the test. Man has to be brought low before God can act. Again, it was a servant who advised Naaman to do as he was told. The number seven is a sign of completion.

(-27)
Naaman's offer of a reward to Elisha and Gehazi's deception and punishment. It is remarkable that Naaman was described as worshipping the one God of Israel while participating in idolatry. The sentence on Gehazi demonstrated that Elisha, like Moses, had power to inflict leprosy as well to heal it (Num. 12.10ff). The name **Gehazi** means 'avaricious'.

### 2 Corinthians 12. 1–10

In this piece of autobiography Paul described a tremendous religious experience he once had. He said he did not wish to boast about it, but because he wanted to relate what God had done, he referred to himself 2 indirectly as **a Christian man.**

It had been an experience of exultation similar to that described by John in the book of Revelation. He had been caught up into the third 4 heaven (the highest in Jewish mythology) and there **heard words so secret that human lips may not repeat them.** What he had learned had been too deep to communicate to others. It was perhaps these visions and revelations which had given Paul's theology its distinctive and inspired originality.

Reverting to the matter of boasting, the apostle continued that he was prepared to boast about what God had revealed, but he would not do this 6 because **I should not like anyone to form an estimate of me which goes beyond the evidence of his own ears and eyes.** For himself, he was content to be accepted for what he had said and done himself, not for the visions and marks of divine favour. Paul here balanced humbly on that delicate divide which separates a joyful account of what God is doing in us from those forms of personal testimony which verge on self-glorification.

It was on a point of humility that the apostle mentioned an unhealed infirmity, **a sharp physical pain.** The alternative in the NEB footnote,

7 a thorn, for the flesh, might mean that his readers knew all about it. The nature of this affliction is not known, though there have been many guesses—epilepsy, malaria, stammering (which could account for his poor showing as a speaker, 1 Cor. 2.1) or an eye weakness (the reference to eyes and poor sight might be inferred from Gal. 4.12–16, 6.11). From this weakness he had three times asked God to deliver him, but the
9 answer had been, My grace is all you need; power comes to its full strength in weakness (the same thought is in Isaiah 40.29).

And so Paul had to come to terms with his affliction. God gave him no healing. The weakness had now become a thing of pride and joy, for it was the means through which the divine presence 'rested upon him'. The Greek means 'tabernacle upon me', the phrase chosen to recall the period when the people of Israel in the wilderness brought the tent of meeting with them as the temporary resting-place of God.

Afflictions, then, were things with which Paul could be content. They were means through which God exercised his power. Hence the paradox,
10 when I am weak, then I am strong.

* Mark 1. 35–45

The passage might be taken as exemplifying a typical day in our Lord's
35 Galilean ministry. Very early . . . he got up and went out . . . to a lonely spot and remained there in prayer. This practice was referred to by Mark again (1.12, 6.46). The authority which Jesus manifested was dependent upon and subordinate to the will of the Father, and this was discovered through times of communion with him in retreat. His prayer is almost always spoken of in connection with his mission.

But there may have been another reason for these withdrawals. When
37 the disciples found him they said, They are all looking for you. People tried to force a secular kind of messiahship on him because they tended to mistake him for a wonder-worker. But the healing miracles
38 were only incidental to his work; his real purpose was to proclaim my message, to announce the gospel. So Mark described him as preaching in the synagogues where the people met, showing that the gospel had
39 come not only with words but also with power by casting out the devils.

It is into this general scene of Christ's ministry that the story of the healing of the leper was set, to focus on the significance of what Jesus did. Leprosy was the name for many skin diseases. The one afflicted was separated from the community, for reasons of ritual cleanness as well as medical isolation. The Mosaic law could do nothing for such a disease, which was regarded by the rabbis as a punishment for sin. But 'what the

41 law could never do . . . God has done' (Rom. 8.3). **Jesus stretched out
his hand**—a gesture of healing that had OT precedent—and declared
the man clean. (For verse 41, the NEB footnote is better, **Jesus was sorry
for him and stretched out his hand.** There was no apparent reason for
Jesus' **warm indignation**, though we notice that his warning about
silence was stern. He may have been indignant because of the note of
40 doubt in the leper's request, **If only you will . . .,** or because he was
angered by the effect of the disease).

The injunction to keep silent about the healing was to guard his reputa-
45 tion. But the man disobeyed him, so that **Jesus could no longer show
himself in any town, but stayed outside in open country.** (Or was
he ostracized because by touching the leper he was regarded as unclean?)
Even so, **people kept coming to him from all quarters**—foreshadowing the universal appeal of the gospel.

# QUINQUAGESIMA
Seventh Sunday before Easter

*Christ, Worker of Miracles*

### Deuteronomy 8. 1–6

The preacher began with a call to obey God, and continued by telling
the people to remember the forty years in the wilderness. It was then that
they had experienced God's fatherly guidance. The Lord had used it as a
time to humble them and to test them, building them up in discipline,
sometimes through scarcity, sometimes through blessings, to reach a
mature understanding of his ways and of his law.

The reference to the manna is interesting because it illustrates a fresh
interpretation of the miracle from the standpoint of a later writer. In
Exod. 16 it was regarded as simply a miracle wrought by God to supply
his people's need; here the miracle is declared to be a lesson from God
3 to teach his people that **man cannot live on bread alone but lives by
every word that comes from the mouth of the Lord.** The Lord's
word is life to Israel. The miracle of the clothes and the shoes which did
not wear out is not mentioned elsewhere in the OT. It is an example of

the way in which the preacher had access to traditions about Israel's past which have since been lost.

The passage looks forward analogously to the season of Lent in various ways—the forty years' in the wilderness as a time of humbling and testing, the quotation used by Christ to refute one of the devil's temptations in next Sunday's gospels, fasting as an act of discipline, and the need for instruction.

## (–10)

The provision of manna is also a prophetic sign of the wonderful land to which the Lord was leading the people, an ideal welfare state. The custom of saying prayers of blessing at meals is behind verse 10. The Lord has blessed the people, so the people in return must bless (thank) God.

## Philippians 4. 10–20

The occasion of Paul's letter to the congregation (*ecclesia*, used in the sense of 'local church') at Philippi, the Roman colony in Macedonia, was to thank them for financial assistance they had given him. Normally the apostle avoided doing anything that might give the impression that he was making money out of preaching the gospel (Acts 18.3f). But he seems to have been on terms of intimate trust with his converts in Philippi, for they had supported him at Thessalonica, at Corinth, and later commissioned Epaphroditus to take further contributions to him. The letter was written to tell them that he had received the gifts and to express his gratitude.

Yet, even so, he endeavoured to make it clear to them that it was their consideration for him and their fellowship with him that gave him joy; they shared the burden of his troubles through what they gave—that was what really mattered to him. Their gifts were inspired by their love for God and were therefore as valid as any sacrificial oblation made in 18 the temple ritual: **a fragrant offering, an acceptable sacrifice, pleasing to God.**

Within this expression of thanks Paul conveyed the sense of his optimism and faith in the goodness of God. He knew what it was to be poor or to be comparatively comfortable, but he gave thanks to God whatever 13 his circumstances, because through Christ he had **strength for anything through him who gives me power.** That is where true riches are; what he wanted was that the Philippians might lay up for themselves treasures 18 in heaven. And through his 'thank you' letter—the phrase **I give you my**

receipt is the common one for acknowledging a financial transaction—
Paul was subtly urging the Philippians to imitate him in dependence upon
God who would supply all they required whatever their social or financial
status.

* John 6. 1–14
The feeding of the five thousand is set in the fourth Gospel against the
background of the Passover—the second of the three references to this
feast in John (the first is at the cleansing of the temple, 2.13, the third
at Christ's passion). It gives the incident the atmosphere of a Passover
celebration, or, rather, a looking forward to the paschal eucharistic
celebrations of the people of God after the resurrection. This impression is
strengthened when we remember that it precedes the great Bread of Life
discourse in this chapter. Some commentators have doubted the miraculous element in the story, saying that it represented an act of mutual sharing by the people inspired by the presence of Jesus. Others have pointed
out that the miracle is credible if Jesus is believed to be the incarnate
Word, through whose agency creation came into existence. Whatever the
explanation, the evangelist seems to be using material from an oral tradition which was independent of the synoptic Gospels.

Jesus did not sit down to teach, as in the synoptics; the teaching came
next morning (6.22ff). The Galilean lake was sometimes called Tiberias
after the Gentile city Herod Antipas had built on the lake shore in honour
of the emperor Tiberius. In John it was Jesus, not the disciples (as in the
7 synoptics) who noticed that the people lacked food. A **denarius** (NEB
footnote) was a day's pay for a hired labourer—bread, even the barley
bread of the poor, was relatively more expensive in relation to other food
in the ancient world than it is today. Pickled fish was added as a relish.
As it was April, the grass was green; it dries up under the hot sun in May
and June.

11    **Jesus took the loaves, gave thanks, and distributed them to the
people** is reminiscent of the Last Supper. The usual Jewish prayer of
thanksgiving was offered over the bread by Jesus, acting as the head of the
table for the meal. When the meal was over, the order to collect what
remained was inspired not by economic considerations but by feelings of
reverence, and may well reflect later Christian concern for the disposal of
the eucharistic elements. The bread which God had provided was the new
manna pointing to Jesus the true Bread from heaven, and it must not be
wasted. Each disciple found his basket full. The feeding therefore becomes
in John a kind of Galilean Last Supper, an acting out of the parable of the

great supper told in Luke 14.15–24. The messianic significance of the
14 occasion was recognized by the people, for they called Jesus the prophet
that was to come into the world (Deut. 18.15, a messianic reference).

# QUINQUAGESIMA
Seventh Sunday before Easter

*Christ, Worker of Miracles*

**Jonah 1. 1–17**
The teaching of the anonymous seer who most clearly of all the prophets
put forward the claims of the Gentile world to a share in the love of God
1 is ascribed to **Jonah son of Amittai.** A man of this name, a native of
Galilee, lived during the reign of Jeroboam II (781–740 B.C.) according
to 2 Kings 14.25; but the book of Jonah was almost certainly written in
2 post-exilic times. **Nineveh** was the capital of Assyria until 612 B.C., when
it was captured by a combined force of Babylonians and Medes. Excavations have shown that it was a huge city with walls seven and a half miles
long; it had the reputation in the ancient world of containing a sinful and
depraved people—a reputation which was no doubt exaggerated by tradition and which served the author's purpose in demonstrating that God is
3 concerned about the salvation of the most wicked non-Israelite peoples.
**Tarshish** is usually identified with Tartessus on the Guadalquivir in
Spain.

The teaching is given in the form of a parable or allegory describing an
episode in the life of Jonah. The prophet, so runs the story, was bidden
by the Lord to go and denounce the city for its wickedness; but Jonah,
like other prophets before him, and like many who are called by God to
specific tasks, rejected the call. What were the people of Nineveh to him,
a Jew? Why should he run risks for the sake of a Gentile city? Besides,
there was always the risk that the wretched city might repent at the last
moment and be saved! So he took a ship in the opposite direction to that
in which he was bidden to go—westwards instead of eastwards.

The action of the sailors in the storm demonstrated the cosmopolitan
nature of their company—each cried out to his own god. But after Jonah
had revealed that he was trying to escape from his Lord, they in their turn

prayed to the God of Israel, who answered their prayer—implying that
the God of Israel was more effective than the gods of other nations.
At his own request Jonah was cast into the sea and the storm subsided.
How the sailors offered a sacrifice to the God of Israel on board ship is a
detail that does not concern the author; nor, indeed, is the species of a
fish that can swallow a man live and eject him still living three days later.
The story is probably drawn from folklore or legend, to bring Jonah
back to the place where he had started from as quickly as possible and to
teach that attempts to escape from the will of God are futile.

### James 1. 2–12

The authorship of this epistle is traditionally ascribed to James, 'the
brother of the Lord', who played such an important part in the life of the
earliest Christian community in Jerusalem (Acts 12.17ff, etc.), and who
was put to death by the Jews about A.D. 62. The elegant Greek style in
which it is written, however, makes it doubtful whether its author could
ever have been a native of Galilee. It is addressed to the Jewish Christians
of the dispersion, especially in the countries adjacent to Palestine, such as
Egypt and Syria. It is more of a sermon than a letter, and its contents may
well reflect the sort of exhortations commonly given in those circles to
congregations and converts under instruction. The section from which this
passage is selected deals with times of trial—probably the trials which face
Christians in all circumstances, for there is no evidence that the people
James was addressing were facing persecution.

2    The Christian can count himself richly blessed (the words **supremely
happy** begin a beatitude) when he faces different kinds of trials, he said,
because such testing discloses what is genuine in his faith, and results in
4 a fortitude which leads him towards perfection. He will then **fall short
in nothing.**

The words led the writer on to say that **if any of you falls short in
wisdom**—knowledge in the things of God—**he should ask God for it
5 and it will be given him, for God is a generous giver who neither
refuses nor reproaches anyone.** But prayer must be offered in faith;
prayer offered in doubt will never be answered, for the man of doubt
lacks the resolution and reliance on God that faith brings. He contrasted
the deep calmness of faith with the stormy restlessness of doubt using the
sea as a metaphor.

Perhaps the thought of testing brought into James' mind the idea that
the rich can be happy when their wealth—always as precarious a possession
as a flower on a hot day—is taken from them. Social status is irrelevant in

the following of the Lord. The OT theme that the poor will be rewarded is developed in the Gospels where that reward is seen in terms of the Kingdom of God (Luke 6.20) and where the rich must humble themselves to receive the same reward (Matt. 5.3ff). Then, like the poor man, he can be proud that the Lord has given him such an opportunity for moral and spiritual progress.

The passage ends with a further beatitude: the man who remains faithful under trials can consider himself richly blessed for, if he succeeds, he will be given the crown of life, the prize God has promised for those who love him.

\* Mark 4. 35–41
The miracle of the stilling of the storm should be seen against the background of the primitive myth that the act of creation involved God in a critical but eventually victorious contest with the forms of chaos and evil which were believed to have their habitat in the waters of the sea. An ability to control the sea, therefore, was one of the signs of divine power: 'Thou rulest the raging of the sea; thou stillest the waves thereof when they arise. Thou didst smite the monster of the deep with a deadly wound'. (Ps. 89.9–10a)

The images of the storm were sometimes used to describe the effect of evil forces in the world—as, for example, the tribulations of the righteous. Because God had smitten the enemy in the deep, he alone could deliver his servant from the storms of evil in this life: 'Save me O God: for the waters are come up even unto my throat' (Ps. 69.1).

Faith in God had to be of a quality that even the raging of all the forces of evil, like a tempest, could not shake it.

> God is our hope and strength:
> a very present help in trouble.
> Therefore will we not fear, though the earth be moved:
> and though the hills be carried into the midst of the sea:
> Though the waters thereof rage and swell:
> and though the mountains shake at the tempest of the same.
>
> (Ps. 46. 1–3)

To be able to sleep in the midst of a storm is a sign of this perfect confidence in God. But for those who are feeling the forces of evil, it sometimes seemed as if God himself is asleep, and has to be roused to save his elect: 'Up Lord, why sleepest thou: awake, and cast us not away for ever' (Ps. 44.23).

Against this background, the miracle demonstrated Jesus' faith in God the Father, his own divine powers, and the poverty of the disciples' confidence. Jesus was asleep on the leather seat used by the helmsman in the stern of the boat. There is a rebuke in the scared disciples' words to their
38 leader: Master, we are sinking! Do you not care? Jesus said to the
39 sea, Hush! Be still! He used the same word to rebuke the demoniac in 1.25, indicating that he also exorcised the evil forces in the tempest. His question to the disciples implied that those who have faith need fear no evil while he was with them. A deep awe of the power of God came over them. Another psalm comes to mind: 'These men saw the works of the Lord: and his wonders in the deep' (Ps. 107.24). The answer to their
41 question, Who can this be? is that only God through his creative word is able to command the wind and the sea. The miracle is yet another sign that the new age is breaking in and that the Kingdom of God is at hand.

Attempts to rationalise the miracle and ascribe it to the normal workings of nature (the Sea of Galilee is subject to sudden squalls which die away as quickly as they arise) miss the point of the story. The answer to the disciples' question tells us all we need to know.

# ASH WEDNESDAY


### Isaiah 58. 1–8

The only fast prescribed in the Mosaic Law is that for the Day of Atonement (Lev. 23.26ff), but other fasts were proclaimed at different times, such as in days of national crisis or disaster. The question at issue in this post-exilic oracle of the Third Isaiah is the effectiveness of fasting: why do the people fast if God does not pay any attention to such observances?

The attitude towards the fast shifts in the course of this passage, indicating perhaps different sources (it is thought that although the oracle reached its final form in post-exilic times, it includes some pre-exilic material). Festivals and fasts were announced by trumpet-calls. The prophet, like a trumpet, was to summon people to hear what God says through him about effective fasting. The people were assiduous in wor-
2 ship: they ask counsel of me day by day and say they delight in

knowing my ways. They sought to hold close to God's will, but their fasts were marred because they had pursued their business on a fast day, and made their labourers work for them. Indeed, the fast day had been an occasion for wrangling and quarrelling, presumably in connection with their business affairs. It had even come to acts of violence.

So far the prophet had complained about serious abuses which had happened on fast days. He had not been concerned with the days themselves as religious institutions but with the question whether the turning to God in prayer—and prayer is the most important element in fast days—was genuine and complete. At verse 5, however, there is a change. The 5 attack was directed against the practice of fasting with some scorn. **Is it a fast like this that I require . . . that a man should bow his head like a bulrush and make his bed on sackcloth and ashes?** is intended to be sarcastic. The divergence suggests a separate source for this verse.

From verse 6 onwards we are told what kind of fasting is pleasing to God. Fasting should include justice for the hungry, the poor, the captives, and the oppressed—the classes who are listed in the prophet's commissioning in 61.1ff ('to bring good news to the humble . . .'). Like the gospel that it foreshadowed, the prophecy brought into the notion of penitential acts charitable deeds towards those in need. The outward observance of a fast is no substitute for obedience towards God, especially where other people are involved. The admonition ended with the promise that God would bless them like a dawn light and their wounds would be healed like new skin over old wounds. Their righteousness would go before them in the caravan, and the Lord's glory would be about their trail.

(–12)

These verses seem to be addressed more to individuals than to the nation, except verse 12 which promises the reconstruction of Israel. Nothing more is said of proper and improper fasting. Good works will be blessed by God—the good works listed are of a representative kind concerning justice and the underprivileged.

1 Corinthians 9. 24–27

The games in the stadium are used several times in the New Testament as an analogy for Christian living, and in this passage the apostle, using contemporary terminology from the language of athletes, summoned the congregation at Corinth to remember that entering the Church through baptism did not guarantee our final perseverance; the Christian must continue in the way he has begun with all his might—and that involves exercising a mastery over oneself. His metaphor is not quite suitable, for he does not mean to imply that only one Christian in a group will win the prize of eternal life; the force of his argument is that we must not assume that, because we have entered the race, we shall automatically win.

Similarly, the analogy of a champion's crown is used to denote the Christian's prize: it is called 'the unfading garland of glory' in 1 Pet. 5.4, 'the crown of life' in Rev. 2.10. The Isthmian games were held near Corinth and archaeologists have discovered a mosaic in the floor of the office of the director of the games depicting a champion, with a palm in his hand, offering thanks to the goddess of Good Fortune (Tyche) and wearing a crown of withered leaves.

In verse 26 the metaphor shifts from that of discipline in training to controlled effort in the race or boxing match itself. For himself he runs, not in such a way that the onlooker cannot tell where he is going (the Greek phrase has a double negative to emphasize that the Christian's goal is very clear), and not like a boxer dealing ill-directed and ineffectual 26 blows. He treated his body severely. **I bruise my body** could be misleading; the JB translation is clearer, 'I treat my body hard and make it obey me'. This does not mean that a man's body is necessarily evil; rather, it means that Paul recognized that the human body is too easily inclined to what is sinful and disobedient to God and has to be disciplined to serve its right master. In speaking of the Christian's being buried and risen with Jesus Christ in baptism, he told the church in Rome, 'Put yourselves at God's disposal, as dead men raised to life; yield your bodies to him as implements for doing right; for sin shall no longer be your master, because you are no longer under law, but under the grace of God'. (Rom. 6.13–14). To call this *self*-discipline is to miss the point: we are to let God master our bodies, offering ourselves in this race, this contest, with all our will. And Paul placed himself under the same warning by envisaging the possibility that, notwithstanding his work as an apostle, he might himself fall from grace and be rejected.

## * Matthew 6. 16–21

The pericope consists of two sections from the Matthean version of the Sermon on the Mount, one on fasting and the other on true treasures.

In addition to the public fasts like the Day of Atonement, private individuals such as the Pharisees and the followers of John the Baptist undertook private fasts as a means of religious and moral discipline. The Pharisee in Jesus' parable of the two men in the temple said he fasted twice in the week (Luke 18.12). Among the Pharisees Mondays and Thursdays were kept as fast days. Jesus assumed that fasting would continue among his disciples, at any rate when 'the bridegroom' was taken from them (Matt. 9.14–15). But he denounced the use of the practice as a means of displaying one's piety and gaining the reputation of being a holy person, and therefore he warned his disciples not to use the customary signs of fasting, the unkempt appearance and the strewing of ashes on the head. On the contrary, Christians who fast must appear to be living normally and joyfully (washed and anointed).

19    Behind the saying about **treasure on earth** is the conviction that the accumulation and hoarding of wordly goods is due to a desire for security, a desire to be rid of anxiety about the future. But Christ argued that, far from removing anxiety, material wealth increases it, because earthly treasures are liable to loss and decay. What his followers should collect is

20 **treasure in heaven.** This heavenly wealth is a permanent possession, freed from the ravages of time and safely out of the reach of thieves. Various sayings of our Lord comment on this—the saying about the pearl of great price, the parable of the rich fool, and the advice to the rich young ruler (Matt. 13.46, Luke 12.16–21, Matt. 19.16–26).

# ASH WEDNESDAY

Amos 5. (4–5)
Among the sins which Amos denounced in Israel, the northern kingdom in the eighth century B.C., were idolatry and the oppression of the people

4 by the capitalists of his day. **Resort to me, if you would live** was said in terms of a summons to a sanctuary, but the prophet realized that the approach to God meant more than an act of worship, and 'to live' meant more than physical survival. It was drawing near to God in their hearts which the people must do. The idolatrous sanctuaries of Bethel, Gilgal and Beersheba would be as nothing.

6–15

6 **Resort to the Lord.** God himself is the only sanctuary for man. To ignore him is to invite the divine fire which is the Lord's instrument against his foes. He who is the author of life would become the author of destruction.

At this point a hymn in praise of the Lord as creator appears in the 8 prophecy. Commencing **He who made the Pleiades and Orion**, it is a later addition, and its position in the text has been adjusted in the NEB so that verses 7 and 10 can run together. It praises God as the maker of the stars, the ruler of day and night, and the one who provides rain. The star groups Pleiades and Orion are mentioned in Job 9.9 and 38.31.

Then the call for social reform is continued in verse 7 in its new position. The justice administered in the courts has been turned by greed into bitter oppression. The task of the court, which often met in the open square inside the gate of Israelite towns and cities ('in the gate', RSV) was to protect the social order by establishing where wrong lay and correcting it. This was particularly important in the case of the weaker members of society who, without power or influence, could not maintain themselves in the social order without the court's upholding of their rights. The proceedings of the court were not as formally organized as in our own western tradition, nor presided over and directed by professional men. All the adult male citizens of a town, who were not disqualified in some way, were eligible to sit as assessors. Any of them could testify as a witness and offer advice as to which norms applied in a case before the court. The competence of such a court depended on the integrity of the assessors in speaking the truth and upholding what was recognized as right in the community. The ninth commandment (Exod. 20.13) forbade false witness. 10 Therefore to **hate a man who brings the wrongdoer to court and loathe him who speaks the whole truth** is to undermine the system.

Amos accused his hearers of exploiting the weak—they were driving the landed peasantry away from their earlier independence into the condition of serfs; the small farmer no longer owned his own land, but was a tenant of an urban class to whom he must pay rent for the use of his land, a rent that was often a large proportion of the grain which the land produced. Out of the proceeds the exploiters had built themselves houses of stones hewn for the building (contrasted with the more usual practice of using stony rubble available on the site) and planted luxuriant vineyards on fields that belonged to the small farmer. The Lord, speaking through the prophet, knows those who use the courts to maintain this corruption. In verse 13 a comment is added that a prudent man—a

figure beloved in the Wisdom sayings (Prov. 10.5, 19, etc.)—will keep
quiet, knowing that to raise a complaint or to plead a case in the courts
13 will be an evil time for him.

Then our passage ends with an exhortation, followed by a conditional
promise. The decision about good and evil is a decision for or against the
Lord and is therefore an invocation of his blessing or his judgement.
But the Lord's relationship with Israel was his own sovereign concern,
and the bestowal of favour and help was in his own will and not what the
recipient might expect.

### James 4. 1–8a

What James denounced was selfishness run riot, causing divisions within
the congregations to whom he was writing. The use of words like
2 **murder, quarrel,** and **fight** suggests that arguments, arising from con-
flicting ambitions and jealousy, have ended in actual blows. This sad
state of affairs made nonsense of his readers' prayers, for their petitions
sprang from unworthy motives and were consequently unanswered.
4 Such prayers cannot be offered in the name of Jesus Christ. **You false,
unfaithful creatures** is literally 'adulteresses!' in Greek: the imagery of
Israel as an unfaithful wife is traditional in the OT (Hos. 1.2ff) and is
carried over into the Gospel ('this adulterous and sinful generation',
Mark 8.37 RSV); here it is applied to the new Israel (as Paul applied it,
'I betrothed you to Christ, thinking to present you as a chaste virgin to
her true and only husband', 2 Cor. 11.2). The adulterous love of **the
world** (the term used in the Johannine sense of creation in opposition
to its creator) is apostasy from God.
5    **The spirit which God implanted in man turns towards envious
desires** is a scripture which now seems to be lost, though it may be based
on Gen. 2.7, when God formed man from the dust of the ground and
breathed into his nostrils the breath of life. There is a real danger that the
spiritual life of man may be turned to evil. Yet resistance to the devil is
effective; the man who humbles himself before God receives all the
8 assistance he needs (quoting Prov. 3.34). **Come close to God** is a
phrase which normally refers to priests approaching the altar: God never
turns his back on those who draw near to him.

### * Luke 18. 9–14

The Pharisees, according to Josephus, were 'a body of Jews with the
reputation of excelling the rest of their nation in the observances of
religion, and as exact exponents of the laws'. Their attitude is reflected

in the confession of Paul in Phil. 3.4ff, 'If anyone thinks to base his claims on externals, I could make a stronger case for myself: circumcised on my eighth day, Israelite by race, of the tribe of Benjamin, a Hebrew born and bred; in my attitude to the law, a Pharisee; in pious zeal, a persecutor of the church; in legal rectitude, faultless'. The dangers in this attitude were recognized by the rabbis: Hillel (c. 20 B.C.) used to say 'Keep not aloof from the congregation and trust not in thyself until the day of thy death, and judge not thy fellow until thou art come to his place'. It is probable that the parable was directed against the self-righteous section within the party rather than the party as a whole.

The two men in the parable stood for the two extremes in Judaism, the Pharisee representing those whose complete devotion to the law set the supreme standard of Jewish faith and morals, the tax-gatherer representing the lowest moral stratum of Jewish life. Both entered the inner main quadrangle of the temple, perhaps at the time of the morning or the evening sacrifice, when every Jew was expected to pray. Both stood for their prayers—the normal posture. The Pharisee's prayer began as an act of thanksgiving, the best form of prayer. To begin with it was not objectionable. He simply thanked God that he was able to avoid deadly sins and
11 perform many acts of supererogation. I fast twice a week; I pay tithes on all that I get. Deut. 14.22 required that only coin, wine, and oil should be tithed, together with beasts, if the man dealt in them. Mondays and Thursdays were fast days for pious Jews. But then in his prayer the Pharisee went on to compare himself with the tax-gatherer, and here his pride came in. The tax-gatherer, on the other hand, was overwhelmed by his sense of unworthiness (and we must not make the mistake of regarding him as a decent sort of chap: he was a scoundrel—his saving grace was that he had come to realize it). From a distance and with downcast eyes he could only ask God for mercy with a penitential beating of his breast.

Jesus' comment shows that what matters is not a man's personal achievements or past record but his present attitude towards God. The Pharisee was so satisfied with himself that God could do nothing for him. He did not see that he needed a physician. The tax-gatherer knew his need, and in that there was hope.

# LENT 1
## Sixth Sunday before Easter

*The King and the Kingdom : Temptation*

**Deuteronomy 30. (11–14)**
The final discourse attributed to Moses by the Book of Deuteronomy
resembled a demand for the people's signature. They had been told of
God's love and care for them. They had been instructed in what he wanted
12, of them in the preceding chapters. The divine command is **not in heaven**
13 . . ., **nor is it beyond the sea; it is very near to you, upon your lips**
14 **and in your heart ready to be kept**—relevant and completely acceptable
if they were true to themselves. Now the people were to answer the question, 'What is your response?'

**15–20**
The choice was between two ways, the way of life and the way of death
(instruction in the two ways passed from Jewish to Christian catechesis;
presenting the choice in terms of white and black made it more obvious
to the catechumen what the consequences of his decision might be).
Although the demand was authoritative, yet obedience should spring
16 from **loving the Lord your God.** The reward of obedience would be
prosperity and an increase in the numbers of their nation in the promised
land. But if they disobeyed and worshipped other gods, they would soon
19 die after crossing the Jordan. The created universe, **heaven and earth,**
is summoned to witness God's demand and the people's response. The
demand is made with a stern warning because of man's tendency to choose
the way of death and evil, what Christian theologians later gave the name
'original sin'. But man is free to make the choice, nevertheless, and he can
20 refuse to **obey God and hold fast to him,** even though that involves
deprivation of **life for you and length of days.**

**Hebrews 2. 14–18**
The opening verses of this passage finalise the argument that the author
has been putting forward at the beginning of this letter; that Jesus Christ
was the true Son of God, superior to all the angels, and that he became
truly human, sharing in full the human experiences of temptation, suffering, and death, in order to be the High Priest of mankind before God the
14 Father in heaven. Thus he **shared the same flesh and blood,** a com-

mon Jewish saying to denote humanity in its frailty and dependence before
God.

Fear of death, and of the consequences of death, is seen as a slavery
imposed on the whole human race. Speculations about terrible punish-
ments awaiting the soul after death abounded in the ancient world. Man
would fall even more into the power of the devil after he had died. The
rabbis wrote of the Angel of Death wielding the power of death, and in the
Wisdom of Solomon it was held that God did not make death, that man
was made for incorruption, and that it was through the devil that death
entered into the world (Wisd. 1.13, 2.23–24). Death, then, was the realm
of the evil one.

The incarnation, said the author of Hebrews, was to liberate men from
this dreadful fate. Precisely how Jesus through death broke the devil's
power over death is not explained. Basically the thought seems to be that
Jesus, through dying and then rising from the dead, passed in his
humanity beyond the power of the devil so that, in his risen life, he was
able to crush the effect that that power had over the rest of humanity.
This is why the author insisted on the full union of the Son of God with
our human nature. The New Testament reflects the tension between the
teaching that Christ has already destroyed death (2 Tim. 1.10) and the
belief that the complete annihilation of the devil awaits the last day (Rev.
12.9) and the last enemy to be destroyed is death (1 Cor. 15.26). This
conquest of Christ over death is pictured in Rev. 1.18: 'Do not be afraid.
I am the first and the last, and I am the living one; for I was dead and
now I am alive for evermore and I hold the keys of death and Hades.'

16  Christ represents the sons of Abraham—not the Jews, but the new
17  Israel. He had to be made like these brothers of his in every way,
so that he might be merciful and faithful as their high priest
before God, to expiate the sins of the people. This is the first mention of our Lord's high priestly office in a letter which elaborates it at
length in later chapters. The office of a high priest is to represent men
in their relationship to God and to reconcile men to God through the
ordered means of the cult. Christ's work is described here in the imagery
of sacrifice, using the concept of expiation—making amends for sins.
Expiation is one of the underlying motives of sacrifice in the Bible, and it
is what the high priest was believed to achieve on the Day of Atonement,
when he offered the sacrifice for the sins of the people. Christ as our High
Priest could intercede sympathetically for men since he himself knew
the temptations to which they are subject. This is another reason why the
author emphasized the Son of God's full participation in human nature.

Christ is not only the leader and the consecrator of his people: he is their mediator as well. And in strong contrast with the Jewish high priests, he
17 is merciful in that he is compassionate towards men, and he is faithful in his obedience to God the Father.

### * Matthew 4. 1–17

After his baptism by John, Jesus was led by the Spirit into the desert to be tempted. We cannot tell whether the location, the suggestions put by the devil, and the threefold form of the temptations are a record of what happened or a stylization of a constant battle that Jesus had throughout his ministry. But this does not matter: neither possibility adds or takes away from the importance of the event in our salvation-history.

Reference to the wilderness is significant. Christ was remaking the journey of the Israelites through the desert where they were tempted. The people succumbed, but Jesus resisted, because he was full of the Spirit. He used three scriptural sayings taken from the story of Israel to counter the temptations (Deut. 8.3, 6.16, 6.13). Deuteronomy was the 'Book of Moses' which gave the scriptural principles on which the chosen people were to occupy the promised land (Deut. 4.1). What sort of a Joshua (Jesus) was Christ to be, as he led the true Israel to the promised land of the Kingdom of God? This was the basic question behind the suggestions put to him by the devil.

3    If you are the Son of God, tell these stones to become bread. Israel—and with her all mankind—forgot her task in life and longed to return to the fleshpots of Egypt. Was Christ to appear before the Jewish nations as the benefactor who provides the messianic banquet in material terms, making bread out of stones? He replied that man is to feed on the word of God, a greater manna than that which appeared in the wilderness. It is true that on one, if not two, later occasions he did in fact provide bread in the desert for thousands of people, but this was in a moment of practical necessity, and the fourth Gospel used the miracle as a sign of the Bread of Life (John 6.49–50).

6    If you are the Son of God, throw yourself down; for Scripture says, 'He will put his angels in charge of you, and they will support you in their arms, for fear you should strike your foot against a stone' (even the devil can quote scripture, in this case Ps. 91.11–12, for his own purposes!). The parapet of the temple on which they were standing is usually thought to be the south-east corner of the huge wall constructed by Herod the Great round the temple in Jerusalem, from which there was a sheer drop of 150 feet into the Kidron valley below. Was

Christ to assume the role of the Messiah of apocalyptic literature, descending from the sky in a miraculous way to draw from the people wonder and awe? Jesus replied that to put God to the test is to fail to trust him. Moses had failed in this way when, in a moment of provocation, he had struck the rock for water at Massah, an act which disqualified him for leadership in the promised land (Exod. 17.2–7, Deut. 32.51). Jesus himself was to be a mightier sign, changing the course of history more than any stunt he might have devised. 'The Jesus we speak of has been raised by God, as we can all bear witness. Exalted thus with God's right hand, he received the Holy Spirit from the Father, and all that you now see and hear flows from him', said Peter (Acts 2.32–33).

9    **All these (kingdoms of the world) I will give you, if you will only fall down and do me homage.** Many hill-tops in Judah offer wide views over the Jordan valley and the mountains beyond, which might well be described as a microcosm of the kingdoms of the earth in their glory. These perhaps Jesus saw, as he saw the drop from the parapet of the temple, in his mind's eye during the temptations. Israel had abandoned herself to the worship of worldly idols. Was Jesus to lead his people as a political messiah to a victory over the foreign oppressor, a new David conquering the Philistines of his day? Jesus refused that kind of earthly lordship in exchange for a genuflection, for he was to be given through his death and resurrection a Kingdom greater than any human empire. 'Full authority in heaven and on earth has been committed to me' (Matt. 28.18).

Because Jesus conformed to the will of God, the trials and temptations which were bringing about the downfall of the old dispensation were conquered at the outset of the new, and the truths which underlay the various elements making up the Jewish messianic expectation were more than fulfilled. The messianic hope was transfigured to a promise of salvation for mankind. Already in the baptism and in the temptations evil was trodden underfoot and conquered.

The time that Jesus was in the wilderness has a symbolic significance. Apart from Israel's forty years' wanderings in the desert, Moses spent forty days on mount Sinai (Exod. 24.18) and Elijah fasted for forty days on his way to mount Horeb (1 Kings 19.8). In biblical imagery these were all periods of purification and preparation before a mighty work of God. Fasting too has a purifying effect; men fasted and prayed before undertaking work in answer to God's call.

Jesus was to face temptation again (Matt. 16.22 and 26.36–46) but this preliminary battle in the wilderness was both a sequel to his baptism in the Jordan (temptation is a common experience of mystics and others after a period of high exaltation) and an overture to his ministry. The idea of temptation is not incompatible with Christ's sinlessness. Temptation is not sin; it is a form of testing. Indeed, it is a sign of Christ's total identification of himself with the human condition. 'Ours is not a high priest unable to sympathize with our weaknesses, but one who, because of his likeness to us, has been tested in every way, only without sin' (Heb. 4.15). So he began his ministry without resorting to the world's ways of making friends and influencing people, taking over when John had been arrested. He proclaimed the gospel of the Kingdom with the summons

16 to repentance, and **the people that lived in darkness saw a great light** (Isa. 9.2).

# LENT 1
## Sixth Sunday before Easter

*The King and the Kingdom: Temptation*

### Deuteronomy 6. 10–17
The divine promises are about to be fulfilled; entry into the promised land is near. The Book of Deuteronomy now begins to express anxiety that the sudden and great change from a nomadic life of poverty to an established life of affluence might entice Israel into forgetting God. So a warning is given to adhere to the worship of the Lord, and it is followed by a threat that God will not allow disobedience to pass unpunished.

The picture is one of taking possession of a land with its cities, houses, water supply, and agriculture all available for the invaders. The stereotyped list of 'real estate' in verse 11, **houses full of good things ...**, is derived historically from a legally binding list, like a land register, used in the ancient Near East for land treaties and other enactments.

14 **You must not follow other Gods ...**, if you do, **the Lord your God**
15 **... will be angry with you.** The anger of God is understood in its more primitive way as personal vindictiveness against the offenders. Later, the wrath of God was seen as an attitude of God towards sin rather than

16 against the sinner. **You must not challenge the Lord your God.** Challenging God would mean putting his worship to the test—adding

the worship of other gods along with the worship of the Lord. This would be equivalent to a complete failure to appreciate the uniqueness of God's
15 claim, seen here in terms of **a jealous god**, and would therefore be an act of defiance against him. The incident at Massah ('Challenge') was when the thirsty Israelites asked the question, 'Is the Lord in our midst or not?' and the Lord instructed Moses to strike the rock and water would pour out of it (Exod. 17.1–7).

### Hebrews 4. 12–16

'The word of God' is not used in this passage in the Johannine sense of the divine Logos but, as it is sometimes used in the OT, as God's messenger. God's word is not dead and empty speech; it is dynamic with life, communicating itself to men. 'The word which comes from my mouth
12 (shall) prevail' (Isa. 55.11). Its effect is that of a **two-edged sword**: it penetrates beneath the surface. Outward behaviour may be exemplary, but it is possible underneath to cherish a spirit of rebellion against God. God's scrutiny penetrates to those depths of the human personality
12 where **life and spirit, joints and marrow, divide**. At the centre is the heart, and the word of God searches that too.

The author contrasted Christ as our High Priest with the Levitical high priest in his cultic office. The high priest in Jerusalem was able only to step beyond the veil in the temple; Jesus passed through the seven heavens (of current mythology) to the throne of God above them: the juxtaposition
14 of the name and title **Jesus Son of God** underlines the union of the human and the divine natures in Christ. This is the faith in which Christians stand.

Anticipating the objection that such an exalted being could not possibly sympathize with the spiritual, intellectual, and moral frailties of human nature, the author asserted that Christ can in fact do this because he has shared in that same nature. He has a real kinship with mankind because
15 he has been **tested every way, as we are** (NEB footnote). The only difference is that he was not guilty of conscious and deliberate acts of rebellion against the Father. Christian confidence, then, rests in the knowledge that the barrier between God and man has been removed by Jesus; all can approach the throne of God—not just the high priest as in the Jewish cult—and all can ask for pardon which God in his mercy so freely gives.

### * Luke 4. 1–13

The Lucan account of the temptation is substantially but not verbally paralleled in Matthew. There are some slight differences:

Luke heightened the impression given by Matthew (and by Mark)
1 that Jesus went into the desert in a state of Spirit possession: **Full of the Spirit.**

The second temptation in Matthew (on the parapet of the temple) became the third in Luke.

In Luke's second temptation (the kingdoms of the world) the author increased the dramatic effect of the devil's revelation by saying it happened
5 **in a flash.**

There is no reference to the ministry of angels in Luke.

(For further commentary on the subject, see Lent 1 Year 1.)

# LENT 2
Fifth Sunday before Easter

*The King and the Kingdom : Conflict*

## 2 Kings 6. 8–17

In this passage, as in the story of Naaman, Elisha is depicted in the setting of contemporary history. The frequency of the raids and the regular repulses of the Arameans suggest border skirmishes rather than a full-scale war. The king of Aram was puzzled because he found that his military plans against Israel were miscarrying and consulted his staff. They told him that Elisha had supernatural gifts which enabled him to predict the king of Aram's manoeuvres and to warn the king of Israel in time to take counter measures. The plan to kidnap Elisha at Dothan, ten miles north of Samaria, was foiled, for one of Elisha's disciples, in answer to the prophet's prayer, was given a vision of the mysterious guard of horses and chariots of fire surrounding the prophet.

Some commentators say that this story belongs to saga rather than history, though the troubles between the Arameans and the Israelites are historical enough. The incident is thought to have taken place when Hazael Ben-adad was king of Aram and Jehu king of Israel, 841–814 B.C. Israelite slaves were attached to Aramean households (as was the Hebrew maid of Naaman's wife) making leakage of information probable, and

Elisha would gather much news on his visits to the communities of prophets scattered about the land. The most important sentence in this
16 passage is, **Do not be afraid, for those who are on our side are more than those on theirs;** it expressed the confidence of a man who had complete faith in the power of God (though sometimes such a man has to
17 pray for others, **O Lord, open his eyes and let him see**).

### (–23)

18 **Strike this host, I pray thee, with blindness.** Elisha's next move was to capture the king of Aram's force. The blindness was not total; it was a form of optical illusion so that they did not recognize Elisha or the trap into which he was leading them. In Elisha's answer to the king of Israel's
22 question, it is better to read the NEB footnote, **Would you destroy those whom you have taken prisoner . . .?** It was not the custom of Israel to murder prisoners of war unless the Lord had pronounced an anathema on a town.

### 1 John 4. 1–6

The passage leads on from the statement in 3.24b: 'This is how we can make sure that he (Jesus Christ) dwells within us: we know it from the Spirit he has given us'. The proof of fellowship with God is the indwelling of the Spirit: 'I will ask the Father, and he will give another to be your Advocate, who will be with you for ever—the Spirit of truth' (John 14.16). Christians are anointed with the Spirit because they are the people of the Anointed One, the Messiah. Christ breathed the Spirit upon the disciples when he appeared in the upper room on the day of resurrection.

1 John was written to counter the influence of those who were creating a division in the Church through heretical teaching. The author warned his readers to test such teachers by their moral obedience to God, by their love of their brethren, and—at this point he applied a third test—to see if they possessed the Spirit of truth. This could be decided if they denied the reality of the incarnation: everyone who possessed the Holy Spirit
2 would say that **Jesus Christ has come in the flesh.** A distinction is made in the author's mind between the Spirit of God and the spirit of man. The spirit of man is that principle of life in a human being which is infused and directed by the Spirit of God when he or she turns to Jesus Christ. When not possessed by the Spirit, the spirit of man is controlled by the spirit of Antichrist.

The concept of a conflict between good and evil in 1 and 2 John, then, is described in terms of an encounter within man between the Spirit of

God and the spirit of Antichrist. The title is not used elsewhere in the NT, but he is called 'the Enemy' in 2 Thess. 2.4 and 'the Beast' in Rev. 13 and 17. He is in the world, but Christians may have supreme confidence in God, for he has conquered the evil one through Jesus Christ. It can be

4 said of Christians, therefore, that **you have the mastery over these false prophets, because he who inspires you is greater than he who inspires the godless world.**

\* Luke 11. 14–26

Jesus was accused of exorcising through the power of Satan. Others had renewed the demand for a sign from heaven to demonstrate his authority —one of the temptations Christ faced in the wilderness. The request (which is only in Luke's version of the controversy) was all the more remarkable for the casting out of a dumb demon *was* a sign for those who had the eyes to see it.

18 Our Lord exposed the fallacy of the accusation: **If Satan is divided against himself, how can his kingdom stand?** The casting out of the demon was an assault on Satan's kingdom; he would hardly drive out one of his own vassals. Then Jesus asked the Jews about their own exorcists (presumably those like the sons of Sceva, the chief priest at Ephesus, Acts 19.13ff). Would they say that their men drove out devils through the power of Satan? Rather, the healing was a sign that the Kingdom of God

20 was among them. It was by **the finger of God** that Christ exercised this power.

The use of this phrase associated Jesus with Moses. When the plague of maggots appeared in Egypt as a result of Moses' striking the dust with his staff, Pharaoh's magicians attributed the wonder to 'the finger of God' (Exod. 8.19). Furthermore, the words on the tablets of stone on mount Sinai were written with the finger of God. God was able to perform the greatest works with what in human terms would be the smallest possible effort—the touch of a finger.

The thought that the finger of God is more powerful than Satan led to the saying about the strong man and his castle. Christ may have imagined a local prince, such as one of the sons of Herod the Great; many of their palaces were heavily fortified against insurgents or raiders. When

23 attacked, the arms and the armour were part of the plunder. **He who is not with me is against me, and he who does not gather with me scatters** shows that there is no neutrality in the warfare against the incursions of evil. One is either for or against God. One either receives the

24 Kingdom of God, or one is defenceless before the evil spirit who **wanders**

over the desert (where demons were believed to dwell) and then returns
in greater strength than before.

15      The meaning of **Beelzebub** is uncertain: it is usually interpreted 'lord
of flies' or 'lord of dung', but may be 'lord of the dwelling', a more
attractive derivation in the light of verses 21–22, which would contain a
play upon the meaning of the word. In this saying he is identified with
Satan or one of his vassals.

# LENT 2
## Fifth Sunday before Easter

### The King and the Kingdom: Conflict

### Isaiah 35. 1–10

The prophet gazed along the way that the exiles would return from Babylon to Jerusalem and in a vision saw the thousand miles of arid desert

2  flowering with great luxuriance—**Lebanon, Carmel and Sharon** were
symbols of fertility and beauty. But more important than the effect on
the desert, it was the people themselves who would be touched by the
glory of God. As the Lord once came with judgement to burn and to
sear, so he would come with redemption to heal and to make whole his

4  crippled people. **Be strong and fear not. See, your God comes with
vengeance, with dreadful retribution he comes to save you**—
the vengeance and the retribution are for the oppressors. Blindness, deaf-
ness, and lameness would be eliminated as the hallmark of God's presence
among them. There would be abundant water in the desert, as mirages
turn to reality, and green pastures would flourish where only the coarser
type of growth survived. Because they would be healed of their unclean-
nesses—causing their physical defects—the pilgrim's way back to
Jerusalem would be a way for the holy people of God, ransomed and
redeemed. There they would be safe from any wild animal.

The theme of the new exodus sounded in this reading suggests that
the passage belongs to the Second Isaiah. The New Testament saw the
theme fulfilled in Jesus Christ: 'that rock was Christ' 1 Cor. 10.1–4,
'I am the bread of life' John 6.48–51.

**1 John 3. 1–8**

The author was writing to refute erroneous ideas about the possibilities of a Christian's falling into sin and about the working of God's grace. Among his readers there were some who were saying that the Christian could not sin, whatever he did, or that it did not matter if a Christian did sin, for this only gave a greater opportunity for more grace (the teaching Paul countered in Rom. 6). The author had to affirm the truth that Christ, because he has conquered sin, drives out the sin of the Christian in whom he dwells, but that the Christian is still in the process of becoming what Christ has made him.

1    The disciples of Jesus were called **God's children**—Christ taught us to address the Father with him as 'Our Father' and declared that whoever did the will of God was his brother, sister, mother (Mark 3.35). This is what the Christian is in reality. Repentance and faith, baptism and the receiving of the Holy Spirit bring the Christian into the family of God, the Church, where he is no longer a slave but a son of God.

   The footnote references in the NEB to verse 2 indicate the various ways of reading it, but they do not alter the meaning of the passage. Verses 1 to 3 say this: We can hope that we shall be like Christ, both now and at the
2 end of time, **when he appears** (NEB footnote), because we know that we are God's children; this means that we must be purified, because Christ is pure, and it also means that we must not expect the world to recognize us as God's children, for it did not even recognize Christ himself when he came—indeed, we should not be surprised if it hates us (3.13). But we know that when the reality of our status as God's children
3 is made manifest at the second coming, **we shall be like him**, because we have lived in purity.

   The argument is amplified in the rest of the reading. Sin is deliberate
4 disobedience to God—**God's law** is synonymous with the will of God as revealed in Jesus Christ. **Christ appeared, as you know, to do away with sins, and there is no sin in him.** The sinlessness of Christ is affirmed throughout the New Testament, though sinlessness does not
6 mean he was freed from temptation. **No man . . . who dwells in him is a sinner; the sinner has not seen him and does not know him.** To sin is to be blind to God.

   Righteousness is always expressed in what a man says and does:
7 **it is the man who does right who is righteous.** It is never independent of conduct. This is how the Christian becomes what God has made him
8 in Christ. **The devil has been a sinner from the first** could mean either from the start of history, if he is a fallen angel, or from the time that

sin entered the world. The work of Jesus Christ is seen in terms of doing battle against the devil in this world and conquering him.

\* **Matthew 12. 22–32**

The Beelzebub controversy is recounted in a slightly different form from that in Luke 11.14–26 (see Lent 2 Year 1). The exorcism of the man who was blind and dumb raised the question in people's minds, Can this Jesus be the expected Messiah? It was widely believed that God would inaugurate the new age by means of a divinely commissioned person, a Messiah, who would be David's successor—that is the meaning of
23 the Son of David—as a leader of the nation. They also believed that the Messiah was already among them and would reveal his identity when the appointed moment came. This was a hope on which fanatical opponents of the Roman regime flourished. But the Pharisees made the accusation that Jesus could control demons in other people because he was himself possessed by Satan. In Jesus' reply to them, Matthew adds 'town' to 'kingdom' and 'household' (compared with the Lucan account) and the saying about the strong man is shortened.
31 The passage goes on to include the warning that **slander spoken against the Spirit,** the ultimate refusal to recognize the manifest work of God, is unforgivable. The gravest aspect of the incident, from Jesus' point of view, was the spiritual condition which his opponents' accusation revealed: they were unable to seek the forgiveness of God because they saw no need for forgiveness. The deliberate misrepresentation of a good deed, performed in the power of the Holy Spirit, is the work of the devil. By their charge the Pharisees have condemned themselves, not Jesus.

The distinction between speaking **against the Son of Man** and
32 speaking **against the Holy Spirit** is not easy to understand. Its most probable meaning is that during the ministry of Jesus (as 'Son of man') it was understandable and excusable not to recognize Jesus as the Messiah, but after Pentecost the ultimate rejection of the recognized and understandable work of the Holy Spirit places a man outside the scope of God's grace. For further details of this incident see commentary on pp. 151–2.

# LENT 3
Fourth Sunday before Easter

*The King and the Kingdom : Suffering*

### Isaiah 59. (1–11)
The problems of Israel in the post-exilic settlements are reflected in this chapter of the Third Isaiah. Sin has separated God from the people:
2 it is your iniquities that raise a barrier between you and your God. There has been bloodshed, lying, and a perversion of the course of justice
5 by men like vipers and spiders: **they hatch snakes' eggs, they weave cobwebs.** There is an emphasis by reiteration in verses 7b and 8 that the paths they follow are crooked. The community lamented that it seemed to be left in darkness.

### 12–20
The lament changed into a confession of sin by the people. They recognized that they had rebelled against God and that the source of that
14 rebellion was in their hearts. **Truth stumbles in the market-place and honesty is kept out of court** expressed the effects of sin in commercial dealings and the administration of justice.
15   **The Lord saw, and in his eyes it was an evil thing, so he inter-vened himself, since there was no man to help,** putting on his armour like a warrior. God cannot tolerate sin for ever, for it is contrary to his nature. The prophet expressed God's reaction in terms of human jealousy and anger exacting reprisals on his foes. The vision had now
18 widened; the **foes** and **enemies** seem to have been the nations hostile to Israel, not just the wicked men within Israel itself. For the effect of
19 God's retribution is that **from the west men shall fear his name, fear his glory from the rising of the sun.** God would reveal himself like the rising sun at dawn, revealing himself to all peoples in the power
20 of his Spirit. And he would liberate **all in Jacob who repent of their rebellion.**

### (–21)
This detached comment on the prophecy assured the people that God would keep the promise he had made that his spirit would rest upon his people.

1 Peter 2. 19-25

This passage on the sufferings of Christ arose out of the author's admonition to Christian slaves who found themselves unjustly punished by their masters—a situation that was not uncommon in the ancient world, where a slave was regarded as the personal possession of his master and subject

20  to his changing whims. The admonition **what credit is there in fortitude when you have done wrong and are beaten for it?** is akin to Christ's own saying, 'If you love only those who love you, what credit is that to you? Even sinners love those who love them. . . . But you must love your enemies. . . .' (Luke 6.32-35). There is nothing extraordinary in bearing patiently a punishment which one deserves—many would boast about the toughness with which they endured it! But to bear undeserved suffering patiently, that is extraordinary conduct and characteristic of a Christian.

The author then moved on to Christ's passion as an example. Christ himself, though innocent, suffered treatment that was totally unjust, and the vocation of a Christian is to imitate him in this—a theme which runs strongly through the NT (1 Thess. 1.6, 'You . . . followed the example set by us and by the Lord', is perhaps one of the earliest expressions of it). He seems to have used a liturgical or credal text—perhaps a hymn—as a means of elaborating his meditation on the passion of Christ, adding a few of his own words to it as a means of applying it to the people he is writing to. This citation is discernible in verses 21-25 in the short rhythmic phrases which are based on quotations or references to the fourth Servant Song, Isa. 52.13-53.12—another NT theme. The slaves were reminded that their Lord Christ, who had been no less blameless than they were, suffered unjustly as the prophet had foretold. If they were

23  tempted to protest their innocence, they were to remember his silence. **He did not retort with abuse . . . but committed his cause to the One who judges justly**: he preferred to leave the vindication of his righteousness to God the Father rather than to take action himself against his enemies.

24  Commentators are not agreed on the exegesis of **he carried our sins to the gibbet**: 'gibbet' translates an archaic Greek word, *xulon*, which literally means 'wood' and was used of a cross. It was therefore associated with the punishment of malefactors. If the preposition 'to' is retained, then the cross becomes an altar on which Christ made the sacrifice for our sins (though there is no other parallel of the cross being considered as an altar in this particular sense in the NT); but if the preposition 'on' (NEB footnote) is read, then Christ becomes the sacrificial scapegoat on

whom the high priest laid the sins of the people in the ritual of the Day
of Atonement (though the scapegoat was not slaughtered but driven into
the desert). But generally what the verses do is to draw together various
ideas from the sacrificial system of the OT to teach that, as in the Servant
Song, 'bearing sins' means taking the blame for sins, accepting the
24 punishment due for them, and so achieving their putting away. In his
own person is literally 'in his body': what Christ did he did as man,
sharing our human nature. His sufferings and death were vicarious;
as our representative, he endured the penalties which our sins merited.

The purpose of his death was that we might abandon sin; his saving
act challenges us to renew our lives in righteousness. So by his 'bruise'
(NEB's wounds obscures the implication that Christ's wounds were more
terrible than the bruise a slave might receive when he was ill-treated)
we are healed—restored to health from the hurt that our sins have inflicted
on us.

The picture of God shepherding his people is found in all parts of the
OT, just as the metaphor of scattered or shepherdless sheep is regularly
applied to Israel when misguided, discomfited, or leaderless. In the prophets the image of the shepherd begins to take on a messianic character
(Ezek. 34.22–23: 'I will save my flock, and they shall be ravaged no more;
I will judge between one sheep and another. Then I will set over them one
shepherd to take care of them, my servant David; he shall care for them
and become their shepherd.') This title passes to Jesus Christ in the NT,
though not directly, only by implication, in the Gospels. It was a favourite
subject in early Christian art in the paintings in the Roman catacombs,
25 mosaics and sculptures. Christ's function as Shepherd includes ruling,
so he is Guardian of his people. The noun *episkopos*, 'guardian', became
the technical name for the Church's chief minister, the bishop, and it was
already in use as such in some of Paul's communities. But here it has no
ecclesiastical overtones; it retains its original connotation, 'one who in-
spects, watches over, protects'. Souls means 'yourselves'.

\* Matthew 16. 13–28
In the fourth Gospel the disciples knew from the beginning that Jesus
was the Son of God and the Christ (John 1.34,41), but in the synoptic
Gospels Peter's confession of faith was the turning-point. It opened the
way to Christ's teaching about the nature of his messiahship; it led into
the prediction of the cross; it was the basis on which instruction about the
Christian community was given.

Caesarea Philippi was twenty miles north of the Sea of Galilee in a

13 pagan (non-Jewish) district. Asked by Jesus, **Who do men say that the Son of man is?** the disciples reply that Jesus was identified with the prophets, John the Baptist restored to life, Elijah who was expected to return before the final day of judgement, or Jeremiah. But when asked,
15 **Who do you say that I am?** it was Simon Peter (given his two names to mark the solemnity of the occasion) who answered: **You are the Messiah, the Son of the Living God.** 'Son of the living God' is only in Matthew and is thought to be a later addition. The title marks Jesus' unique nature and filial relation to the Father, demonstrating that his messiahship was something far greater than and radically different from Jewish expectation.

Israel had not responded to Jesus' proclamation of the Kingdom of God, but Peter's confession revealed that the disciples were beginning to form that core which Christ needed for the carrying forward of the gospel after his death, resurrection, and ascension; and so Peter's act of faith was the foundation on which the Church could be built. It gave Peter a place of distinction among the band of disciples: his name proclaimed his
18 office, he was *Petros* (Greek), *Cephas* (Aramaic), **the Rock.** The congregation (here and in Matt. 18.17 called *ekklesia* a 'church') within Israel would not be conquered by the power of death; Christ gave the keys, a figurative expression denoting the trust put in a steward by a master of the house, to the apostles to exercise authority within the Church.
19 'Bind' and 'loose', translated in the NEB as **forbid** and **allow**, are rabbinic terms for disciplinary procedures in being bound (sentenced) to excommunication and in being loosed (absolved) from it. The injunction to secrecy was common sense. Until Jesus could establish by teaching and suffering what it meant to be the anointed one, and what this meant for the faith and life of his disciples, to tell people that he was the Messiah would arouse false hopes among nationalist Jews and cause trouble.
21 **From that time** indicates the turning-point we have just mentioned. Jesus had been proclaiming the Kingdom of heaven to the people. Now he began to prepare his disciples for what they would see him undergo on the cross in terms of the suffering Servant of God from the Second Isaiah. But he also prophesied his resurrection. This prediction of the passion and resurrection of Christ in compact phrases suggests that they became the summary of the apostolic Church's message; they occur three times in this gospel (16.21, 17.22f, 20.18f). Peter's reaction was that of a Jew caught up in the more conventional kind of messianic expectation in which it was unthinkable that the Christ should suffer. The intensity of
23 Jesus' reply, **Away with you, Satan,** indicates the courage it took to face

death. Peter momentarily played the devil's role, placing a stumbling-block of disobedience in front of Christ.

25 Jesus invited his followers to be ready for self-sacrifice, even to death. Whoever cares for his own safety is lost; but if a man will let himself be lost for my sake, he will find his true self. This is the death and resurrection as it applies to the Christian. Using the apocalyptic vision of the coming of the Son of Man from Daniel 10, Christ then applied the advent of that mysterious figure both to the final judgement and to the

28 saving events which some of those standing here would see—the resurrection, the ascension, the gift of the Spirit, the mission of the Church.

# LENT 3
## Fourth Sunday before Easter

*The King and the Kingdom : Suffering*

Isaiah 45. (14–17)

15 The nations will come to give homage to the God of Israel, the de-liverer. Idol-worshippers are to be shamed, but Israel will be saved

17 for all eternity.

18–25

The universalism of Second Isaiah was rooted in the belief that God

18 made the earth and fashioned it . . . a place to dwell in. The refrain

18 I am the Lord, there is no other is repeated in verses 21 and 22. Addressing Israel, God disputed the implied assertion that he had left his chosen people in the lurch and that his words (his earlier prophecies) had led to darkness and nothingness. On the contrary I the Lord speak

19 what is right, declare what is just.

20 Gather together, come, draw near, all you survivors of the nations. The word 'survivors' presupposes a lost campaign, from which those concerned have made their escape. Thus the people summoned to appear before the Lord were those who had fled from a battle in which they had been defeated. They were invited to put their cause before the Lord: Urge your case, consult together; they were chided for their

21 idolatry: **There is no other god than I, victorious and able to save.**
But the amazing thing was that this victorious God did not glory in
his triumph; there was no jubilation on his part over the defeated gods
of the nations. Instead, he invited those among the nations who had
survived the catastrophe to participate in the salvation which he offered.
His aim was that each individual should freely accept him as the one God
23 who saved them: **to me every knee shall bow, and by me every tongue
shall swear.** The final verse promised victory and glory for Israel among
the nations as God's chosen.
The text is quoted in Rom. 14.11 and in Phil. 2.10–11 to add scriptural
proof to the teaching that Jesus Christ came to save all men and that all
men would appear before the judgement seat of God.

### Colossians 1. 24–29

This passage contains one of the most daring of Paul's assertions—
namely, that in his own body he is 'making up all that has still to be
undergone by Christ for the sake of his body, the Church' (JB). It is daring
because the NT is clear that Christ suffered once and for all and that his
self-surrender was unique and complete, the fountainhead of all reconciliation and a free gift to us that cannot be earned.
Yet Christians have to suffer in this world, in varying and often, it
appears, in unfair degrees. What Paul did, by his profound insight into
the nature of Christ's union with his people in the Church, was to realise
that what we suffer in this world is a means of being united with Christ
in his suffering. Baptism is a once-for-all sacramental participation in the
death and resurrection of Christ. If we are risen with Christ (3.1), we live
a life transformed by the power of Christ's saving acts. This does not
protect us from the ravages of life which afflict us; yet because Christ
triumphed over the suffering and death with which he was afflicted, we
too shall triumph over them. The things we suffer can, in a sense, be the
means by which the Body of Christ fulfils her part in Jesus' saving acts.
This is creative suffering, suffering accepted to effect an ultimate good.
24    Paul did not usually speak of **his** (Christ's) **body which is the church**
in a universal sense. Nor was it usual for him to designate the Church as
Christ's body; it is *Christians* who are the body of Christ in the Pauline
letters. Here, then, is something more than a mere metaphor. **His body
which is the church** expresses the solidarity which Christians have with
Christ and with one another. Paul saw himself as the Church's servant
(*diakonos*, 'a minister') for the benefit of the Colossian Christians; his
task (*oikonomian*, 'a stewardship', a household word) was the 'mystery'

(RSV) of God's secret purpose, now divulged to his people. Its content
27 was **Christ in you, the hope of glory to come,** so that the character of
Jesus is reproduced in believers through the Holy Spirit individually
and corporately to manifest Christ present **among** them (NEB footnote).
The thing had happened which it was impossible for most Jews ever to
conceive: the Gentiles have a Messiah! Paul's purpose was that they should
grow in Christ. This they would never do if they followed the false
teaching which he has had to combat among them; they would only
mature if they grasped the wisdom of God in which he had instructed
them. The favourite image of the athlete appears in the final sentence as
Paul described how he toiled in the power of Christ to this end.

### * Luke 9. 18–27

Jesus' first direct instruction about his destiny is set in the context of
prayer. He was praying before he asked his disciples whom they thought
19 he was. **Some say John the Baptist, others Elijah . . .;** the various
answers revealed, among other things, that there was some substance to
Herod's fear that Jesus would continue the Baptist's movement. It was
20 Peter who confessed Jesus to be **God's Messiah.** The charge not to di-
vulge this to anyone has the atmosphere of the messianic secret—the
identity of God's Anointed one in Jewish expectation was known only
to God until he chose to reveal him—but it is probably due to the practical
fact that Jesus did not at that time wish to be known. To be hailed as a
Messiah of that kind would involve political complications which might
prevent the proclamation of the gospel.
22    **The Son of man has to undergo great sufferings.** The title in the
synoptic Gospels is confined to Jesus' own utterances; it seems to have
been the name by which he chose to designate himself, in contrast to his
hesitation in accepting the name of Messiah. And he used it here to show
that the Jewish concept of messiahship must undergo a radical change
before it could be applied to him. His rejection and death was not what the
Messiah was supposed to undergo. The association of the idea of the
suffering Servant of God with the Anointed one was one that was made by
Jesus himself.
23    Some commentators have suggested that the expression, **he must
take up his cross,** belongs to the post-resurrection era, since it could
hardly have had the meaning of total self-denial before Christ's own crucifixion. Death by nailing to a cross was the Roman method of dealing with
rebels. If Jesus had used these words to his disciples, they would probably
have misunderstood him as meaning that they must risk their lives in

acts of open rebellion against the Roman occupation forces. Whether this is correct or not, Christ's invitation has a vital spiritual application. The Christian disciple is called to die daily to himself and to live in the risen

26 Lord. A man's response determines his fate before the **Son of Man** on the last day. The original Christian conception of the coming judgement is one which included God active within it and in which he would send his angels to gather his elect from the four corners of the world. It was founded on God's promise to gather his own together (Zech. 2.6 LXX). The **Son of Man** is an addition to this scene and is associated with it in later Jewish apocalyptic. Compared with the other synoptic writers, Luke slightly modifies the massive drama of the scene in a few words.

27    **I tell you this: there are some of those standing here who will not taste of death before they have seen the kingdom of God** also causes commentators difficulties. It could mean that Jesus, within the limitations of his human knowledge, expected the establishment of the Kingdom in the near future. Or it could mean that Jesus foretold that some would see the power of the Kingdom in the resurrection, the ascension, the gift of the Spirit, and the mission of the Church.

# LENT 4
Third Sunday before Easter

*The King and the Kingdom: Transfiguration*

### Exodus 34. 29–35

Behind the narratives of the transfiguration of Christ in the Gospels is a conscious parallelism with the theophany on mount Sinai when Moses received the covenant from God. Part of the story of this theophany forms the OT reading for today. Aaron and the people saw Moses coming down from the mountain with the two tablets on which the words of the coven-

29 ant had been written, and **the skin of his face shone** because he had been talking with God. The miracle of this encounter, as far as Jewish theology was concerned, was that Moses had been able to see God and speak to him without perishing in the process, for it was thought that the glory of God was such that no man could see God and live. The Hebrew word 'to radiate', *qaran*, is derived from *qeren*, a horn, and this gave rise in later

art forms to a depicting of Moses with horns to simulate the glory of God shining from his face. The radiation frightened the people, so Moses had to put a veil or a priest's mask over his face. The task of Moses in speaking with God and conveying the divine commands to the people expresses exactly the offices of priest and prophet, both of which merge in the life of the great patriarch.

Verses 29–33 and 34–35 belong to separate Priestly traditions. The latter is part of the story of Moses' going into the tent of meeting to commune with God, but it has been transferred to the encounter on Sinai.

The Exodus story also describes the tabernacle and the tent which sheltered it. The divine presence, the *shekinah*, descended as a pillar of cloud upon this tent, and Moses spoke with God there. It is probable that the story was influenced by the Jewish traditions surrounding the celebration of the feast of Tabernacles, the last of the three great annual pilgrimage festivals—the other two being Passover and Pentecost. The feast of Tabernacles arose out of the custom of erecting tents in the vineyards at harvest-time in order that the work of gathering the fruit could be continued from dawn to dusk without interruption. The law was ceremonially read aloud by the Levitical priesthood to the people during these celebrations (Deut. 31.9–13). Later, the giving of the law on mount Sinai was associated with the feast of Pentecost, but its connection with the feast of Tabernacles was never wholly lost. The erection of tents in the vineyards and the gathering in of the harvest prompted Jews to look forward to the end of time, when they would be encamped with the Lord for ever, surrounded by the fruits of his goodness. Then God would be enthroned as ruler of all his people (Isa. 32.15–18, Ezek. 47.12, Hos. 12.9–10, etc.).


2 Corinthians 3. 12–18
Paul had been speaking about the splendour of 'the divine dispensation of the Spirit' which has replaced the dispensation of the law given on mount Sinai (3.4–11, see Epiphany 5 Year 1). Compared with the latter, the splendour in which the Christian shares never fades. Nor must the Christian try to hide that splendour, as Moses had to by putting a veil 12 over his face. With such a hope as this we speak out boldly.

With the reference to the veil, Paul's thought switched to the Jews of his time and he saw their lack of response to the gospel as the result of 14 another kind of veil being dropped over their minds. When the lesson is read from the old covenant (he was referring to the reading of the

OT in the synagogue services) they failed to recognize that the old covenant with its binding law had been abrogated in Christ. Quoting Isa. 61.1-2, he reminded the readers of his letter that it is in repentance that this kind of blockage is removed. It is possible that Paul believed that wherever the OT referred to 'Lord' it meant Christ and that it was Christ whom Moses encountered in the tent of meeting. But Christ is the Spirit—the apostle does not seem to distinguish between the two here—and the Spirit gives the true interpretation of the OT.

18   **We all reflect as in a mirror the splendour of the Lord; thus we are transfigured into his likeness, from splendour to splendour.** Because Christians have the Spirit they can, unlike the Jews, behold the glory of God, and they reflect that glory as a mirror reflects the sunlight. Consequently, they are themselves changed by their beholding.


\* **Matthew 17. 1–13**
The transfiguration is one of the events in the Gospel which reveals Jesus as the Messiah of God and the bringer of salvation. Moses and Elijah, representing the law and the prophets, stand by him as witness to the truth that in Christ the promises of God made in the OT have been fulfilled. The details of the event recall the apocalyptic vision of a man clothed in white linen which Daniel received after keeping a fast for three weeks (in the Bible a fast is, among other things, a means by which men prepare themselves to receive a revelation from God). 'The wise leaders shall shine like the bright vault of heaven, and those who have guided the people in the true path shall be like stars for ever and ever' (Dan. 10.5, 12.3). The whiteness of the garments, the charge to keep the messianic secret, the conversation with Moses and Elijah (one dead, the other ascended into heaven), the metamorphosis of Christ (*metamorphomai*, 'to be transformed'): all these emphasise the eschatological nature of the event. For a moment, eternal reality had broken through into the present order.

1    **Six days later Jesus took Peter, James, and John the brother of James, and led them up a high mountain.** The detail of the time after the confession of Peter at Caesarea Philippi is unusual. It may be a historical reminiscence, or it may be due to Exod. 24.16–18. 'The glory of the Lord rested upon Mount Sinai, and the cloud covered the mountain for six days; and on the seventh day he called to Moses out of the cloud. The glory of the Lord looked to the Israelites like a devouring fire on the mountain-top. Moses entered the cloud and went up the mountain; there he stayed forty days and forty nights.' The feast of Tabernacles

lasted seven days. Peter, James, and John also shared the agony in the garden with Christ (26.37). The mountain is the place where God traditionally reveals himself to men in the OT (Elijah as well as Moses, 1 Kings 19.1–12, see Lent 4 Year 2).

4    **If you wish, I will make three shelters here, one for you, one for Moses, one for Elijah.** Peter's offer could mean that he wanted to make permanent a vision which could only be temporary, the purpose of all shrines. Or it could be a distant echo of the celebrations of the feast of Tabernacles, where the tents were erected for harvesting and where it was believed God would come and 'tabernacle' with his people (*skene*, a 'tent' or 'tabernacle').

5    **A voice called from the cloud, 'This is my Son, my Beloved, on whom my favour rests; listen to him'.** The cloud is a sign of the divine presence, the *shekinah*, in the story of the Exodus, and it was from it that God spoke at the transfiguration. The voice was heard on two other occasions, at the baptism (3.17) and at the beginning of the passion (John 12.28, see Lent 5 Year 1). Like the baptism, the transfiguration was an epiphany in which the veil which separates the invisible from the visible and the future from the present is removed for a moment and the truth revealed. The voice may have been quoting Deut. 18.15, 'The Lord your God will raise up a prophet from among you like myself (Moses), and you shall listen to him'. The disciples fall on their faces as Daniel had done before the vision of the heavenly man and, also like Daniel, they were touched by Jesus who told them to stand up.

The parallelism between mount Sinai and the transfiguration is underlined more strongly by Matthew than the other evangelists. Only Matthew
2 notes that Christ's face, like the face of Moses, **shone like the sun,** a detail used by Paul immediately before today's epistle (2 Cor. 3.7), and only Matthew adds the phrase from Isa. 42.1, **on whom my favour rests** thus linking the event with the song of the Servant of God. For this writer, Jesus Christ is the second Moses, the Servant of God who through obedience and suffering was able to offer himself for the salvation of man. It is these implications, together with the rich eschatological content of the narrative, which have led some commentators to believe that behind this story is the memory of one of the resurrection appearances of our Lord.

Further details indicate that Matthew was presenting Jesus as the new
10 Moses. The scene is followed by a question about Elijah: **Why then do our teachers say that Elijah must come first?** The teachers are the doctors of the law whose traditional interpretation of Mal. 4.5, 'I will send

you the prophet Elijah before the great and terrible day of the Lord comes', had been to give Elijah a mighty role as the one who would
11 **come and set everything right.** Jesus' reply was that Elijah had already come. John the Baptist had fulfilled Elijah's task; so the implication is
12 that he (Jesus) was to fulfil Moses'. **The Son of Man is to suffer at their hands,** a prophecy that his own fate would be the same as John's as well.

## LENT 4
## Third Sunday before Easter

*The King and the Kingdom: Transfiguration*

### I Kings 19. 1-12
Alone and unsupported, and in need of encouragement for his faith, Elijah set out to escape the vengeance of Jezebel, and reached Beersheba, the southernmost part of Judah. The broom-bush is found in the beds of wadis near the Dead Sea; it has a delicate white flower with a maroon
4 centre. His prayer, **Lord, take my life,** reflects the Semitic conception that life (lit. 'life-breath') proceeded directly from, and properly belonged to, God. Though a man wished to die, he was not at liberty to commit
6 suicide. But the Lord had other plans for him. The **cake baked on hot stones** refers to a round flat cake of bread, still baked in this way by
8 Arabs in the desert. **Forty days and forty nights** is the conventional round number of Semitic folk-lore; Elijah's journey was influenced by the tradition of Moses' sojourn for the same period on the mount of God. Horeb, which simply means 'desert', was the holy mountain of the covenant and the law-giving, Sinai. It was the place where the true God revealed himself (Exod. 3.1ff, 33.18—34.9) and where the covenant had been concluded. Elijah entered that cave where Moses had crouched when the glory of God appeared (Exod. 33.22).

The storm, earthquake, and lightning, which in Exod. 19 had manifested the presence of God, did not contain the message that Elijah needed; they were only the heralds of the Lord's coming. The whisper of a light breeze signified that God is a spirit and that he converses intimately with his prophets; it does not mean that God's dealings with men are necessarily gentle and unnoticed—as indeed the career of Elijah was to demonstrate!

The story brings together the figures of Moses and Elijah; both experienced a theophany of God on the holy mountain, and by it Elijah understood that he was to continue the work of Moses in maintaining the covenant and restoring the ancient faith of Israel.

### (–18)

Elijah was sent to anoint Jehu king of Israel, Hazael king of Syria, and Elisha as his own successor. In 2 Kings Hazael was anointed by a messenger of Elisha (8.7–15), Jehu did not become king until later (9.1–13), and Elijah did not immediately appoint his successor. The Lord told Elijah that a terrible fate awaited those who were unfaithful in Israel, but a remnant of seven thousand would be saved.

### 2 Peter 1. 16–19

This passage represents the main part of 2 Peter, claiming that the apostolic teaching is firmly founded on a historical revelation which in itself confirms what earlier prophecy had foretold. The author, a Jewish Christian familiar with Hellenistic cults, represented himself as the apostle Simon Peter and appealed to the experience of the transfiguration in support of his case.

16   The **tales artfully spun** were the legendary stories about the gods current in Hellenistic mythology. Christianity is based not on similar mythology but on truths which are supported by tangible and objective evidence. **The power of Jesus** is the divine might which he possessed as risen Lord; **his coming** is the appearance at the transfiguration which, for this writer, looked forward to the final advent of the Son of God at the end of the world. (*Parousia* was a word taken from Hellenistic cults to describe the epiphany of the gods; it entered Christian vocabulary via
16  Hellenistic Judaism.) Behind the phrase **we saw him with our own eyes in majesty** are two words (*epoptes*, eye-witnesses; *megaleiotes*, majesty) also from Hellenist cults: the former denoted those initiated into sacred mysteries; the second the revelation of divine power. On the other hand, the writer showed a typical Hebrew reserve about using the
17  divine name and referred to **the sublime Presence**; the synoptic Gospels, we note, make no mention of God in their accounts of the transfiguration and represent the voice as coming from the cloud. **This is my Son, my Beloved, on whom my favour rests** has been affected

in the manuscripts by parallels in the Gospels. (See NEB footnote.) It
17 comes close to Matthew's version, but differs from it by adding **on**
18 **whom my favour rests**. The mount of transfiguration is now **the**
**sacred mountain**, a specific spot hallowed by the religious memory of
the Church.

The transfiguration disclosed Christ's divine nature and ratified it by
the heavenly voice, confirming his power and future coming. The writer
19 saw it as confirming also **the message of the prophets**, meaning here
not just the prophetic books but the whole of the OT, which he assumed
looked forward to the glorious coming of the Messiah and his subsequent
establishment of his Kingdom. 'God's word', he said, is truly 'a lantern
unto my feet, and a light unto my path' (Ps. 119.105), and Christ is the
morning star (Num. 24.17), illuminating men's minds, until the day of the
Lord comes.

* Luke 9. 28–36
The gospel continues last Sunday's reading.
For a general discussion of the meaning of the transfiguration, see
above pp. 164–6.
28    The differences in Luke's account are as follows: Luke has **about**
**eight days** after the previous discourse, while Mark and Matthew have
six days.

The order of the names of the second and third disciples are changed
round so that Peter and John come together, as in the early chapters of
Acts.
29    **The appearance of his face changed and his clothes became**
**dazzling white**. Luke avoided using the verb 'transfigured' (Greek
*metemorphothe* Mark 9.2), perhaps because for his Hellenistic readers it
might have had associations with pagan cults.
30    He described Moses and Elijah as **two men** before mentioning their
names, thus enabling him to link the two witnesses with the two men
at the resurrection (24.4) and the ascension (Acts 1.10).
31    Moses and Elijah spoke of Jesus' **departure, the destiny he was to**
**fulfil in Jerusalem**. *Exodus* means 'departure' but is also a euphemism
for 'death'. Furthermore, Luke must have had in mind the exodus which
Moses had led from Egypt and during which he had died. The transfiguration thus pointed forward to the paschal death and resurrection
of Christ.
32    The disciples **had been in a deep sleep**, following the Biblical tradition of sleep before a vision.

33    Peter's suggestion about making **three shelters** is rationalized by the explanation that the figures were moving away.

34    The disciples **were afraid as they entered the cloud**, Luke suggesting that their awe was due, not to the enveloping of the cloud, but to consciousness of the divine presence.

35    Luke added **my Chosen** to identify Jesus more clearly as the new Moses of God, from Ps. 106.23, 'Moses his chosen'.

# LENT 5
## Second Sunday before Easter

*The King and the Kingdom: Victory of the Cross*

### Isaiah 63. 1–9

The first six verses are in the form of a dialogue between the prophet, speaking as a watchman upon the walls of the city, and the Lord. Like a sentry, the prophet challenged the mysterious figure who approached

1 **from Edom, coming from Bozrah, his garments stained red.** The figure replied that he was the one who is to announce that righteousness has triumphed. The second challenge from the prophet asked about the

2 figure's clothes, **like one who treads grapes in the vat.** This is a simile which goes back to God's action in judgement, even the judgement of his own people: 'The Lord trod, like grapes in the press, the virgin daughter of Judah' (Lam. 1.15). As a sign of God's judgement of the nations, it was used in Joel 4.13, to be taken up in Rev. 14.19 and 19.15, 'The winepress was trodden outside the city'. At this point the Lord identified himself as the victor who had trampled his enemies under his feet. The enemy was Edom, who had refused to allow Israel to travel up the king's highway past Bozrah on their way to the promised land (Num. 21.14–21), but by implication it is the forces of evil which have been overcome.

5 **I looked for a helper but found no one:** the Lord was alone in his struggle to vindicate his people; no help came from his elect.

7    **I will recount the Lord's acts of unfailing love** begins a psalm of praise for all that the Lord has done for us. He had chosen them,

8 **they are my people,** and he had become their saviour in all that befell

9 them. He did not send a messenger but delivered them himself (lifted

**them up and carried them** pictures the Lord acting like a parent or a shepherd).

(–16)

10 **His holy spirit** is the will of God directing a man inwardly. The term prepared the way for the revelation of the Holy Spirit as a Person within the Trinity. It was the people's rebellion that turned God into their enemy, until they repented. The memory of the exodus leads to verses
16 of warm appeal to God, calling on him as a **father** and a **kinsman** (NEB footnote).

### Colossians 2. 8–15

In early Christian history the Colossian Church had a reputation for dabbling in wild theological speculations—a reputation which it acquired from its foundations, judging by Paul's letter. Its members mixed mythical ideas with beliefs about the angelic powers who were supposed to
8 control the universe. **Elemental spirits,** *stoicheia,* could mean simple forms of doctrine (**elementary ideas,** NEB footnote). It was against such deviations from Christian teaching that Paul uttered the warning in this passage.

He began by asserting the divinity of Christ in the sense that God's power is fully integrated in him and not dissipated over other spiritual
9 beings. **It is in Christ that the complete being of the Godhead dwells embodied.** This has an incarnational meaning, but it also has the sense of 'dwelling in the body of Christ, the Church' (**corporately,** NEB footnote). One sense leads to another in Paul's theology, and the double reference could explain the use of the present tense in the verb 'dwells', as in 1 Cor. 15.12ff. Every power and authority in the universe is subject to Christ as Head, even the elemental spirits of the world.
11    **In him also you were circumcised, not in a physical sense, but by being divested of the lower nature; this is Christ's way of circumcision.** Paul saw the act of circumcision as a tiny analogy of the crucifixion; as the body of a Jewish baby boy was offered for the surgical act in obedience to the law, so the human body of Christ was offered for the sacrificial act of crucifixion in obedience to the will of God. This perfect obedience was the climax and implementation of Christ's own baptism in the Jordan and led, through Calvary and death to resurrection and life. The passion of Christ, commemorated on this Passion Sunday, is a consequence of this 'circumcision'.

Through baptism each Christian is brought into this 'circumcision'.

Earlier in this epistle Paul had spoken of this union in terms of Christ as the Head and the Church as his body (1.18) and of his own sufferings as a share in the sufferings of Christ (1.24). Now he underlined the way in which the Colossian Christians were joined to Christ, not through bap-
12 tism as a mechanical ritual act, but **through faith in the active power of God, who raised (Jesus) from the dead** and who appointed baptism as the sacramental sign by which men and women in penitence and faith are united with Christ.

The 'deadness' of the Colossians was evident in two ways: first, they
13 were **morally uncircumcised** in that they were outside the covenant of Israel; and, secondly, they were in the grip of their sins. It was only in Christ that, in spite of this, they were now part of the true Israel of God.
14 For Christ has **cancelled the bond which pledged us to the decrees of the law.** The image is that of an I.O.U., an undertaking to obey the law of God imposed by a man's conscience. The law, disobeyed by man, stands as his accuser to God. This incriminating document Christ has destroyed by letting himself be nailed to the cross (did Paul know of the notice put on the cross proclaiming Jesus as King of the Jews?).

The passage ends with a picture of Christ, like a triumphant warrior, leading in a victory procession the hostile powers of the spiritual universe as a parade of the captives—a common feature of parades in the ancient world which marked the successful conclusion of a campaign.

* **John 12. 20–32**
After the entry into Jerusalem (12.2–19) a group of Greeks who went up to worship at the festival approached Philip, presumably because they thought that, being the disciple with a Greek name and a Gentile background, they could count on his sympathy. They were Gentiles who were sufficiently attracted to the religion of Israel to attend the synagogues of the dispersion and to adopt some of the practices of Judaism, including the making of pilgrimages to the holy city for the feasts. Like the Gentiles at Colossae to whom Paul wrote, they were seeking Christ but were still some distance from him. Philip went to tell his fellow-townsman Andrew, and they both went to Jesus.

We hear no more of these Greeks, for at that moment John inserted
23 into his Gospel Jesus' declaration, **The hour has come for the Son of Man to be glorified.** Hitherto in this Gospel Christ had said that his hour had not yet come. Perhaps the homage of the Greeks foreshadowed the worldwide homage that was to be given to our Lord, and this was a sign that the climax of his ministry was at hand. He explained the mean-

ing of his passion and death in terms of a grain of wheat which, falling
into the ground and dying, bears a rich harvest of new life. The disciples
25 had to learn that the way to life is through renunciation: **the man who
loves himself is lost, but he who hates himself in this world will
be kept safe for eternal life.** It is the Johannine parallel to Mark 8.34,
'Anyone who wishes to be a follower of mine must leave self behind; he
must take up his cross and come with me'; except that in the fourth
Gospel there is a further saying that the disciple who shares in Christ's
suffering will also share in the honour which the Father gives him.

There is no agony in the garden in John. In its place comes the incident
in verses 27–32. Christ wondered whether to ask that the cup of suffering
27 might be taken from him, **Father, save me from this hour**; but no
sooner had the thought entered his mind than he banished it with a fresh
surrender of his will to the Father ('Not what I will, but what thou wilt',
Mark 14.36). Instead, he glorified God and experienced a theophany,
28 **a voice sounded from heaven: 'I have glorified it, and I will glorify
it again.'** (This is the third time the Father addresses the Son from
heaven; the first time was at the baptism, the second at the transfiguration.)
God had already glorified his name through the ministry of Jesus, and
he would glorify it again in his death. Thunder is recognized as the voice
of God in the OT (Exod. 19.19, Ps. 24.3). The voice spoke, said Jesus, for
the benefit of the crowd.

31    Jesus continued his discourse, the repetition of Now giving it a certain
emphasis, and declared that his death was the moment of crisis for the
world (*crisis*, 'judgement') whereby the power of evil would be broken.
By rejecting Jesus, men condemn themselves, but by the providence of
God this very rejection is made the means of salvation. Though Jesus trod
'the winepress of the wrath and retribution of God' (Rev. 19.15) in the
sense that he bore the effect of sin in dying on the cross, yet when he
was lifted up, in the glory of the cross and in the ascension, he would
draw all men to himself. Behind this saying is the image of the serpent
whom Moses lifted up in the wilderness for the healing of the people.

# LENT 5
## Second Sunday before Easter

*The King and the Kingdom: Victory of the Cross*

### Jeremiah 31. 31-34

As the Jews came to recognize that God demands moral obedience rather than a formal obedience in rituals, they came to see that the performance of a ritual sacrifice was an empty and hypocritical gesture without the proper disposition of the heart in the worshippers. The sacrifices in their various forms—peace offerings, burnt offerings and especially sin and guilt offerings—must express true repentance and obedience in the lives of the people. The sacrifice of bulls which Moses celebrated to inaugurate the covenant between God and his people on mount Sinai was only valid as a ritual if the people kept their promise, 'We will do all that the Lord has told us'. The blood of the covenant was merely a seal on the act of obedience which they had already made (Exod. 24.3ff).

With the failure of the old covenant, Jeremiah was one of the prophets who came to see that what men needed was a new heart and a new spirit before they could be obedient to the law of God. So the prophet looked
31 forward to the time when God would **make a new covenant with Israel and Judah.** In this new covenant the desire to obey him would be set so deeply within their hearts that there would be no question of their
34 wishing to disobey. **All of them, high and low alike, shall know me, says the Lord;** and in this sentence to know the Lord means that they would have a 'knowledge' which is akin to what the Christian means by 'faith'. In these circumstances the new covenant would be superior to the
33 old, for the sins of the people would be forgiven, and **I will become their God and they shall become my people.** Prophecies of this new and eternal covenant appear also in Ezek. 36.25-28 and Isa. 55.3, etc.

### Hebrews 9.11-15

The author interpreted the work of Jesus Christ in terms of the sacrificial ritual of the temple in Jerusalem, which had probably ended by the time this letter was written. In this ritual Christ is high priest. The variants,
11 **high priest of good things already in being,** or **high priest of good things which are to be** (NEB footnote), make the difference between saying that the perfect relationship with God, which is the aim of the Christian life, is wholly an other-worldly experience, and claiming that to

some extent at least we are able to enter into that relationship here and now.

11    The tent of his priesthood is a greater and more perfect one; the NEB identifies the 'tent' as the sanctuary within which Christ exercises his high priestly office, namely, the heavenly sanctuary. (JB translates, 'He has passed through the greater, the more perfect tent'.) Made by men's hands was probably a phrase used by Jewish writers in the Hellenistic world to describe idols, and in the NT is used by Jesus and by his followers of the temple at Jerusalem (Mark 14.58, Acts 7.48). Jesus did not offer blood in order to gain access to this heavenly sanctuary;

12    he gained it through the sacrifice of his own blood. Thus he has entered the sanctuary once and for all and secured an eternal deliverance.

But how is Christ's sacrifice effective for all times? Starting with the ritual sacrifices of the old covenant, the author acknowledged that these

13    were partially effective, at least in matters of external purity. The blood of bulls and goats was used in the sacrifices on the Day of Atonement; the sprinkled ashes of a heifer were used for making 'water of impurity' for the cleansing of persons and vessels and clothes ritually polluted by contact with a dead body (Lev. 16.14f., Num. 19).

If these are effective in rituals, he said, how much greater is the

14    power of the blood of Christ; he offered himself without blemish to God, a spiritual and eternal sacrifice. He who in self-sacrifice offered himself to God in his full and perfect humanity, was himself eternal by nature. Because of this, the salvation which he procured for us by his blood is everlasting. As the external sacrifices were effective for ritual cleansing, so the personal self-sacrifice of one who is eternal will cleanse us spiritually and fit us for the service of the living God. The original words suggest a sacred ministry of a liturgical kind, though of course the author sees the whole of a Christian's life embraced within this phrase.

* Mark 10. 32–45

32    The road, going up to Jerusalem, may well have been crowded with pilgrims on their way to celebrate the Passover. Jesus and his disciples were about to enter Jericho, and they would see beyond that town the road ascending up towards the mount of Olives many miles away and nearly four thousand feet higher. In the eyes of this evangelist, Jerusalem was the centre of hostility to Christ and also the goal of his journey. Our Lord was determined to fulfil his work—Luke recorded that he

'set his face resolutely towards Jerusalem' (9.51)—and the disciples seem
32 to have understood something of what was involved, so that they were
filled with awe; while those who followed behind were afraid.

The third prediction of the passion is more detailed than the previous
two (8.31, 9.31). Some have said that it was a piece of the Church's
33– teaching after the event: The Son of Man will be given up (betrayed)
34 ... condemned ... handed over to the foreign power ... mocked,
spat upon and flogged ... killed ... rise again. Certainly it reads
like the programme of Good Friday and Easter Day. But we need not
suppose that Christ, even within the limitations of his humanity, had no
idea what his fate might be when he reached the city.

33 The disciples had not understood what the title Son of Man meant.
Perhaps they still thought in terms of an earthly kingdom, to be established when Jesus reached Jerusalem. It was from this hope that James
37 and John made their request, to sit in state with you. They wanted to
be Christ's chief courtiers. But Jesus challenged them first about facing
38 suffering, allegorized in terms of a cup and a baptism. The former was
used in the OT as a symbol for suffering and for the stern judgement of
God; the latter as a metaphor for being dipped beneath a wave of afflictions. The link with the Eucharist and Christian initiation may well be
behind the record of Christ's challenge. Perhaps in the circumstances in
which Mark wrote, to accept baptism and become a communicant was
to accept the danger that one might be called on to suffer and die for one's
faith. The disciples accepted the challenge, but Jesus then told them that
40 to sit at my right or left is not for me to grant; it is for those to
whom it has already been assigned by my Father (NEB footnote).
Later tradition assumed that the two places of honour were not assigned
to the brothers because Peter and James 'the Lord's brother' emerged
as the leaders of the Church.

43 Whoever wants to be great must be your servant. This had
already been said (9.35), but had to be repeated when Jesus saw signs of
ambition among his followers. He called for humility and self-giving
within the Christian community on the pattern of his own life as a servant.
45 For him, that service led to the surrender of his life as a ransom for
many. God had ransomed his people in OT times—saved them from the
effects of their disobedience and sin. The Son of Man in Daniel 7.14
was exalted to a position where he would be served by all peoples. But
for Jesus that lay in the future. On his way up to Jerusalem, he knew that
his destiny involved suffering; and since he is the representative of his
disciples, in all succeeding generations each Christian must learn first to

44  be the willing slave of all. The idea of vicarious suffering was current
in contemporary Judaism as a result of the martyrdoms experienced at
the time of the Maccabees some two centuries previously (2 Macc.
7.37–38), and in Isa. 53.12 there is a phrase which suggests that the
Servant of God 'bore the sin of many'.

## PALM SUNDAY
The Sunday before Easter

*The Way of the Cross*

### Zechariah 9. 9–12
The second part of the book of Zechariah (9.1 to 14.21) consists of a collection of oracles of uncertain date but much later than the earlier part.
It is possible that they come from the Greek period, following the con-
quests of Alexander the Great (336–323 B.C.). This passage is part of a
prophecy that the Messiah will come in an even greater conquest than
that of Alexander—Aramean, Phoenician, and Philistine cities are mentioned in the first half of the chapter—but he will come in humility,
demonstrated by the ass on which he will be riding. (The poetic parallelism in the Hebrew text caused Matthew to understand that there were two
animals.)

10      He shall banish chariots from Ephraim means that the northern
tribes will be reunited with Judah when the messianic kingdom is established. The Messiah's victory is a humble one; his cause is won by the
power of God, not by the force of arms. Yet his kingdom will embrace
lands greater than the empire of David, from sea to sea (Mediterranean
to the Dead Sea—or the Arabian Sea?—and from the River, the
Euphrates, to the far south.) The ancient custom of riding on a donkey
was not always significant of humility; it could also be a sign of dignity.

### 1 Corinthians 1. 18–25
The contrast between the mind of God and the mind of man is nowhere
demonstrated more vividly than in the teaching (*logos* is translated 'word'
RSV, 'doctrine' NEB, 'language' JB) of the cross of Christ, the historic
act of Christ's crucifixion and all that stemmed from it. The apostle
18  saw it in terms of the end of man: for those on their way to ruin
(the present tense suggests that the end of a person may be anticipated

by their reactions to the gospel now) the effect is the opposite to these who are on the way to salvation. The two ways, going in opposite directions, manifest the contrast between the mind of God and the mind of man. Paul reinforced this by quoting the OT (Isa. 29.44 LXX); the prophet had predicted the overthrowing of the world's wisdom—the wisdom of those who sought the meaning of life in religious-philosophical ideas of a human origin. Salvation, deliverance on the last day, is not gained by gnosticism of this kind; it comes by faith, the 'folly' of accepting the teaching of the cross as presented by Paul and his companions.

The whole passage has a rhetorical polish which suggests that the apostle was using material which he had worked over before. In the traditions of contemporary schools of rhetoric, he asked a series of
19 questions in the style of a diatribe, **Where . . .?** to underline how narrow and foolish, contrasted with the wisdom of God, is the mind of man as exemplified by the wise man, the scholar, the disputant.

Paul was not deprecating human wisdom as such, for he said elsewhere: 'All that may be known of God by men lies plain before their eyes; indeed, God himself has disclosed it to them. His invisible attributes, that is to say his everlasting power and deity, have been visible, ever since the world began, to the eye of reason, in the things he has made' (Rom. 1.19–20). God reveals himself through creation. What Paul was saying is that even with the reason that God had given man when he created him, man did not recognize God. So when God acted to save man, he exposed what the world considers wisdom as the folly it truly is.

Nor did the apostle criticize the Jews for seeking signs or the Gentiles (the word is used in the sense of non-Jews, foreigners in general) for seeking the meaning of life. Jesus Christ performed miracles which pointed to the reality of his mission and explained the meaning of life. What Paul condemned was that attitude which refuses to recognise the way God wants things done. The Jew saw the will of God epitomised in the law; the Greek saw the highest form of wisdom in human speculations; but the wisdom of God is in the proclamation of the cross of Christ— the total salvation event in Christ from the passion to Pentecost—through which divine power flows into the world as never before.

The cross was **a stumbling block to Jews** because it was an offence
23 to their understanding of the law of God; it was **folly to Greeks** because, from the human viewpoint, it appeared a senseless waste of a good life. Yet although it was in direct contradiction of human ideas of wisdom and power, it achieved what human wisdom and power could never achieve. It made the gospel more than a theological system; it made it the power

of God in the world, so that our proclamation of the good news of
salvation in Jesus Christ must be expressed as much by what we are and
what we do as by what we say.

## * Matthew 21. 1–11

The Mount of Olives, rising from the deep narrow cleft of the Kidron
valley opposite the eastern wall of the city of Jerusalem, is featured in
Jewish eschatology, both as a place where the Messiah would appear, and
as the place of the general resurrection. On it the prophets were supposed to be buried, and around it are hundreds of tombs and sepulchres.
When this evangelist reported that many of God's people arose from sleep
after the resurrection and entered the holy city (27.53), we can assume
he meant they came from these slopes. Bethphage and Bethany are on the
other side of the Mount of Olives from Jerusalem, just off the road from
Jericho. Bethany was an obvious place for a pause on Jesus' pilgrimage
2 from Jericho, and **the village opposite** was Bethphage, about a mile
away. The arrangements for borrowing the donkey may have been made
beforehand, as were the later arrangements for using the upper room
(26.18), but Matthew narrated the incident as if it were an act of fore-
5 knowledge. Characteristically, he added, **This was to fulfil the prophecy,** and then quoted Zech. 9.9.

The quotation of Zechariah is taken from the Hebrew text where there
is a poetic parallelism. Matthew took this to mean two animals, as the
RSV and JB translations indicate. The NEB adjusts Matthew's mistake by
5 translating, **Here is your king, who comes to you in gentleness,
riding on an ass, riding on the foal of a beast of burden.** Mark and
Luke refer only to one animal.

In describing the messianic king's humble mode of entering the city,
Zechariah had in mind the unpretentious and unwarlike nature of his
rule. Jesus, by performing this action, deliberately associated himself
with that prophecy and gave it a profounder meaning. The details of the
triumphal entry into Jerusalem are capable of a more prosaic explanation
—that for some reason Jesus needed a lift to reach Jerusalem, and that
happy pilgrims on the road cheered his progress—but there seems little
doubt that in fact it was a gesture staged by him to demonstrate that he
was the Messiah.

The shouts of the crowd came from Psalm 118, one of the Hallel Psalms
(113—118) sung at Passovertide. 'Save us, we beseech thee (*Hosanna*), O
Lord . . . Blessed be he that cometh in the name of the Lord' (verses
25–26). *Hosanna* had become a liturgical acclamation of joy. The use of

branches from trees was common in festival pilgrimage processions. The
9 welcome they gave to Jesus as **Son of David** indicated that they recognized him as the Messiah. (Matthew was particularly careful to base
Christ's claim to messiahship on his ancestry from king David.) But when
the people from the city came out to see what the excitement was about,
11 the crowd simply said that **This is the prophet Jesus, from Nazareth
in Galilee,** as if Matthew wanted to draw attention away from the
political implications of Jesus' messiahship to the imminence of the
Kingdom in his teaching. Despite its humble pose, however, the entry
into Jerusalem by Jesus and his subsequent action (in the synoptic Gospels) in cleansing the temple threw a challenge before the Jewish authorities which they could not ignore.

\* **Matthew 26.1–27.61**
See parallel passages in Mark and Luke, Monday, Tuesday, and Wednesday before Easter.


                                                      YEAR 2

# PALM SUNDAY
The Sunday before Easter

*The Way of the Cross*

## Isaiah 52. 13–53. 12
The last of the four songs of the Servant of God in Isaiah has been an
important source for the Church's understanding of the sacrifice of Jesus
Christ, not only because its concepts were used to interpret what Christ
achieved through the cross, but also because Jesus himself seems consciously to have identified himself with the Servant in pursuing his mission.
Through this song the prophet explored the mystery of vicarious suffering—the righteous Servant who shared in afflictions to such an extent that
in so doing he carried the cause of that suffering, the sin of the people.
The identity of this Servant is unknown; it is best not to limit that identification to one individual or to the corporate personality of Israel, but to
include both.

The passage reports what the people said, 53.1–11a, within a framework
of something God said, 52.13ff and 53.11b–12 (or perhaps 53.11–12,
following the capital letter in the NEB).

God introduced the work of his Servant with the word **Behold,** a

word used by this prophet when introducing a vision. The misfortunes
of the Servant were to be reversed; he would share in the glory of God
13 himself, **he shall be lifted up, exalted to the heights.** What God does
for him would have consequences throughout the world: just as the
rulers of the nations had recoiled at the sight of him, so they would be
15 amazed, **For they see what they had never been told and things
unheard before fill their thoughts.**

The picture of the Servant of God which is drawn in 53.1–11 is of one
who was so disfigured by suffering that others rejected him and then
despised him. He experienced that involuntary yet cruel retreat of men
2 from one of their number who is so disfigured that to them he **lost all
the likeness of a man**—he ceased to resemble a human being. In the
OT the beauty of a person is a sign that God blessed them; there was
nothing beautiful about the Servant, so it was assumed he was a man
without a blessing.

4 **Yet on himself he bore our sufferings,** is the confession of men who
had changed their opinion of the Servant. The rhythmic interplay of the
words 'he' and 'we' is noteworthy. They had never dreamed that the one
5 who suffered was **pierced for our transgressions, tortured for our
iniquities.** Thus, the healing gained for others by his stripes included
also the forgiveness of their sins and the removal of their punishment.
The Servant's exaltation brought them to realise this.

The report, interrupted by this confession (verses 4–6), continues
with the details of the Servant's sufferings, but this time they are the result
of physical violence, not disease. His silence in the midst of suffering,
7 **he did not open his mouth,** and his complete isolation, **cut off from
8 the world of living men,** are poignant details which increase the horror
of the passion. The report then goes on to tell of the Servant's death and
burial, either as a result of illness or violence. Shame followed him to his
grave, for he was buried with malefactors.

10 Finally, verses 10–12 report his deliverance. The Servant who **made
himself a sacrifice for sin**—the word is used for a **guilt offering** (NEB
footnote) was restored by God to be vindicated and rewarded by prosperity, a long life, children and grandchildren. How this would come
about is not explained. But at the end of the song came the words which
were to find their way into Christian teaching on the cross of Christ,
12 **he bore the sin of many.**

## Hebrews 10. 1–10

Law is used by the author of Hebrews in this passage in the sense of the cult of Judaism, not of the moral code which Paul referred to in his epistles (though obviously both cult and code are but different sections of the same law). These ritual practices, said the author, were only a dim reflection of the good things which were to come when the promises were fulfilled. Levitical sacrifices cleansed only ritual offences; they never succeeded in removing the real sins which formed a barrier between God and his people. If they had been effective in removing that barrier, it would not have been necessary for the priests to repeat them year after year—they would have done that once and for all. The cult, on the contrary, only succeeded in making men remember their sinful state (the

3 word for **brought to mind** is *anamnesis*, the same word Christ used at the Last Supper when he spoke of the Eucharist as a 'remembrance' (Luke 22.19); it implies something vividly and consciously made present again.) Sins cannot be removed by animal sacrifices—the author may

4 have in mind the ritual of the Day of Atonement, though **the blood of bulls and goats** suggests the whole complex of ritual oblations made in the former temple at Jerusalem (assuming the author wrote after A.D. 70).

He next quoted Ps. 40.8–10, as the words of Christ before his incarnation, spoken to the Father, giving the reason for his coming into the world. They underline the Son's obedience in carrying out the human task which the Father had destined for him. The author's quotation is made more striking by a difference in the Hebrew and Greek versions of verse 8 of this psalm. The Hebrew version reads, 'But mine ears hast thou opened' (Revised Psalter), but the Greek version of the LXX reads,

5 **Thou hast prepared a body for me.** The LXX text enabled the author of Hebrews to show how the OT teaches God's rejection of the ritual sacrifices, his preparation of a human body for the speaker in the psalm (the Son), and the promise of obedience to God's will on the part of the speaker. All kinds of expiatory sacrifices were rejected. The speaker in the psalm also quotes an earlier scripture, Deut. 6.5 or Jer. 15.16. Instead of sacrifices, the coming Messiah should offer to God the body which was to be given to him. The author commented on this to show how the cult is now cancelled with the sacrifice of Christ.

The last verse asserts that the unique and completed sacrifice of Christ, the offering of his human life in obedience to the will of God, has

10 **consecrated** (made holy, belonging to God) the Christian community.

* Matthew 21. 1–11 and * Matthew 26.1—27.61
See Palm Sunday Year 1.

# MONDAY BEFORE EASTER

Isaiah 42. 1–4
See Epiphany 1 Year 2.

Acts 10. 34–43
See Epiphany 1 Year 1.

\* Mark 14. 1–26

1 **The festival of Passover and Unleavened Bread** was the junction, long before NT times, of two ancient celebrations. The Passover was a springtime festival at which the slaughter of the lambs within the temple precincts and the eating of them in household groups in homes, lodgings, and tents around the city was understood as an enactment of the exodus from Egypt (Exod. 12). The festival of Unleavened Bread, on the other hand, seems to have originated as a kind of new year celebration, in which all old leaven was removed from the house and only leavened bread was eaten for the following week as a sign of renewal. The preparations were made on the 14th day of the month Nisan, which fell between March and April, as the Jewish calendar being a lunar one the date had to be constantly adjusted. On that day all leaven was removed from the house and destroyed. In the afternoon the lambs were slaughtered before the great altar in the temple. After sunset which, according to the Jewish way of reckoning was the beginning of the next day, i.e. the 15th Nisan, the people assembled in their families or groups of friends to make a solemn meal of roasted lamb, a lamb having been brought from the temple by a member of the family or group. Since the festival of Unleavened Bread was combined with this meal, unleavened bread and cakes were eaten, and the celebrations continued for one week during which all the bread was prepared without leaven.

There are problems concerning the dating of the events of the passion in the synoptic Gospels and in John. The differences between the Jewish reckoning of a day (from the previous evening) and the Roman one (from midnight to midnight), and the custom of including in any numbering
1 the day from which the count was made (so that **two days off** means Wednesday–Thursday, not Tuesday–Wednesday–Thursday, as we would calculate today), solves some of the problems, but not all of them. However, we will not go into details here. Suffice it to say that in 14.1–11

the evangelist is telling us what happened on the Wednesday before the crucifixion, and in 14.12–72 what happened on the Thursday.

3    During these days Jesus was staying **at Bethany, in the house of Simon the leper,** evidently well known in the evangelist's circle, for he made no further attempt to identify him. **The small bottle of very costly perfume, oil of pure nard** was a long-necked container full of an unguent made from a rare Indian plant and much prized in the ancient world. The breaking open of the neck indicated the woman's extrava-
5    gance. **300 denarii** (NEB footnote) equalled a year's wages for a working man. The ointment was poured over Jesus' head: perhaps the woman was an enthusiast who hoped that Jesus would rule over the nation, for the anointing of the head was part of the coronation ceremony of a king (1 Kings 1.38–40, etc.). Christ's rebuke of those who criticized her was not an expression of indifference to the needs of the poor; he saw that the woman's act was a spontaneous gesture of her sense of the honour due
8    to him. **She is beforehand with anointing my body for burial.** Christ accepted the gesture and made it a prophetic sign; there was no time to anoint his body after the crucifixion. The Messiah ('the anointed
9    one') had to die. **Wherever in all the world the Gospel is proclaimed, what she has done will be told as her memorial.** If this is a later addition, as most commentators say it is, it is nevertheless true. The anointing at Bethany has become part of the passion narrative.
10    **Judas Iscariot, one of the Twelve, went to the chief priests to betray him to them.** What was Judas' motive? It could hardly have been financial. Was he disillusioned with Jesus when he saw his Master rejecting an earthly messiahship? Was he trying to force God to reveal his purpose by a miracle? Or was he tricked into believing that the chief priests would protect Jesus from his enemies?

For verses 12–26 see Maundy Thursday Year 2.

# MONDAY BEFORE EASTER

Lamentations 3.19–33
See Epiphany 5 Year 2.

Philippians 2. 1–13
The passage commences as Paul was gathering together every thought, feeling, and Christian experience that he could find to move his readers to respond to his urgent plea for unity. He said he spoke to them, not out 1 of any authority of his own, but as one who shared with them the **common life in Christ**, the incentive of Christ's love, the participation (*koinonia*) in the Holy Spirit which is given to every believer, and the human feelings which they had for one another. After summoning these aids to his appeal, he disclosed the appeal itself: the establishment of the unity of love among themselves.

3 **You should humbly reckon others better than yourselves**— the basis of unity—led him to quote a hymn which tells of the humility of Jesus Christ, not as a quality which Christians should copy (though this is how Paul used it here) but as a theological propositon. The hymn is thought by some to have been written in Judaistic or Hellenistic circles, or a mixture of both, and to have been quoted by Paul because it suited his argument at this point in his letter. Others have argued that the hymn was composed by the apostle himself independently of the letter. Whatever its origins, it has provided scholars with a fascinating fragment of primitive Christian theology, echoing a Christology of a period long before the Church embarked on her definitions of the person of Jesus Christ.

The hymn consists of two strophes, the first ending at the words 8 **death on a cross** (which may have been added by Paul as he copied the 11 hymn into his letter); the second at **to the glory of God the Father.** (JB prints the hymn with shorter lines, though without committing itself to the strophe divisions.) The first strophe is concerned with the descent of Christ to earth, the second with his ascent to heaven.

The first strophe speaks of Christ's pre-existence in his divine nature, of his incarnation, and of his humiliation, expressed in an obedience extending to the acceptance of death. Christ's pre-existence had been expressed elsewhere in the NT in terms of the Word of God (John 1.1–14) and of the Wisdom of God, and in saying **the divine nature was his from the first** the hymn also asserted his pre-existence. The follow- 6 ing line, **he did not think to snatch at equality with God,** probably

means that he renounced his divine claims in order to tread the way
6–7 of humility and obedience. **The divine nature** is contrasted with **the
nature of a slave.** Christ is almost like an angel sent by God into the
world—though Hebrews 1 carefully distinguishes Jesus as higher than
the angels. Later doctrines of the Holy Trinity and the Incarnation were
built on these words, but the words themselves cannot be interpreted in
terms of later dogmatic definitions. (An attempt to interpret the incarnation in the light of the phrase 'emptied himself' (JB) ran into difficulties.)

The second strophe speaks of God's action through Christ. God
9 exalted him and gave him the name of Lord, *Kurios,* **the name above all
names,** a title acclaimed by the whole universe, the spirit-powers of the
heavens, of the earth, and of the underworld. It is in his manhood that
Jesus is exalted. The salvation of God embraces the entire cosmos, and
homage is offered the newly-crowned King by the mighty spirits who rule
over the three realms. The worship of Jesus is by the spirit-powers
10 governing the universe, not by men. **At the name of Jesus** does not
mean that knees should be bowed when the name is pronounced; it
means that Jesus as the mediator is the one through whom created beings
offer their worship to God. It is to God that every knee should bow.

So the hymn tells the great story of Christ who, through the voluntary
choice of self-abasement, accepted the suffering of the cross and was
crowned by God to rule over the whole universe.

With this dramatic and imaginative composition before their eyes,
the apostle urged his Philippian congregation to struggle on, enduring
to the end, fulfilling the hope of the gospel and winning through to the
attainment of final blessedness. They would be strengthened by the
knowledge that God was always present with them. This is the sense in
12 which they were to be **in fear and trembling**—not frightened about the
outcome but in awe at God's power that works through them.

  \* **Luke 22. 1–38**
Only points of special interest in the Lucan narrative of the passion will
be noted here.

3    **Satan entered into Judas Iscariot.** Luke did not attempt to speculate
on Judas' motives. The events of the passion were set in motion by
supernatural powers.

15–    **How I have longed to eat this Passover with you before my
16 death! For I tell you, never again shall I eat it until the time when
it finds its fulfilment in the kingdom of God!** Jesus not only linked
the last supper with the Passover but also pointed forward to its fulfilment,

as Paul did, 'Every time you eat this bread and drink the cup, you proclaim the death of the Lord, until he comes' (1 Corinthians 11.26). Luke reversed the order of the bread and the cup; he also concentrated on the significance of the meal as a foretaste of the coming Kingdom of God.

29    **I vest in you the kingship which my Father vested in me.** Jesus is 'covenanting' or 'appointing' (RSV) or 'conferring' (JB) a kingship on his disciples in the sense that they will enjoy a status, not immediately, but after his death and resurrection.

31–    **Simon, Simon . . ., you must lend strength to your brothers.**
32    The prophecy of Peter's denial—attributed here, like Judas' betrayal, to Satan—is linked with a prophecy of the apostle's future importance in the Christian community.

38    **We have two swords here.** The carrying of a sword on the sabbath would have been sufficient provocation for an arrest. When Jesus said,
38    **Enough, enough!** he may have meant that it was sufficient for this purpose. He would now be 'counted among the outlaws' as Isaiah had prophesied.

# TUESDAY BEFORE EASTER

Isaiah 49. 1–6
See Christmas 1 Year 2.

Hebrews 4. 14–5. 10
The ritual function of the high priest on the Day of Atonement (*Yom Kippur*) was an important one. The day was kept by the people on the tenth of the seventh month (*Tishri*, September–October) with fasting and penitence to seek God's mercy for their sins.

The ceremonies were laid down in Leviticus 16. Discarding his normal vestments, the high priest bathed and put on a linen robe. In the temple precincts he killed a bullock as a sin-offering for himself and his assistants, and entered alone into the holy of holies to sprinkle blood round the Mercy-seat. Then he returned to the people, who presented him with two goats. One of these he selected as a sacrifice and killed it, sprinkling the blood in the holy of holies and on the altar where the daily oblations were made; on the other he laid his hands, confessed over it the sins Israel had committed in the past year, and prayed for forgiveness. This animal, the scapegoat, was then taken into the wilderness—the abode of evil—and destroyed. The significance of the first sacrifice was that the life-blood of the goat was supposed to unite God and his people in the transaction; the significance of the second was that the animal carried away the people's sins to the place where sin belonged.

The faults confessed by the high priest were the sins of ignorance committed unwittingly by himself and the people—a healthy recognition that in a religion of law men can still sin, even when they have obeyed every precept. Wilful transgressions such as murder, adultery, sabbath-breaking, and suchlike had to be dealt with under the ordinary provisions of the law; the sacrificial system itself could not effect atonement for them.

The author of Hebrews expounds Jesus Christ's ministry and sacrifice in terms of this cult. The death, resurrection, and ascension of Christ were the means whereby he entered the holy of holies—heaven itself. His people, unlike the Jews, are able to enter the holy of holies with him:
4.16 we may boldly approach the throne of our gracious God, where we may receive mercy and in his grace find timely help.

But the analogy is extended in three other details. First, to be a true high priest a man must be a proper representative of those in whose
5.1 name he officiates. He must be taken from among men. Christ fulfilled
4.15 this condition, says the author, because of his likeness to us.

5.4      Secondly, a high priest must be called by God, as indeed Aaron was. To demonstrate that Christ was called in this way, the author quotes two messianic proof-texts from the OT: Ps. 2.7, Thou art my Son; today I have begotten thee, showing that God addressed Christ as his Son, begotten in the 'today' of eternity; and Ps. 110.4, Thou art a priest for ever, in the succession of Melchizedek, thus declaring that the Son was appointed to an eternal priesthood superior to that of Aaron and the Levites, for Abraham, father of the Jews, had paid homage to the mysterious priest-king of Salem (Gen. 14.17–20).

Thirdly, a high priest must be able to sympathize with the human condition since his task is to plead to God on man's behalf—his petitions would be less sincere if he was not involved with the people in their plight. Christ, says the author, did not share in man's sin like the Jewish
4.15 high priests, but he had been tested in every way and was able to sympathize with human suffering more perfectly than the high priests

5.8  because he had learned obedience in the school of suffering. Through pain of body and anguish of mind he had paid the price of obedience to God. Since that had been accomplished, Christ was now perfected as the one high priest who is able to secure the forgiveness of sins and salvation for men. What the Jewish high priest had attempted to obtain on the Day of Atonement, Christ had successfully won.

The author assumes that his readers were familiar with the story of the
5.7  agony in the garden of Gethsemane, when Jesus offered up prayers and petition, with loud cries and tears, to God who was able to deliver him from the grave. Because of his humble submission his prayer was heard and God raised him from the dead.

5.2  To say that the Jewish high priests were beset by weakness was (unintentionally) an ironic understatement, considering the unsavoury history of the holders of the office, including Annas and Caiaphas!

* Mark 14. 27–72

Jesus' prediction of his disciples' desertion is supported by a quotation
28  from Zech. 13.7. Appearances of the risen Lord in Galilee are recorded in Matt. 28.16–20 and in John 21, but it may be that Jesus was using the name as a symbol of the whole world. In the OT Galilee meant 'land of the heathen' (as in Matt. 4.15). After his resurrection, Jesus would go before his disciples into all the world. Peter's protest, characteristic of him, is
30  answered by another prophecy, Before the cock crows twice, you yourself will disown me three times. Cock-crow in the east is between midnight and one or two o'clock in the morning.
32  Gethsemane—the name probably means 'oil-press' or 'olive grove'— is on the slopes of the mount of Olives facing the eastern wall of Jerusalem.
34  Taking the leading three disciples, Jesus told them My heart is ready to break with grief. The story of the passion at this point is in great contrast to the version in John, where Jesus saw the future with calmness and assurance (12.27). Did Jesus actually say this prayer? (The only
36  witnesses were asleep.) Abba, Father, an intimate Aramaic word, was the way Jesus himself had taught his disciples to address God. Not what I will, but what thou wilt is almost the same as the Lord's Prayer. It is not surprising that Jesus underwent such agony. Heb. 5.7 is another testimony to it. His prayer at this point must have been like this, asking God for deliverance from death but in obedience accepting whatever was
38  to happen. Pray that you may be spared the test, he told his sleeping
41  disciples. Then, after the third time, he announced, The hour has come. The Son of Man is betrayed to sinful men. There is irony in the

statement. The last thing that was expected of the Messiah was that he should be betrayed and suffer.

44 A signal would be necessary in the dim light among the trees, and Judas had arranged this. A kiss on the head or on the hand was a normal form of greeting between a rabbi and his pupil. The incident of the
51 young man is a mystery. It could have been a piece of autobiography slipped in by Mark himself, though there is nothing to support this popular guess.

Mark told of three interrogations of Jesus: one before the Sanhedrin at night (verses 55–72), during which Peter denied his Lord; a second in the morning (15.1), and a third before Pilate (15.2–15). At the night meeting attempts were made to secure his condemnation on the basis of an alleged threat by Jesus to destroy the temple, but the proceedings resulted in a charge of blasphemy and a condemnation because Jesus,
62 asked if he was the Messiah, replied, I am; and you will see the Son of Man seated on the right hand of God and coming with the clouds of heaven. The 'I am' implies Christ's deity; the rest of the sentence, based on Dan. 7.13 and Ps. 110.1, is a clear assertion of Christ's messiahship. The tearing of the robes was a sign of mourning at the supposed profanation of God's name.

The story of Peter's denial must have come from the apostle himself and is a remarkable illustration of the way in which the Gospels do not attempt to whitewash the reputations of the first leaders of the Church.

# TUESDAY BEFORE EASTER

### Genesis 22. 1–12

The story of the testing of Abraham's faith is told from two levels: from the level of heaven, where God decides to put Abraham to the test to see if he is worthy of his promise, and from the level of earth, where the narrator unfolds the step-by-step response of Abraham to God's command, with an attention to detail which is striking and moving: e.g., Abraham himself carried the fire and the knife, objects with which a boy might injure himself, and permitted his son to carry the wood for the sacrifice. The testing shows the lengths to which a man is called to go in obeying God. The patriarch had already taken the drastic step of leaving his ancestral home. Now he is summoned to offer in sacrifice his only son, born in extreme old age, his one hope of being the father of descendants as numerous as the sands upon the sea-shore, as God had promised him. Abraham had cut himself off from the whole of his past; he must apparently be tested to prove whether his faith in God was such that he was willing to give up the whole of his future. It was as if God was saying to Abraham as he was later to say in Christ to Peter, 'Do you love me more than these?'

2    It is not known where **the land of Moriah** was. A Syriac version has 'the land of the Amorites'; the LXX has something different. The variations probably indicate that at an early period in the handing down of the story, different sanctuaries competed for the honour of being the traditional place for this event. Nor is the name Jehovah-jireh, 'the Lord will provide' (verse 14), identifiable with any known mountain. We notice that at one place in the narrative God addressed Abraham directly whilst in other places he used an angel: the differences reflect later stages in ideas about the divine transcendence, when it was believed that God would use messengers in communicating with humans.

Behind the passage is the practice of redeeming the first-born of Israel. This expressed itself ritually in the offerings made for the first-born son of a family, such as Joseph and Mary made after the birth of Jesus (Luke 2.22ff). All firstfruits belonged to God, including the first son; but, unlike other firstfruits (animals, etc.), children were not to be offered in sacrifice but were 'redeemed' and an oblation of animals or birds was made in their place (Exod. 13.11). The Fathers of the Church saw in the story a prophecy of the cross. Abraham handed over his son to death in obedience to God and received him back alive; God the Father handed over his only-begotten Son to death for the sins of the world and raised him back to life. The words of Abraham, 'God will provide himself the lamb for a burnt offering' (verse 8 RSV) reveal the sacrifice of Isaac as a type of the sacrifice of Christ.

**Colossians 2. 6-15**
See Lent 5 Year 1.

* **Luke 22. 39-71**
Only points of special interest in the Lucan narrative of the passion will be noted here.

43    **There appeared to him an angel from heaven bringing him strength.** Usually in this evangelist angels are messengers, but here they

are employed to denote the severity of Jesus' anguish of spirit (*agonia*, from which our word 'agony' is derived).

67–  **If I tell you, you will not believe me; and if I ask questions,**
68  **you will not answer.** To defend himself properly, Jesus needed an opportunity to explain and discuss, but his inquisitors had neither the patience nor the inclination for that.

# WEDNESDAY BEFORE EASTER

Isaiah 50. 4–9
Although the third of the songs of the Servant of the Lord is technically a lament, it breathes entire confidence that prayer will be answered. He
4  had been given **the tongue of a teacher** and other charisms for ministry among the people of Israel, **the weary**; he had been given an insight
4  into the divine mind as revealed in prophecy and fulfilled in event. And he did not disobey what God told him to do and to say, even though obedience entailed suffering. He accepted the consequences of his work
7  in the knowledge that **the Lord God stands by to help me**. It was in this complete confidence in God that he was enabled to see his suffer-
7  ings as the fulfilment of the divine will. So he could say, **I have set my face like flint, for I know that I shall not be put to shame, because one who will clear my name is on my side.** In the thought of Israel the shame which suffering brought to the sufferer—because it was regarded as a punishment for sin—was almost as hard to bear as the pain itself.

This confidence was then expressed by the prophet in terms taken from
8  legal processes. **Who dares argue against me? . . .** The Servant summoned those who opposed him and persecuted him to stand on trial with him, for he was convinced that God would justify him and that no one could condemn him.

(–11)[1]
Another voice urged the people to obey God's will as spoken by the Servant. Those who obey him are like men finding light in dark places.

[1] The commentary on these additional verses relates to the use of the passage on Trinity 12 Year 1, but is more conveniently printed here with the commentary on the major portion of the reading.

11 Those who ignore him walk into their own destruction. To **lie down in torment** means to die in condemnation.


1 Peter 2. 18–25
See Lent 3 Year 1.


\* **Mark 15. 1–41**
Pontius Pilate was procurator of the imperial province of Judah from about
A.D. 26 to 36. He showed little tact in his administering of an unusually
difficult province—various riots occurred during his time in office because
of his blunders—though he could not have been a complete failure, for
Tiberius kept him in office for ten years. The silence Jesus kept when
2 interrogated by him, except for his ambiguous **The words are yours**
(or, **It is as you say**, NEB footnote), is notable. Pilate's agreement to
the condemnation of Jesus was political expediency. Tiberius would
12 not have been pleased if he had released **the man you call king of the
Jews**.

The mocking of Jesus is believed to have taken place in the Antonia,
a fortress on the north-west corner of the temple, which has been located
by archaeologists. This could have contained the **praetorium** (NEB
18 footnote). The salute, **Hail! King of the Jews!** was a parody of *Ave,
Caesar, victor, imperator*.

21     **Alexander and Rufus** were evidently well known in the circles for
which Mark wrote. Crucifixion was a form of execution practised by the
Romans on rebels, slaves, and criminals of the lower classes. At the place
of execution there were stakes driven into the ground, or suitable trees,
and the victim was forced to carry the *patibulum* or cross-beam which was
then fixed to the upright support.

The narrative of the crucifixion is given soberly by Mark. OT quotations
or allusions appear in verses 24 (Ps. 22.18), 29 (Ps. 22.7–8), 34 (Ps. 22.1),
and 36 (Ps. 119.21). There is strong evidence to suggest that Jesus used
Ps. 22 as his prayer on the cross. The Aramaic *galgalta* means 'head' or
'skull'. Since the fourth century this has been identified with part of the
site covered by the Church of the Holy Sepulchre, and there is some
archaeological material to suggest that there was a slight hill here which
23 was outside the walls of the city in the first century. The **drugged wine**
may have been offered by women in Jerusalem who performed this act
of mercy for condemned men.

# WEDNESDAY BEFORE EASTER

**Numbers 21. 4–9**

The discontent of the people with the frugal life in the desert did not bring divine assistance, as it had done earlier in their wanderings, but divine punishment. The confession that this punishment provoked, 7 **We sinned when we spoke against the Lord,** enabled Moses to intercede with the Lord, who told him how the snake-bites could be cured. Release was linked with a test of obedience to the Lord's instructions. Behind the story is perhaps the primitive concept that one can annul the power of dangerous animals by making an image of them and offering them worship, though of course any such concept is banished from this narrative. The incident was interpreted in apostolic´ times as a prophecy of the lifting up of Christ on the cross for the healing of the world.

**1 Corinthians 1. 18–25**

See Palm Sunday Year 1.

* **Luke 23. 1–47**

Only points of special interest in the Lucan narrative of the passion will be noted here.

8 **When Herod saw Jesus he was greatly pleased.** Only Luke records the appearance of Jesus before the tetrarch Herod Antipas, an appearance engineered by Pilate because the Sanhedrin accused Jesus of beginning his agitation in Galilee, which was in the jurisdiction of the tetrarch. In this account of the trial, Luke pictures Pilate endeavouring to save Jesus more insistently than in the other synoptic Gospels.

28 **Daughters of Jerusalem, do not weep for me.** Though the women were apparently weeping for Christ, Jesus saw their tears as a prophetic sign of the future suffering of the people in Jerusalem (A.D. 66–70). He quoted Hos. 10.8 and then uttered a proverb, **If these things are done** 31 **when the wood is green, what will happen when it is dry?**—if this can happen to a preacher, what will happen when violent revolutionaries become active?

34 **Father, forgive them; they do not know what they are doing.** Though uttered as a prayer for his executioners, Christ's words were an absolution for the whole Jewish nation. The unconditional nature of God's forgiveness is a feature of the teaching of this Gospel.

43 **I tell you this: today you shall be with me in Paradise.** Jesus'

promise to the criminal was in the language he could understand. Paradise, meaning 'garden', was the reward granted by God for the just. The man had faith that Jesus would one day 'come to his throne'.

46    **Father, into thy hands I commit my spirit.** A phrase from the righteous sufferer in Psalm 31.6, prefaced with Jesus' usual mode of addressing God, 'Father'.

# MAUNDY THURSDAY

**Isaiah 52. 13–53. 12**
See Palm Sunday Year 2.

**1 Corinthians 11. 23–29**
In dealing with the disorders which took place in the Christian assembly at Corinth, Paul reminded his readers of Jesus' acts and words at the Last
23  Supper. The tradition came to Paul **from the Lord himself**: this can mean either that the story came to the apostle directly from God by revelation, such as that which brought about his conversion on the Damascus road, or (more probably) that the narrative was handed down to Paul through the teaching processes of the Church. Hellenism as well as Judaism had its collections of **tradition** which were passed down by word of mouth until they were committed to writing—that is how the Gospels themselves came to be written—and it would be within the scope of Paul's belief about the people of God and their union in Christ to say that a tradition handed on by them to him would be as 'from the Lord himself'.

The narrative of the institution of the Eucharist in this letter is the oldest written account of the event in the NT; it is nearer to the narrative in Luke than those in Mark and Matthew. In the manner of a prophet, Christ identified the bread over which he had said the blessing and which
24  he had broken as his body: **This is my body, which is for you; do this as a memorial of me.** The lamb eaten at the Passover meal was called the 'body of the Passover lamb' in Jewish teaching, and Jesus at the Last Supper seems to have applied this concept to the meal he was sharing with his disciples and his own sacrificial self-offering on the cross. The Jews at Passover time celebrated their deliverance from Egypt: the Passover Haggadah declared, 'He brought us out from slavery to liberty, from sorrow to joy, from darkness to great light, from servitude to redemption'.

Christ similarly delivered the new Israel from the servitude of sin; and the Eucharist was their means of both celebrating that redemption and
24 participating in it. That is why Christ said it is **for you**.
25     The command to **do this** is linked with the idea of memorial. *Anamnesis* has a meaning far deeper than the English understanding of an act of remembrance. What Israel remembered at Passover time was what God had done for them, his mighty acts of deliverance from Egypt, his guidance through the wilderness into the promised land; but the events commemorated were made present in the people's celebration of them. Similarly, the Christian celebration of 'Christ our Passover' made real among the worshippers the mighty acts of God in Christ which were associated with the Last Supper itself. Christ had given himself on behalf of his people, and they shared in the benefits of his passion in eating a loaf at a meal held in his memory.

The cup of blessing was passed round in a Jewish meal for the final prayer, and it was at this point that Christ said, **This cup is the new**
25 **covenant sealed by my blood. Whenever you drink it, do this as a memorial of me.** The direct identification of the wine itself with the blood of Christ was made in the Marcan-Matthean tradition (Matt. 26.27; Mark 14.24). Perhaps the tradition which Paul here quoted came from a strongly Jewish-Christian source, where any idea of partaking of blood, even as a sacramental sign, would have been avoided; the change to a direct identification in Matthew and Mark may have been due to a later modification in the tradition of the Last Supper when the saying over the loaf influenced the form of the saying over the cup.

Behind the saying over the cup are the OT passages Exod. 24.8 and Jer. 31.31–34. To drink the cup is to enter into the new covenant established in Christ's blood. When the covenant on Sinai was made, Moses sprinkled the people with the blood of the sacrificial victims, saying, 'Behold the blood of the covenant which the Lord has made with you'; and Jeremiah, after the failure of the old covenant, foretold the establishment of a new covenant between God and man, which would include the forgiveness of sins and personal union with God himself. So the shedding of Christ's blood marked the inauguration of a new covenant in which men's sins are forgiven and union with God is re-established. The Passover background to the Last Supper provides a way of interpreting the Supper and the cross from Israel's salvation-history.

The command to 'Do this' is repeated, and the apostle went on to assert that the celebration of the Supper is a proclamation of Christ's death—and all the benefits which accrue to it for the Church—until the return of

Christ to judge the world. Paul expected this to be in his own time; the Supper linked men and women across time and space with the saving grace of God in Christ until the Second Coming.

29 The passage concludes with a warning about worthy reception—or rather, reception after penitential self-examination. **He does not discern the Body** has at least two interpretations (the use of the capital letter in the NEB acknowledges this): it can mean Christ's Body in the sacramental sign, and/or his Body in the assembled Christian community. The precise meaning is not easy to define, but it implies a separation from Christ and his Church for those who are guilty of desecrating the sacrament.

\* **John 13. 1–15**

The public proclamation of the gospel by Jesus had ended. His hour had come—the hour for which he had come into the world, and which was through suffering, death, and resurrection, to manifest the glory which he shared with the Father. It was also the hour when he was to leave his disciples in the world (always seen as transitory and unsatisfying, even hostile, by this evangelist) where they, too, would experience suffering and death. So he gave them a sign to show them that, following in his path of love and humility, they also might share in his resurrection and glory.

To wash the feet of guests was the normal duty of servants before a meal; it was unusual for the host to perform the task while a meal was being eaten. Perhaps Jesus only thought of it after they had commenced the Last Supper. He may have discerned the way in which Satan was taking possession of Judas' mind and wanted, in one final gesture of love, to save him from falling into sin. We can assume that, even though Judas' betrayal fitted in with Christ's destiny, the disciple still had the free will to be loyal if he had wished to be. Anyway, Jesus enacted a parable of self-sacrifice for others. The sign is all the more striking because the evangelist recorded that as he was enacting it, Jesus was conscious of his divine authority and of the way of glory which was his from God.

6 Peter's character comes through clearly in the dialogue. **You, Lord, washing my feet?** As in Matt. 16.22, when he rejected the suggestion offered, he could not be in fellowship with him. Peter's impetuosity brought him into conflict with his leader. Jesus firmly pointed out that unless Peter had the humility to accept the service which his Saviour offered, he could not be in fellowship with him. Peter's impetuosity 9 swung in the opposite direction. **Then, Lord, not my feet only; wash my hands and head as well!**—the hands and head are the other *foci* of man's thought and action. But the bathing which Jesus offers—his

10 sacrifice for sin—is complete. **A man who has bathed needs no further washing.** The NEB footnote alternative **needs only to wash his feet,** can be interpreted as a reference to the sacramental sign which Jesus offers in the feet-washing. The sacrifice of the cross cleanses a man; he needs only to appropriate it through the washing which Jesus institutes.

The feet-washing becomes therefore a type of Christian baptism. The laying aside and taking up of Christ's garments have been interpreted over the centuries as an analogy of the laying aside and the taking up of his human nature in his death and resurrection; the feet-washing is a sacramental sign of participation in that death and resurrection without which we cannot have fellowship with him; it is also the baptismal sign which we need because through Christ we have been made clean. The words of institution are not included in the Johannine account of the Last Supper; they are implicit throughout the Gospel through the discourse of chapter 6 (the feeding of the five thousand and the 'bread from heaven' discourse, see Easter 1 Year 2). But in their place is this incident which can be interpreted as an institution of baptism, without which a man may not share in the Lord's fellowship and the Lord's table.

The concluding words of the passage charge the disciples, and through them the Christian Church, to continue the ministry of love and service to one another (a Johannine characteristic is that a Christian's duty is

13 first to other members of the Church). **You call me 'Master' and 'Lord', and rightly so, for that is what I am.** The Jewish pupil never addressed his master by his name but always as *Rabbi umari*, 'my teacher and my lord'. The title is uniquely suitable for Jesus Christ since he was the

14– disciples' Teacher and Lord par excellence. **Then if I, your Lord and**

15 **Master, have washed your feet, you also ought to wash one another's feet. I have set you an example: you are to do as I have done for you.**

The Christian duty of love and service is echoed in Phil. 2.5 ('Let your bearing towards one another arise out of your life in Christ Jesus') and 1 Pet. 2.21 ('Christ suffered on your behalf, and thereby left you an example'). 'Washing the feet of God's people' (1 Tim. 5.10) was one of the qualifications for being a widow in the true sense of support from the Christian community; it was a mark of service and hospitality.

# MAUNDY THURSDAY

Jeremiah 31. 31–34
See Lent 5 Year 2.


## 1 Corinthians 10. 16–17

The passage comes at a point in Paul's letter where he was concerned to prevent the Corinthian congregation thinking that participation in pagan worship did not matter for Christians. He had earlier dealt with the problem of meat offered to idols. Now he contrasted the worship of the Church with the worship of pagans and Jews. Sacrificial worship in pagan temples frequently ended in a banquet at which some of the meat offered to the god was eaten, and the meals tended to end in orgies. Immorality and excesses associated with pagan worship, therefore, were a sign of evil influences. 'I will not have you become partners with demons', he told them (verse 20). Those joined to the Lord in the Eucharist could not be joined to Satan in other kinds of worship. From the Jewish background of the Christian faith Paul wanted his readers to learn a lesson. God had fed his people in the wilderness, but punished them for their idolatry. This then is the argument within which our passage is set.

16  **The cup of blessing** is a technical word, referring to the cup which was blessed and passed round at the end of a meal among Jews, and which was the third of the four cups used in the Passover meal. The prayer said over it was, 'Blessed art thou, O Lord our God, who givest us the fruit of the vine'. It was from this prayer that the eucharistic prayers of the church developed. The Christian bishop or the one who presided at the Eucharist, like the host at the Passover, said a prayer of thanksgiving to God over the cup of wine.

Most pagan banquets were thought of, not crudely as eating the sign of the deity, but as banqueting with him and being united with him. Paul applied this to the Eucharist. The cup of wine over which the blessing has been offered ('The cup of blessing for which we give thanks
16  to God' TEV) is a **means of sharing in the blood of Christ** in the sense of sharing in all the benefits that the blood of Christ secures for us. Simi-
16  larly, the head is a **means of sharing in the body of Christ**, the sign here being a sacramental sign of Christ himself and, through him, the members of his Body. The Christians are made one in this sharing of bread and wine, for they are participants in the work of Christ; as Paul had said earlier in the letter (5.7–8), the Christian Passover has been offered

in the person of Jesus Christ, and Christians are celebrating not only the feast but themselves as the unleavened bread with which it is celebrated.

* Mark 14. 12–26

We have already noticed the problem concerning the dating of the events of the passion in the Gospels (see p. 182). Whether or not the Last Supper was a Passover meal has been debated by scholars for a long time. For our purposes, the matter is academic. No one disputes the paschal nature of the Last Supper.

13    Two of his disciples (Peter and John in Luke 22.8) were given a rendezvous with a man carrying a jar of water. Identification would not be difficult, as women rather than men carried these jars in the East, though the larger stone water-jars were carried by men (John 2.7). Was the room used by Jesus in the house that belonged to the mother of John Mark (cf. Acts 12.12)? If it was a proper Passover meal (and not a *kiddush*, a social religious gathering of the kind held by groups of pious Jews in preparation for celebrations such as the Passover) the disciples would have had to prepare the lamb, unleavened bread, bitter herbs, a sauce called *charoseth*, and cups of wine.

Jesus presided over the meal as the head of the group. At the Passover the father of the household presided. The ritual involved blessings, wine drunk at four different intervals, explanations over the elements of the meal, and the singing of the Hallel Psalms (Ps. 113—118). The unleavened bread symbolized the past misery (the 'bread of affliction'), the bitter herbs symbolized past slavery, and the lamb recalled God's 'passing over' Egypt, and so on. Even if the Last Supper was not a Passover meal, there would be nothing unusual in Jesus' giving explanations of its elements. The room would probably be furnished with rugs and cushions and a low table, at which the guests would recline.

Mark did not identify Judas as the betrayer, but Jesus accepted his fate 21 willingly: **the Son of Man is going the way appointed for him in the scriptures.** No scriptural text is mentioned, but the words are a reminder that there is God's purpose behind the tragic events; they are part of 'the deliberate will and plan of God' (Acts 2.23).

The account of the institution of the Eucharist is brief and simple. Interest is focused on its religious significance, not on historical details. Early liturgical traditions in the Church may have preserved and shaped 22, some of its phrases. **Take this; this is my body. . . . This is my blood,** 24 **the blood of the covenant, shed for many.** Jesus was soon to leave his disciples and the visible union between them was to be broken until the Kingdom of God comes in its fulness. He therefore provided a visible means of an invisible union by associating the broken loaf and the shared wine with his body and blood. Those who partake of the loaf are brought into communion with him and with each other; those who drink of the wine participate in the atoning sacrifice of his death through which he inaugurated the new covenant. Questions about the mode of Christ's presence in the bread and wine did not arise. The ancient world was familiar with symbols which effected, or helped to effect, that which they symbolized.

The words used by Jesus when he prayed over the bread and the wine were probably something like these:

'Blessed art thou, O Lord our God, king of the world, who hast brought forth bread from the earth.'

'Blessed art thou, O Lord our God, king of the world, who hast created the fruit of the vine.'

23  *Eucharistesas*, **offered thanks**, is the origin of the word Eucharist.

The OT passages which supply the background to the phrase, 'blood of the covenant', are Exod. 24.4–8, the covenant on Sinai with its inaugural sacrifice of blood, and Jer. 31.31–34, the prophecy of a new covenant.

# GOOD FRIDAY

*The Death of Christ*

**Exodus 12. 1–8,11**
The Priestly account of the institution of the Passover. According to the scheme in the book of Exodus, these instructions were given in Egypt.

2  **This month is for you the first of months** introduces what was to be a new way of calculating the beginning of the year. Exod. 23.16 says that the harvests lead up to the end of the year (our October); **this month**, the month of the Passover, is called in other sources the month Abib (the Babylonian Nisan), our March–April. The origins of these different ways of calculating the beginning of the year are unknown.

**The whole community of Israel** is the Hebrew *'edah*, the basic

meaning of which is 'to appoint'. With *qahal* it is used to describe the assembly of the people, and it was rendered in the LXX by *ekklesia*, 'church'. Why the head of the household should select the lamb without
3 blemish, a male which is one year old, **on the tenth day of this month** is not apparent. Like the third and the seventh days, it may have had some
6 ritual significance. The animal was slaughtered **between the two evenings** (NEB footnote), that is, between sunset and the sight of the first
7 star. The smearing of the blood **on the two door-posts and on the lintel of every house in which they shall ea** the lamb had the practical purpose during the exodus of indicating which houses in Egypt were occupied by Israel. The ritual manipulation of blood had a highly religious significance and was a prerogative of the priests in later Israel. In the Passover ritual this priestly office was performed by the head of the household.

The Passover was a nocturnal feast. To bake without leaven means speedy baking before a hurried departure, as on the last night in Egypt; bitter herbs are lettuce or chicory, to be dried and carried on the journey.
11 **It is the Lord's Passover.** Hebrew *Pesah*, Greek *Pascha*. The meaning of the word is uncertain; it could mean 'protect', 'save', 'be lame', 'placate', etc. 'Pass', 'pass over' and 'share' are suggested by the contexts in which it is used.

The Jewish Passover became a rehearsal for the Christian Passover in which Christ, the Lamb of God, was sacrificed on the cross during the paschal celebrations in Jerusalem to bring salvation to men. The Eucharist, in which Christians offer a prayer of thanksgiving over bread and wine and consume the elements in sacramental communion with God and with each other, is the Church's means of celebrating the new Passover of Christ.

### Hebrews 10. 11–25

The priests of the temple in Jerusalem were occupied each day in offering sacrifices, standing before the altar; but Jesus Christ, our one High Priest, made one offering of himself on the cross, and this single sacrifice is effective for the remission of sins—which the former oblations could never be. Ps. 110, used earlier in this letter, was quoted again: Jesus **took his seat at the right hand of God, where he waits henceforth until**
12– **his enemies are made his footstool.** The session of Christ, contrasted
13 with the standing attitude of the priests, denotes not only Jesus' divine status but also the completion of his work. His enemies are the forces of evil still active in the world. By that single offering Christ has achieved 'the eternal perfection of all whom he is sanctifying' (JB); the sentence

embraces the work of Christ in its completion and also in its continual process in the lives of Christians.

The fact that God's forgiveness has been obtained by Christ's sacrifice is proved by quotations from Jeremiah's prophecy of the new covenant, already used earlier in the letter. The new covenant promised by God is
17 established and the past forgotten as well as forgiven—their sins and wicked deeds I will remember no more at all.

We are admitted into the sanctuary through the sacrifice of Jesus
20 Christ by the new, living way which he has opened for us through the curtain, the way of his flesh. The way is new because Jesus inaugurated it; it is living because it was inaugurated through the death and resurrection of the living Lord ('I am the way; I am the truth and I am life; no one comes to the Father except by me', John 14.6) The way of his flesh is a difficult phrase to interpret. JB has 'through the curtain, that is to say, his body'. Perhaps the most satisfactory solution is to understand it as referring to Jesus' flesh *and* blood, which he shared with us as humans and which he offered in sacrifice. It is this sacrifice which is the curtain through which we are admitted into the sanctuary.

The rest of the passage works out the consequences of this offering in
22 Christian living. We approach the sanctuary in sincerity of heart and full assurance of faith, through our baptism, we are firm in the
23 confession of our hope, and we study how each of us may best rouse others to love and active goodness within the Christian com-
25 munity, spurred on because you see the Day drawing near. Faith, hope, and love—the primary virtues—are the three bases on which this exhortation stands.

\* John 18. 1—19. 37
Only points of special interest in the Johannine narrative of the passion will be noted here.

6    When he said, 'I am he', they drew back and fell to the ground. Linked with the 'I am' sayings of the fourth Gospel, this incident underlines the divine authority of Christ.

11   This is the cup my Father has given me; shall I not drink it? This is a suggestive variation of the prayer which Jesus offered in Gethsemane, according to the synoptic narratives. Only John calls Gethsemane 'a garden'.

13   They took him first to Annas. Matthew and Mark reported that Jesus was brought before a specially convened meeting of the Sanhedrin on the night of his arrest; Luke said that Jesus was held in Caiaphas'

house during the night. Annas had been relieved of the office of High Priest in A.D. 15, but he still remained influential in Jerusalem, for five of his sons held the office, including Caiaphas, who was High Priest from A.D. 18 to 36. According to the fourth Gospel, Peter's denial also took place here. The variations in the details are not incompatible. The special meeting of the Sanhedrin could have been summoned to meet near Annas' house, and Jesus taken to Caiaphas' house afterwards.

29    **What charge do you bring against this man?** John did not mention the morning interrogation of Jesus by the Sanhedrin, but he indicated that the Jews brought Christ to Pilate because they were not allowed to put anyone to death. They were evasive about the charge, however; the synoptic Gospels are clear that the Jews' initial complaint against Jesus was that he had blasphemed. In John's account Pilate questioned the Jews outside the building and Jesus inside.

38    **Pilate said, 'What is truth?'** He showed by this question that he was not on the side of truth. However, he admitted Jesus' innocence and attempted to secure his release.

19.12    **If you let this man go, you are no friend of Caesar.** Every Roman administrator aspired to be *amicus Caesaris*, to have influence in the imperial court. The Jews' threat ended Pilate's attempt to save Jesus, and he formally handed him over in the public tribunal outside the governor's residence. John timed the crucifixion a day earlier than the synoptic Gospels, when the lambs were being slaughtered, and at a later hour, noon instead of nine o'clock in the morning (to coincide with the killing of the lambs?).

26    **Mother, there is your son.** Only John reported that Jesus' mother was at the cross. Christ's words to her, and to the disciple whom he loved, have been interpreted by the Church as addressed to all Christians, Mary herself symbolizing the community of the redeemed.

28    **I thirst.** The incident of giving drugged wine to Jesus was characteristically given deeper significance by John. The true meaning of this word from the cross is to be found in Ps. 63.1, 'O God, thou art my God, I seek thee, my soul thirsts for thee'.

30    **It is accomplished!** In the fourth Gospel Jesus' life and work were seen moving towards an appointed destiny. The last word from the cross drew these threads together in fulfilment.

# EASTER EVE

### Haggai 2. 6–9
Dated in the second year of Darius king of Persia (522–486 B.C.) these prophecies are concerned with the rebuilding of the temple in Jerusalem after the exile. The prophet thought of the remnant of the people as standing on the threshold of a new age, ushered in with the shaking of
6 **heaven and earth, sea and land,** and the nations bringing their tributes to the restored and glorified temple.

### 1 Peter 3. 17–22
The first verse, and perhaps the second, of this controversial passage may rest on a catechetical formula or early hymn, summing up in a few words the purpose of the death and resurrection of Christ. In the interval between his death and resurrection Christ preached to the dead—the ones who perished in the flood being specially mentioned as grave sinners in an exemplary, not exclusive, sense. Reference to Christ's Passover and Noah's ark led the writer to say that baptism is not just a washing;
21 **it brings salvation through the resurrection of Jesus Christ.** It is a pledge of God's forgiveness and admission to the new life.

### * Matthew 27. 57–66
According to this evangelist, the burial of Jesus' body was undertaken by
57 Joseph of Arimathaea because he had himself become a disciple of Jesus. Mark recorded that Joseph was a member of the Sanhedrin. The appeal of the chief priests and the Pharisees to Pilate is surprising, since next day, the morning after that Friday, was the sabbath. One would suppose that they would have done this the night before. Pilate provided a guard from the Roman troops. As an additional precaution, the Jews put a seal on the stone of the tomb so that any unauthorized opening could be detected.

### * John 2. 18–22
See Epiphany 3 Year 2.

# EASTER DAY
*The Resurrection of Christ*

### Isaiah 12. 1-6
The prophet had announced a new exodus for the people of God (11.12ff), and since Moses and the Israelites sang to the Lord after their deliverance from the Egyptians at the Red Sea (Exod. 15.1ff) the prophet provided two short psalms as a response to the announcement of the new exodus. Israel would praise God again for removing his anger from them and showing them his strength, for delivering them from great danger and setting himself over them as their defence. The provision of water from the rock in the wilderness during the first exodus is recalled in verse 3:
3 **You shall draw water with joy from the springs of deliverance.**

The second psalm (verses 4-6) includes all the elements of the people's
4 response to God—proclaiming his word (**make his deeds known**), praying and praising him, and giving thanks to him, because of the assurance of his presence in majesty.

On this day the psalms become a hymn for the risen Christ to sing to his people.

### Revelation 1. 12-18
Part of the introduction to John's letters to the seven churches. The seven lamps, familiar to anyone who saw a seven-branched candlestick in a Jewish synagogue, represent the seven churches to whom the letter
13 was addressed. Standing among them is **one like a son of man** (lit. 'a man', i.e. a human being), Jesus Christ in his risen humanity vested with the glory of deity. This is depicted in terms of the robe and girdle of the high priest (Exod. 28.4), the white hair of the Ancient of Days (Dan. 7.9), the flaming eyes of divine knowledge (eyes that pierce the hearts of men), the feet of burnished brass like Ezekiel's cherubim (Ezek. 1.7), and the voice like the sound of rushing waters, from the same prophet (Ezek. 43.2), demonstrating his strength and inspiring fear at his majesty. The seven stars are the seven angels, the heavenly counterpart of the seven churches (the imagery is perhaps taken from the seven known planets of the time), hanging like a necklace of jewels in the right hand of the figure.

It is, however, not helpful to analyse too closely the details of John's vision. Based on the angel of Daniel (10.5-6), it gathered together divine manifestations from various parts of the OT and put them together to give readers a picture of the risen Christ in order to call forth from the readers the same response of awe and wonder which the prophet himself experienced in his trance.

It was believed that no one could see God and live. John fell on his feet at the vision (as the women fell at the feet of the risen Christ), but 18 the figure lifted him up: **Do not be afraid. I am the first and the last, and I am the living one; for I was dead and now I am alive for evermore, and I hold the keys of Death and Death's domain.** Christ has not only resumed his eternal life which he had with the Father before the world began; he has also through his resurrection entered upon a new and victorious life in which death itself is conquered. Hades, *Sheol*, was the place of departed souls in Jewish mythology.

**\* Mark 16. 1–8**

The resurrection of Christ is the centre of salvation-history, the dramatic event prepared for and promised by God for thousands of years. With great simplicity Mark told the first effect it had on some of Jesus' followers. It was not the disciples who discovered the empty tomb but the women who, practically unnoticed throughout his Gospel, had followed Jesus to his crucifixion and watched from afar. The spices had been brought after sundown on the sabbath in preparation for the embalming of the body. A visit to the grave for the purpose would be entirely natural. The stone across the sepulchre would keep out marauders and animals.

The great moments of the Gospels are often marked by angelic activity, though the evangelist did not stress the supernatural nature of the figure 5 seated at the tomb. He is **a youth wearing a white robe.** Some commentators have suggested that it was Mark himself, who had arrived earlier at the tomb and realised the fulfilment of Christ's sayings that he would rise from the dead. The young man's only function was to explain that Jesus had been raised up and to send a message to the disciples through the women. Jesus had promised to meet his disciples in Galilee, the scene of much of his earthly ministry. The special mention of Peter among the disciples is a feature of this Gospel.

The fear and awe of the women is the fear and awe of humanity in the presence of a mighty act of God; eventually they recovered from their tongue-tied terror sufficiently to tell the disciples what had happened, but if the evangelist ended his Gospel at the words, **They said nothing** 8 **to anybody, for they were afraid,** he left this to be understood in the continuous teaching of the Church down to his own day. The real evidence of the resurrection for his readers was the presence of the Christian community to which they belonged and the knowledge of the risen Lord in their own lives.

# EASTER DAY

*The Resurrection of Christ*

Isaiah 12. 1-6
See Easter Day Year 1.

1 Corinthians 5. 7b-8
The Christian community at Corinth had been divided through internal rivalries and disgraced by a case of incest among its members. In pressing for the removal of the offender from the fellowship, the first known case of an excommunication from the Church, the apostle explained that Christians must be pure, like the unleavened bread of the Passover celebrations. (Unleavened bread was used because leaven was considered to be ritually impure.)

Christians live in a state of perpetual Passover celebration, because they have been saved by the Lamb God himself provided, prophesied to Abraham before the offering of Isaac (Gen. 22.8) and announced by John the Baptist at the beginning of Christ's ministry (John 1.29).
7 Indeed our Passover has begun; the sacrifice is offered—Christ himself. Our life consists of a continuous thanksgiving to God for his mighty act of love and deliverance in Christ, a thanksgiving expressed not only in the prayers and ritual of worship but in the way we conduct ourselves in our ordinary lives.

\* Matthew 28. 1-10
Matthew based his account of the resurrection on Mark 16.1-8 (see Easter Day Year 1), but with alterations and additions. In Mark the women approach the tomb to complete the work of anointing the body of Jesus, which remained to be done after the hasty burial before the sabbath began. On arrival they find the stone which sealed the tomb already removed and they see inside a young man in white who tells them that the resurrection had already occurred before sending them off with the message for the disciples. In Matthew there is no mention of the anointing;
1 the women came to look at the grave. But what they see is a terrifying accompaniment of the resurrection, an earthquake and the descent of the angel to roll away the stone and sit on it. The guards who had been placed over the tomb collapse with fear.

The Marcan narrative is resumed in verse 5 when the angel announces the resurrection which Jesus had foretold (12.40, 16.21, etc.), and that the disciples are to meet him in Galilee. Then in verse 8 Matthew used his own sources to tell of an encounter with the risen Christ which the women had on their errand. When Jesus greets them, they fall prostrate— the position of adoration, but also of fear in the presence of deity—and he repeats the message about meeting him in Galilee. Matthew was not so much concerned to explain how the resurrection happened as to describe the event in terms of an OT theophany. The God of Israel, as of old, was now bringing deliverance with his mighty hand and outstretched arm.

1    The other Mary was Mary the mother of James (Mark 16.1).

# EASTER DAY

# ADDITIONAL READINGS

### Exodus 14. 15–22

The passage tells of the most critical moment in the history of Israel. The flight from Egypt had been halted at the Red Sea (JB uses the alternative name, 'Sea of Reeds'). Behind them was the pursuing army of Pharaoh. 'We would rather be slaves to the Egyptians than die here in the wilderness', they said (14.13). In the crisis the Lord spoke directly to Moses.

The various traditions which go to make up the Pentateuch contribute to the details of the story. The oldest, the Jahwist source, says that the Lord sent a strong east wind to drive back the waters of the Red Sea; the Elohist source says that the angel of God and Moses' rod were the means for the expression of God's power; the Priestly source says the gesture of Moses' hand made the waters as a wall on either side of the Israelites. But whatever each tradition contributed, the event was regarded in the OT as the mighty act of God on behalf of his people and was constantly referred to by prophet and psalmist. It takes the same focal importance in the OT as the resurrection of Jesus Christ takes in the New. And it provides the interpretation of the resurrection as the new exodus, an escape from death and slavery through the waters of baptism—the free gift of God's faithfulness and love.

### 1 Corinthians 15. 12–20

Four of the epistles in Eastertide are taken from this chapter of 1 Corinthians, in which the apostle taught about life after death. Easter 3 Year 1

(1 Cor. 15.1–11) affirms as in a creed the Christian faith in the resurrection of Jesus. This passage deals with the resurrection of Christians.

Belief in our own resurrection, said the apostle, is rooted in faith in Christ's resurrection. Arguing against some who attempted to set limits to the resurrection of Christians or who did not believe that it was possible, he pointed out that, if what they said was true, then the Christian had nothing to preach and nothing to believe. **Our gospel is null and void,** 14 **and so is your faith.** The apostles would then be shown to be lying against God, because they had said of him that he had raised Jesus from the dead. Faith would be a delusion, sins would not have been forgiven, 19 believers who had died would be lost for ever, **and we of all men are most to be pitied** because, believing that in the risen Christ we had everything, in the dead Christ we would have nothing.

But in fact Christ has been raised from the dead. Furthermore, he is the first instalment of that crop which promises the ultimate offering of the whole: since he has been raised, the rest of mankind can also be raised in him.

20   The image of **the firstfruits of the harvest of the dead** may have been in Paul's mind because of references to the Passover which he had made in this letter. A feature of the Passover celebrations was the presentation of the sheaf from the first cutting of the corn in the fields as a promise of a greater harvest to come.


\* John 20. 1–18

1 **While it was still dark** would be somewhere between 3 and 6 a.m. Although only Mary of Magdala is mentioned, the 'we' of verse 2 suggests that there were others with her, as in the Synoptic accounts. The stone covering the entrance of the small cave-tomb, a natural rock formation or artificially constructed as a sepulchre, had been removed, and she suspected a grave robbery. She ran to tell Peter and **the other disciple,** 2 **the one whom Jesus loved,** traditionally recognized as John.

The visit of the two disciples to the tomb confirmed the discovery. More than that, it demonstrated that the disappearance of the body was 5 not the result of a robbery but of a supernatural act: **the linen wrappings,** which would have been disturbed or taken away if there had been a theft of the corpse, were lying in such a way as to suggest that the spiritual and glorified body of Christ had passed through them without disturbing them. Only the cloth which had wrapped round the corpse's head appeared to have been removed to some distance. This cloth would in any case have been separate from the winding-sheet, and John's words may mean no more than that it was observed to be still in this separate position. As a result of seeing the empty tomb and the grave clothes, John came to a faith in the resurrection which Peter apparently had not reached at that time. But the teaching of the OT as interpreted by the early Church, an interpretation initiated by Jesus Christ himself and guided by the Holy Spirit, about the resurrection now took on a meaning for them.

12    The **two angels** play a less important role in the fourth Gospel than the figure(s) in the tomb in the synoptic Gospels. They merely provide Mary of Magdala with an opportunity to explain why she is weeping. It was to her that the risen Christ appeared first. She did not recognize him at once; she thought he was the gardener. In an allegorical sense he was 'the gardener' who came to reopen the garden of Eden for sinful man. The Fathers expounded the incident in this way, though it is not obvious that the evangelist thought of it so. Then, when Mary did

16    recognize him, she used the term **Rabbuni**, the word for the divine Lord, a stronger term than Rabbi—recognizing him in an act of faith like that of Thomas later that day (20.28. See Easter 1 Year 1).

The fourth Gospel does not picture the ascension as a separate event, though the words of Christ to Mary as she clung to him indicate that the completion of Christ's glorification took place when he returned to his Father's side. The way is prepared for the Johannine Pentecost (20.22. See Easter 1 Year 1). Although Jesus Christ accepted the disciples as

17    **my brothers**, he still made a distinction between his relationship to the Father and theirs by mentioning the Father twice as 'my' and 'your'. The unique relationship of 'God's only Son, he who is nearest to the Father's heart' (1.18) remained.

The fourth Gospel's presentation of the resurrection is in striking contrast to that of the Synoptics, especially Matthew. There is no mighty act in which the hosts of evil are routed and the power of God vindicated. Rather, the resurrection takes place quietly and irresistibly, like the rising of the sun at dawn, when the shadows of the night are slowly removed and the freshness of the garden sweetens the beginning of a new day.

## THE RESURRECTION APPEARANCES

When the narratives of the resurrection given by the four evangelists are compared, it can be seen that they display far more differences than do the narratives of the passion. From this, biblical scholarship has deduced that the stories in question were given a stereotyped form at a later stage than the passion narratives. The passion was a single event, the core of the apostolic preaching; the resurrection appearances were many ('He showed himself to these men after his death, and gave ample proof that he was alive: over a period of forty days he appeared to them and taught them about the kingdom of God' Acts 1.3.) Neither Paul nor any of the evangelists attempted to give all the events. They made their choice, no wider than was necessary to proclaim fittingly the one great message. Under these circumstances a fixed form of narrative about the resurrection was not established so quickly, and several lines of tradition were formed with divergences in detail. These divergences go back to the first Easter morning when the women went to the tomb.

We need not elaborate the divergencies here, but we should note that the four accounts agree on the main themes: the empty tomb, the appearance of an angelic messenger, and the message—the Lord is risen and is alive. And behind the narrative is the awareness that we are in touch with events beyond this world, events which can only be grasped by men with a vivid faith in the living God, who works with power to fulfil his holy and gracious purposes. The gospel of the resurrection can only be interpreted within this faith; then the rise and power of the early Church can be explained.

# EASTER 1

*The Upper Room Appearances*

## Exodus 15. 1-11
The song of Moses and the Israelites, offered to God in thanksgiving for the safe crossing of the Red Sea, is one of the great canticles of the OT. It is a later composition than the song of Miriam, which is repeated later in the chapter (verse 21) and with which it begins: **Sing to the Lord, for he has risen up in triumph; the horse and his rider he has hurled into the sea.** The song may have received additions over the years as it was used at festivals—the Passover, the New Year, or some other occasions. Although the song tells of the destruction of Pharaoh's army, its underlying theme is joy at the Lord's faithfulness and power and

2 care for the people he has chosen: he has shown himself my deliverer
('my salvation' RSV and JB). The horse and his rider refers to chariots;
6 the Egyptians did not fight with mounted cavalry in this era. The right
hand of the Lord, the image used to describe God in his mighty activity
for his people, cast the Egyptians into the watery abyss, the abode of
chaos in Jewish mythology.

9 I will pursue, I will overtake, I will divide the spoil echoes the
eagerness and over-confidence of the Egyptians, heightening the dramatic
11 ending of their chase. Who is like thee, O Lord, among the gods?
assumes the existence of other deities (unless the NEB footnote, in might,
is followed) and contrasts their importance with the power of God.

(–18)

12 The earth engulfed them. It was the sea which swallowed up the
Egyptians, unless the miracle was due to some volcanic movement which
lifted the seabed for the Israelites and pulled the Egyptians down by
13 sinking again as they crossed in pursuit. Thou hast guided them by
thy strength almost certainly referred to the ark, which headed the caravan on its way to Canaan. Thy holy dwelling-place could be Zion or
14 the whole of Canaan. The nations which heard and trembled were the
neighbouring peoples and their leaders who were affected by the exodus;
the list corresponds to those mentioned as being on the route in Deut.
17 2.1–9. The mount . . ., the dwelling-place . . ., the sanctuary could
be Canaan, or Zion, or the temple, or all of them.

1 Peter 1. 3–9

After the opening salutations, 1 Peter begins with a benediction common
in the scriptures: 'Blessed be the God and Father of our Lord Jesus
Christ' (RSV). Similar formulas are found in the psalms (e.g. 'Blessed be
the Lord, even the God of Israel: who alone doeth wondrous things'
Ps. 72.19) and in the Eighteen Benedictions, recited in the synagogues
three times a day. Benedictions of this kind were prayers of praise and
thanksgiving for what God had done (they are the forefathers of the
Church's eucharistic prayers), and in this letter the thanks offered is for
the new birth made possible through the resurrection.

The NEB breaks up the long Greek sentence of verses 3–5 into three.
3 A living hope by the resurrection is the inheritance to which
4 we are born. We receive a foretaste of that inheritance in this life but its
fulfilment will not be ours until the end of time; until then, it is guarded
by God in heaven, where it is untouched by those forces which ruin

4 earthly possessions. The use of the three words **destroy or spoil or wither** emphasizes the difference between the Christian's possessions and his heavenly inheritance. This inheritance, unearned like all property which passes from parents to children, is the state of salvation and blessedness which will be ours in the Kingdom of heaven.

1 Peter seems to have been written with strong connections with the baptismal liturgy, and the benediction with which it opens reads like a thanksgiving for baptism and its effects in the lives of believers. But whereas Paul taught of the effects of baptism in terms of dying and rising with Christ (Rom. 6.4–14) and being made new (Gal. 6.15), Peter taught it in terms of a new birth, of Christians as newly-born children of God. The concept of baptism as a new birth is found in our Lord's own teaching on accepting the kingdom of God 'like a child' (Mark 10.15). His warning to Nicodemus that 'unless a man has been born over again he cannot see the kingdom of God' (John 3.3) is a further strand in the tradition, as is 'the water of rebirth' ('the washing of regeneration', RSV).

6    The **great joy** which the living hope brings cannot be diminished by the trials of this life. The Christians in Asia to whom the letter was addressed may have been experiencing persecution at the time; these, the writer assured them, were opportunities through which faith is being tested, like gold in a fire. The analogy was used by Paul, though he spoke of it as the testing on the day of judgement when a man's work is scrutinized by God (1 Cor. 3.13). The comparison is found in the OT. The Christian can be happy in the face of trials because of his hope in the risen Christ, and, like Paul, the author of 1 Peter saw its result in the blessedness of the Christian at the end of time.

This further reference to Jesus reminded the writer that he was
8 speaking to those who had never seen Christ in the flesh. **You have not seen him, yet you love him.** But this was no disadvantage. The exultation which God's blessedness gives is a 'joy in harvest'—**the**
9 **harvest of your faith,** resulting in **salvation for your souls.** The writer's use of the word 'soul' is Semitic; it depicts the living self or person. He was saying the same thing as Paul, 'Faith is our guide, we do not see him' (1 Cor. 5.7), and as the risen Christ said to Thomas, 'Happy are they who never saw me and yet have found faith' (John 20.29).

* John 20. 19–29
The appearance of Christ in the upper room to his disciples was remembered as the first and most authoritative of his resurrection appearances. Paul recorded an appearance to 'the Twelve' (1 Cor. 15.5) and Luke gave

an account of it (24.36ff) which is very similar to this one. The number of
the disciples was not indicated by John. The fact that it was Sunday looks
forward to the Christian custom of assembling on the first day of the
week to celebrate the resurrection of Jesus and meeting him in the
breaking of bread.

20     **Peace be with you** is a conventional Jewish salutation, but its repetition sends us back to Ps. 147.14, 'He (the Lord) maketh peace in thy
borders', and the Aaronic blessing of Num. 6.24–26: 'The Lord bless
you and watch over you; the Lord make his face shine upon you and be
21  gracious to you; the Lord look kindly on you and give you peace.' **As the
Father sent me, so I send you** recalls the earlier discourses in this
Gospel. Then Christ bestowed the Holy Spirit upon the disciples and gave
them authority to pronounce the remission of sins.

Evidently we encounter here divergent traditions about the gift of the
Spirit, the Luke–Acts tradition which places the gift on the day of Pentecost fifty days after the first Easter Day, and the Johannine tradition
which places it on the day of resurrection and as the immediate gift of the
risen Lord to his Church. We must not, however, discount the possibility
that both traditions may be right: a gift of the Spirit may have been
bestowed by Christ at his first appearance, but was not manifested until
seven weeks later—though this raises problems about the Johannine
ascension. The meaning is clear: the Passover of Christ has inaugurated a
new creative act of God for man, a completion of God's work which began
in Gen. 1.1. Later patristic teaching saw the resurrection as the work of
God on the *eighth* day of creation, the work with which he completed the
salvation of man after his seventh day of rest (when Christ's body was
in the tomb). God breathed into the dust and gave man life at creation
(Gen. 2.7); in the act of recreation Christ breathed on his disciples and
gave the Holy Spirit. Ezekiel's prophecy of the wind bringing resurrection life to dry bones was fulfilled (37.9).

In these few verses the evangelist gathered together the fulfilling of
Christ's promises earlier in the Gospel: 'I will not leave you bereft: I am
coming back to you. . . . Because I live, you too will live; then you will
know that I am in my Father, and you in me and I in you' (14.17–18);
'Peace is my parting gift to you, my own peace, such as the world cannot
give' (14.27); 'If I do not go, your Advocate will not come, whereas if I
go, I will send him to you' (16.7); 'I shall see you again, and then you will
be joyful, and no one shall rob you of that joy' (16.22); 'As thou (Father)
hast sent me into the world, I have sent them (my disciples) into the
world' (17.18).

The authority to pronounce the remission or retention of sins is parallel with a similar commission in Matt. 16.19, 'I will give you the keys of the kingdom of Heaven; what you forbid on earth shall be forbidden in heaven, and what you allow on earth shall be allowed in heaven', repeated in Matt. 18.18. Some exegetes distinguish between the two by ascribing power to make rules for the Christian community to the Matthean commissioning and the authority to pronounce the absolution of sins and to excommunicate to the Johannine version. (The matter has been further confused by the fact that the Johannine commissioning has been used in the rites of ordination to the presbyterate in the Western Church since the twelfth century and has been interpreted by some Roman Catholic and Anglican theologians as a necessary part of the sacramental 'form'.) The two commissionings may go back to a single authorization of the apostles by Christ based on Isa. 22.22, 'I will lay the key of the house of David on his shoulder; what he opens no man shall
22 shut, and what he shuts no man shall open'. **He breathed on them.** 'Breath' in Hebrew is the same word as 'spirit'; the giving of the Holy Spirit by Jesus could be described in the same terms as the giving of the breath of life by God.

Matthew recorded that 'some were doubtful' (28.17) about Christ's resurrection. John named one of those involved—Thomas, who was not so much a cynical doubter as one who required proof. When a week later Thomas was offered the proof by Jesus, he did not in fact require it, but
28 confessed his faith in Christ immediately by calling him **my Lord and my God**. The affirmation of Christ's divinity made at the beginning of the Gospel, 'the Word became flesh' (1.14), is now accepted as a result of the resurrection. But true faith is not based on what the eye sees or the hand handles but on an experience and knowledge of the risen Lord.

# EASTER 1

*The Bread of Life*

### Exodus 16. (1–3)
The Priestly source of the book of Exodus states that the Israelites had been on the march a month before the complaints began among them. The slavery in Egypt looked attractive to them compared with the hard-

ships their liberation brought them; they looked back with longing at the
3 place **where we sat round the fleshpots and had plenty of bread to
eat.**

### 4–15
The Jahwist source was responsible for the first two verses of this section
(4–5), recording that the Lord promised a rain of bread to Moses in the
wilderness of Sin. It reflects the concern to observe the sabbath in the
4 provision of two days' bread on Fridays. The Lord gave them **each
day . . . a day's supply**—the phrase is reminiscent of the Lord's Prayer.
The day-to-day dependence on God for the provision of manna was to be
part of the divine testing or disciplining of Israel.

The Priestly source resumed the story in verse 6. The people were
reminded that it was God himself who had brought them out of Egypt.
13 **Quails** would be supplied in the evenings for food and **manna** in the
15 mornings. The order, evening before morning, is based on the Jewish
custom of reckoning the evening as the beginning of the following day.
The glory of the Lord would be revealed in the brilliant appearance of
fire veiled in cloud—the Priestly source's usual description of the manifestation of God in connection with the Tent of Meeting.

Both quails and manna are found naturally in the Sinai peninsula.
Quails are small game birds belonging to the same family as pheasants
and they sometimes fall exhausted to the ground during the season of
migration when the wind changes against their flight. The name manna
15 may come from the Hebrew **What is that?** (NEB footnote, **man-hu**).
It has been suggested that the name was given to the secretions of certain
insects, small white drops which are light in colour and weight and sticky
and sweet; they harden at night, but melt in the sun.

### (31–35)
31 The manna is compared to **coriander seed**—small, round, and grey-
white. Moses directed that about an omer, 6½ lb., should be 'reserved' in
a jar before the Testimony, the Ark, in the sanctuary as a memorial for
future generations.

### 1 Corinthians 15. 53–58
Paul answered the question, What will happen to Christians who survive
until the Second Coming? and, in so doing, explained that they, like
all those who have not survived, will be changed, taking off what is mortal
and perishable and putting on (like clothing) what is immortal and

impérishable. 'We know that if the earthly frame that houses us today should be demolished, we possess a building which God has provided—a house not made by human hands, eternal, and in heaven. In this present body we do indeed groan; we yearn to have our heavenly habitation put on over this one.' 2 Cor. 5.1–2 is a commentary on verse 53. The image of taking off the physical body and putting on the resurrection body serves to emphasize the continuity of the person through the change. Then, quoting Isa. 25.8 and Hos. 13.14, the apostle declared that the end would celebrate the final triumph, the annihilation of death and God's universal reign. Death is the last enemy to be overthrown. Its defeat is not accomplished yet; it still has its sting—sin. But final victory is assured.

Reference to sin led Paul on to that which gives man the realization of sin and provides a base from which further sin operates—the law. Not that the law is sinful—on the contrary, it is the holy law of God (Rom. 5, 6 and 7 expound this); rather it is that the law, though holy, provokes a man to sin by rousing in him the urge to be disobedient to it or to take 57 advantage of it. But God **gives us the victory through our Lord Jesus Christ**, and this victory is available to all who are in him. Paul was so sure of this that he was able to say that the victory is being given at this moment (**he gives us**, NEB: JB's 'giving us' must be understood in the same tense). The Christians in Corinth might go about their task of building up the Church, whatever the cost, confident that their labour was not in vain.

## \* John 6. 35–40

The 'bread of life' discourse follows the Johannine account of the feeding of the five thousand, and at the point where our passage begins, Jesus had been challenged to show the crowd a sign that they might believe him. 'Our ancestors had manna to eat in the desert', they had said (verse 31). Jesus reminded them that it was the Father who gave bread 35 in the desert, not Moses, and announced, **I am the bread of life.**

For the Jews who heard that statement, it must have been a solemn nd impressive claim. 'I am', *ego eimi*, is an OT phrase representing the majesty and person of the one true God (Exod. 3.14); applied to Jesus by himself, it is an assertion of his unity with God and total participation in the work of God. The gift of the manna in the OT and the feeding of the five thousand are parables pointing to Christ's gift of himself to men as the true bread. As Wisdom invited men to her table ('Wisdom has spread her table. . . . "Come, dine with me" ' Prov. 9.1–5) so Jesus, prefigured in the OT's personification of Wisdom, invited men to feed and drink on himself. He is available to satisfy once and for all the hunger and thirst of those who come to him and believe in him. Although ideas about the Eucharist in Christian life developed from this bread of life discourse, it is not the sacrament of continuing fellowship with Christ which is foremost here, but the act of conversion, turning to Jesus as the source of supply for all men's needs.

36    **But you, as I said, do not believe although you have seen me** appears to interrupt the progress of thought, but in fact it prepares for the succeeding verses: Jesus recognized that some men, although they see the signs, still do not believe in him and recognize in him the answer to their

37 needs. **All that the Father gives me will come to me.** Men come to him, not drawn by their own instinct, but brought to Christ by the Father. This is the strange paradox of the divine initiative and the human response. The Father draws men to Jesus, but if men do not believe in him, they do not escape the blame for their unbelief. Sometimes John, like Paul, stressed the divine initiative so much that he seemed to lose sight of a human response. But Jesus went on to declare, **The man who comes to me I will never turn away.** The eternal salvation of men is the will of God, and it was for this purpose, and this purpose alone, that Christ became incarnate, suffered, died, and rose again.

40    **Everyone who looks upon the Son and puts his faith in him shall possess eternal life.** To 'look upon' is to perceive with the eye that leads to knowledge of God and to faith in Jesus. Eternal life is a present possession and a future hope—the concept covers both a 'realized eschatology' which sees eternal life in the here-and-now and a 'futurist eschatology' which looks forward to the end of time. Later, Jesus was to claim that what the Father had sent him to do had been accomplished, 'Not one of them is lost' (17.12).

# EASTER 2

*The Emmaus Road*

### Isaiah 25. (1–5)

A psalm of thanksgiving for all that the Lord has achieved for the redemption of his people. It may have originated in the overthrow of an
2 enemy town—**thou hast turned cities into heaps of rubble**—but has been taken into a far wider concept of the Lord's strength and triumph and his protection of the poor and needy.

### 6–9

The mountain is the throne of the Lord of Hosts where he has spread
6 out a magnificent feast, a messianic coronation banquet, **for all the peoples** (the universal extent of the invitation is noteworthy). He rules triumphantly. Everyone will be joyful, for all mourning will be taken away and even death itself will be abolished. The idea of the end of death is a novel one in the OT. There is no suggestion of a resurrection or a heaven here, but the text was quoted by Paul to explain the effects of Christ's rising from the dead (1 Cor. 15.26, 54).
9 **See, this is our God for whom we have waited to deliver us** is a hymn of praise. We have been waiting for the Lord's salvation; now let us rejoice in it.

The prophecy of the messianic banquet was used by Jesus in the parable about the wedding feast (Matt. 22.2–10) and the sacrificial meal was linked with the day of the Lord in other prophetic writings (e.g. Zeph. 1.7 and Ezek. 39.17–20).

### Revelation 19. 6–9

The passage brings us the vision of the wedding feast of the Lamb from the Apocalypse. Because God has broken down the last resistance to his
6 universal reign, the vast crowd of martyrs take up the Easter cry **Alleluia**, a transliteration into English via Greek of the Hebrew 'Praise the Lord!' The faithful are rewarded by an invitation to the wedding feast.

Prophetic tradition had pictured the people of God as a bride (Hos. 2.19; Isa. 54.1–8) and, in this vision, the new Israel, the Church, is now made ready in fine clean and shining linen given to her—a sign of the purity of the Church washed in the blood of the Lamb, demonstrated by
6 the righteous deeds of God's people. **The Lord our God, sovereign**

over all, has entered on his reign! may be an early Christian acclamation used in worship, like many of the hymns and prayers in the Revelation of John.

* ### Luke 24. 13-35

The story of Christ's appearance to two of his disciples on the road to
Emmaus comes from one of Luke's independent sources in the stream
18 of apostolic tradition. One of the disciples was named **Cleopas**, a
shortened form of Cleopatros; he may have been the husband of a certain
Mary (John 19.25). Perhaps his home was at Emmaus. It is not possible
nowadays to identify with any certainty where this village was, though
the most likely site is on the Jaffa road four or five miles north-west of
Jerusalem.

When the stranger asked the disciples what they were talking about,
they gave him a summary of what had happened using words and
phrases which echo catechetical and credal passages in other parts of the
20– NT: **Jesus of Nazareth, a prophet powerful in speech and action**
23 **before God and the whole people** . . . **our chief priests and rulers**
**handed him over to be sentenced to death, and crucified him** . . .
**the third day** . . . **some women** . . . **went early to the tomb, but**
**failed to find his body.** . . . These are common elements in the early
preaching of the Church. When the apostles spoke to the Jews about the
death of Jesus, they usually stressed the guilt of the Jewish leaders (Acts
2.23, 3.13–14, 4.10, etc.) and recalled the 'miracles, portents, and signs'
that God had worked through Christ (Acts 2.22). They also portrayed
Christ as another and greater Moses, and the references to a prophet
powerful in speech and action and the man to liberate Israel should be
seen in this light.

The early preaching of the Church went on to proclaim the resurrection
of Christ; and this is what the stranger talked about to the two disciples
as they completed their journey. He reminded them that the Messiah
26 **had to suffer before entering upon his glory**, and beginning with
27 **Moses and all the prophets** . . . **explained to them the passages**
**which referred to himself in every part of the scriptures.** The
great turning-point in the Christian understanding of the OT had been
reached. From now on these writings would be seen through their fulfilment in the Passover of Jesus Christ and the gift of the Holy Spirit at
Pentecost. Luke did not try to 'prove' the resurrection; as he neared the
end of his Gospel, he drew together, with the skill of an artist, the threads
of prophecy and event which focus on Jesus.

And so the disciples invited the stranger to join them at supper, and as he took the bread, said the blessing, and broke it, they recognized him. The meal at Emmaus was a mirror of the Last Supper and an early Eucharist. The ministry of the word was followed by the ministry of the sacrament, as Luke was to describe the celebration in the apostolic community in Jerusalem and Troas (Acts 2.42,26; 20.7). The Holy Spirit had begun to reveal Christ to the disciples as the scriptures were expounded—

32 Did we not feel our hearts on fire as he talked with us on the road and explained the scriptures to us?—but it was not until the prayer of thanksgiving was offered and the bread broken that Christ was fully revealed. When the Eleven and the rest of the company in Jerusalem

34 heard it, they made the Easter proclamation: The Lord has risen.

# EASTER 2

*The Good Shepherd*

### Ezekiel 34. (1–6)

The title of 'shepherd' was commonly applied to kings and leaders in the ancient East. This is understandable when we remember that in a society which was dependent economically on stock-rearing, the king or leader was ultimately responsible for decisions relating to the care of the flocks and the movement of the tribe from one grazing area to another. In identifying her rulers with the office of shepherd, and in regarding herself as a flock under their care, Israel was simply copying the outlook of her neighbours.

That outlook left its mark on the Old Testament. The great men of Israel were nearly all shepherds. Abraham was introduced as one rich in cattle and sheep (Gen. 13.2). Moses was recognized as a shepherd of the people (Exod. 2.17, 3.1ff; Num. 27.17). David was a shepherd-hero: as a shepherd he defended his flock against lions and bears, and he proved himself to be worthy of being a shepherd of the people by taking on in single-handed combat the Philistine champion, Goliath (1 Sam. 17.31ff).

Gradually the concept of Israel as a flock under the care of shepherds acquired a profound, religious significance. Prophets and psalmists looked back on the early history of the people as a parable of the nation's spiritual destiny. For them the Passover and the Exodus represented the beginning of a spiritual pilgrimage which had not yet been completed, even though Israel's nomadic days were over and the temple was established in Jerusalem. Once the people had fled from the slavery of Egypt and had been led by God through the wilderness to the promised land. Now they were still seeking the freedom of God's children in his kingdom, led by the shepherds whom he had chosen.

The prophet denounced the rulers of Israel for exploiting the people for their own profit and for neglecting their duties as those appointed by
3 God for the care of his people. **You consume the milk, wear the wool, and slaughter the fat beasts, but you do not feed the sheep.** Because of their neglect, the people were scattered throughout the world.

7-15
10 God declared that he himself would now intervene: **I am against the shepherds and will demand my sheep from them.** He would put himself in charge of the flock and that would be the end of all misrule.
13 **I will bring them out from every nation, gather them in from other lands, and lead them home to their own soil.** The reference to collecting the people from other lands may refer to the Jews of the dispersion, or it may be a vision of the universal application of the law of God which is seen in some parts of the OT.

1 Peter 5. 1–11
Part of a letter addressed to a Christian community bewildered by a crisis, a 'fiery ordeal', which has engulfed them (4.12). The actual situation of the recipients of the letter is not clear, but the crisis—a sudden local persecution or some other threat to the wellbeing of the community —prompted the author to exhort those who exercised pastoral care among them to be particularly watchful to their charges.

Although there was no definite pattern of ecclesiastical government in New Testament times, Christian congregations often modelled themselves on the organization of the Jewish synagogues, both in Palestine and in the dispersion, and set up a bench of elders selected on the basis of their seniority and experience to care for the local Church. This was a natural development, since many early Christians, being Jews by birth, were familiar with synagogue administration. The bench of elders was responsible for leadership, pastoral supervision, and financial and disciplinary arrangements, and they may have been presided over by a chairman.

To some such presbyteral bench the author addressed himself **as**
1 **a fellow-elder and a witness of Christ's sufferings, and also a par-**

taker in the splendour that is to be revealed. Leaving aside the problem of apostolic authorship implied in these phrases, the words spell out the truth that the Christian pastor—and indeed the individual member of the Church—finds that his life of discipleship involves him in the responsibilities, the sufferings, and the glory of Christ. What the good shepherd accepted on our behalf, we experience in different ways as Christians.

2    The elders were shepherds of the flock of God: early in the second century the title was conventionally applied to the Church's ministers, especially the bishops. The author reminded them that the motive of their ministry must be voluntary self-dedication, so that they might be an
3    example to those allotted to your care—the phrase which, translating the single word *kleroi*, suggests that each elder had some group or 'parish' for which he was responsible. In this way they would be rewarded by
4    the Head Shepherd when he manifested himself at his second coming.
5    The younger men seem to be those who depend upon the pastoral oversight of the elders. Perhaps this sentence, the first part of verse 5, is a detached fragment which has little importance. It leads into the exhortation given by the author to all his readers to be humble because God favours the humble (a quotation from Prov. 3.34, LXX). We are reminded of the *Magnificat* with its verse about the humble being lifted high.

11    The final three verses of our pericope, ending with the Amen, may have been quoted from a catechetical formulary or a baptismal hymn. The purpose of the letter was to recall the recipients to the 'new birth into a living hope by the resurrection of Jesus Christ from the dead' (1.3), and some scholars have detected a baptismal—maybe a paschal—liturgy
8-9    behind the epistle. The succession of imperatives—Be on the alert . . . Stand up . . ., remember—and the charge to renounce the devil, may echo a catechetical tradition, adapted by the author in his attempt to sustain the readers in their critical situation.

\*  John 10. 7–18
The expectation of Israel that the Lord himself would be their shepherd found fulfilment in the ministry of Christ. The parable of the lost sheep (Luke 15.4–7, the gospel for Trinity 3) took its inspiration from this theme. But the christological implications of the shepherd image are explored more deeply in today's gospel. The Lord had said to Ezekiel, 'I myself will ask after my sheep and go in search of them'. Thus Christ's assertion that he was the good shepherd was a claim to messiahship. He

echoed the prophetic condemnation of the bad shepherds by saying that all
8 who came before him were thieves and robbers, and he declared the
uniqueness of his office by saying that only through him do men have
access to God. Because of what Christ has done as the good shepherd,
9 individual members of his flock shall go in and out and find pasturage
—that is, they will enjoy the freedom of trusted servants and they will
enter into eternal life.

David, as a shepherd, risked his life for his sheep; Christ, as the good
shepherd, did more than this—he laid his life down in an act of willing
and sacrificial surrender for the love of his people. The deliberation with
which Christ foretold that he would do this is one of the characteristics
of the fourth Gospel; it is found in several passages in the book (for
example, 'Jesus had always loved his own who were in the world, and now
he was to show the full extent of his love', John 13.1, the beginning of the
gospel for Maundy Thursday); and the phrase 'lay down my life' occurs
no less than four times in today's extract. This willing and sacrificial
surrender of his life was vindicated in the resurrection, ascension, and
session of Christ at the right hand of the Father, the source of all that the
Church celebrates during the great Fifty Days. This is why the figure of
the good shepherd is also a figure of the risen Christ. Jesus had completed
his Passover (and here we come close to the theme of the Lamb of God,
another image from the sacrificial cult of a sheep-rearing community)
and had entered into his inheritance which he now shares, through baptism, the Eucharist, and the Spirit-filled life, with his Church.

14  Christ declared I know my sheep, and my sheep know me, as the
Father knows him and as he knows the Father. 'Knowledge' such as this
is more than an intellectual apprehension; it is a mutual acceptance and
understanding which grows out of the experience of intimate personal
contact and which, when it matures, becomes love. It is because he knows
his sheep in this way that the good shepherd is willing to lay down his
life for them. But the love of God is so great that it extends to sheep
outside the flock of Israel, to men and women of all nations; and Christ
revealed that his ultimate aim was to bring them all into unity with God
16 and with each other so that they formed one flock under one shepherd.

# EASTER 3

*The Lakeside*

### Isaiah 61. 1–3

The situation in Judah after the return from the exile did not manifest that new age which had been expected; the enemies of the nation still remained and life within the rebuilt city of Jerusalem was hard and meagre. In this passage the Third Isaiah, in a personal act of witness, announced that the spirit of the Lord had come upon him to bring a message of good news to the people. The divine breath, thought of in terms of a power from God which could invade man's personality with an intensity that gave him the authority and the ability to speak in God's name, had

1 descended upon him to bring this message (**anointed me** is used here figuratively, though an actual anointing of oil was used in certain circumstances to signify the divine spirit descending on a man for his work, e.g. the anointing of kings, 1 Sam. 16.13).

The series of infinitives catalogues the purpose for which the messenger was sent. His apostolic mission was **to bring good news to the humble**

2–3 (the pious, faithful ones); **to comfort all who mourn** for their failings which seem to have caused the Lord to desert them; **to proclaim liberty** to those whose life is restricted like a prisoner's; to declare a **year of the Lord's favour**, a reference to the year of jubilee in which debts were remitted and slaves freed, and a **day of the vengeance of our God**, an event in history when God would vindicate his people. The signs of repentance—tears, ashes,—would be replaced by joy and festal array.

3 The prophetic symbol, **Trees of Righteousness**, is the title given to those who receive the word of the prophet, for they will be established in strength and stability like oak trees.

The Hebrew verb meaning 'to announce good tidings' has been translated by the Greek verb corresponding to the noun *evangelion*, from which English-speaking Christians derive the word 'gospel,' 'good news'. It is used in the prophets and psalms to declare the good news that God was fulfilling his promises, was acting, or was about to act.

### (–11)

The change which the Lord's favour would bring would result in the

5 rebuilding of the city. Manual labour would be done by **foreigners and aliens** while the people themselves would exercise a spiritual leadership

6 as **priests of the Lord**. Everlasting joy would replace their former shame,

8  the robbery and wrong-doing suffered by Jerusalem at its capture. The
9  Lord promised a new salvation and all people would acknowledge
   in them a race whom the Lord has blessed.
10    Let me rejoice in the Lord with all my heart: the prophecy moves
   into the people's song of thanksgiving to the Lord for what he has done
   for the people using the image of Israel as a bride decked in her
   jewels.

### 1 Corinthians 15. 1–11

There were those in Corinth who held that there was no resurrection of
the dead (verse 12), so Paul had to tackle this erroneous opinion by going
1  back to the gospel that I preached to you when he first came to Corinth.
   It was this gospel, he reminded them emphatically, which they had
   received, on which they had taken their stand, and which was even at that
   moment bringing them to salvation. Two aorist tenses are followed by a
   futurist present—the salvation, though still to come, is assured.
      Verses 3, 4, 5 and perhaps 6, represent the early gospel proclamation,
   the *kerugma*, which Paul and the other apostles preached; the words may
   not be Paul's own but part of a received text which he used in common
3  with other Christian preachers. I handed on to you: he was not the
   originator of the tradition but a link in the chain which handed it on. The
3–4 three short clauses, Christ died for our sins . . ., was buried . . ., was
   raised to life on the third day compactly state the early form of the
   Christian creed. The apostle did not indicate which scriptures were fulfilled—probably he meant the general fulfilment of the scriptures in
   Christ's Passover rather than specific texts. The apostolic Church only
   gradually recognized in the details of Christ's passion a fulfilment of
   particular verses in the OT.
      Paul then went on to list in outline the appearances of the risen Jesus
   to various witnesses: Cephas, whom the Corinthians already knew (he
   had a group of admirers, 1.12, 9.5); the Twelve, a term not used by
   Paul himself so probably taken from his source; and five hundred of
   our brothers, some of whom had died in the twenty years since the
5–7 event: James; all the apostles, a wider group than the Twelve in
   Pauline terminology. This list does not tally exactly with the accounts in
   the Gospels, but it is not incompatible with any of them. It is unlikely that
   the stories of the resurrection appearances would have been in a tidy
   shape by Paul's time.
7     Paul's reference to all the apostles enabled him to lead into the
9  reminder that the risen Jesus appeared to him also, who was not fit

8 **to be called an apostle.** The phrase, **It was like an abnormal birth,**
is difficult to interpret: its most likely meaning is that Paul's birth
into the Christian faith and into Christian apostleship was untimely in
that it was almost freakish. He may have been repeating words used by
those at Corinth who questioned the authenticity of his apostleship
(9.1ff and 2 Cor. 10–13). Even so, he said, through God's grace he had
laboured more abundantly than all the apostles. As the apostle to the
Gentiles he had broken new ground with the gospel to those who had
not heard it.

Verse 11 returns to the subject in hand. The resurrection of Christ is
the focal point of all Christian preaching; every apostle announced that
fact, and the Corinthians accepted it when they were converted.

\* **John 21. 1–14**
A post-resurrection story found in the appendix of the fourth Gospel,
rooted in the tradition of the Galilean appearances of Christ. Seven
disciples were involved in a miraculous catch of fish not dissimilar to that
recorded in Luke 5.1–11. Night was the best time for fishing, but they
caught nothing. As with other resurrection appearances, this one happened
early in the morning, Jesus was not immediately recognized, Peter and
the beloved disciple figure prominently in the story, and there was a meal.
The narrative recalls other occasions when Jesus fed with his disciples,
saying the blessing and distributing the food—notably at the Last Supper
and at Emmaus.

The allegorical imagery in the story is noteworthy. Thus the net
represents the Church gathering into her unity under the word of the
risen Christ men and women of all races and all types; with the Lord's
guidance, the apostles bring them to him on the shore. The number of
153 must be significant, though no one is certain why it is so: it may be
that naturalists at the time thought there was that number of species of
fish and so the number represented the universal mission of the Church;
or that $153 = 17 + 16 + 15 + \ldots + 3 + 2 + 1$, the number 17 being
chosen because $10 + 7 =$ the mark of perfection and completeness.

The narrative teaches that Jesus can feed his disciples without their
aid (he is 'the bread of life'), but that they cannot fish without his assistance. The details of the meal had an effect on early Christian art, where
the Eucharist was pictured as a meal presided over by Christ with fish and
bread on the tables, like the paintings in the Roman catacombs, dated
from about 200. (The Greek word for 'fish', *Ichthus*, makes up the initials
for 'Jesus Christ God's Son Saviour')

# EASTER 3

*The Resurrection and the Life*

### 1 Kings 17. (8–16)
An incident in the cycle of Elijah stories. The woman was the widow of
Zarephath (Sarepta, 7 or 8 miles south of Sidon) who made a shelter for
the prophet on the flat roof of her house. The generosity with which this
Phoenician woman was prepared to share her little flour and oil is remarkable. The miraculous supply of food was her reward for believing
16 the word of the Lord foretold through Elijah.

### 17–24
Another story in the saga. Although the narrative does not actually state
that the widow's boy died, we are to understand this from the statement
17 that his breathing ceased, breath being the sign and source of life. His
mother blamed Elijah. She believed that the death of her son was God's
punishment to her for some sin she had committed in the past; the prophet, a person in whom the spirit of God dwelt, had brought the sin to
light because his presence in the house had made it impossible for the
evil to remain hidden any longer. Had he not been there, she might have
escaped the penalty.

Then Elijah carried the boy up to his shelter on the roof—a simple
matter of hygiene, removing him from the stuffiness and debris of the
household to the airy conditions above (this may have been a factor in his
recovery); and, invoking the Lord, stretched himself upon the child.
The act illustrates the belief that the life force in Elijah was so strong that
it could communicate itself to the body of the child, organ to organ. If
the NEB text is preferred, it might be interpreted as an early example of
'the kiss of life'. The breath of life, the spirit of God, was infused into
the body of the child, restoring him to life. The miracle confirmed for the
woman her belief that the prophet was a true man of God.

### Colossians 3. 1–11
To be risen with Christ is the Pauline equivalent to being born again in
baptism: 'When we were baptized into union with Christ Jesus we were
baptized into his death. . . . In Christ Jesus the life-giving law of the
Spirit has set you free from the law of sin and death' (Rom. 6.3, 8.2).
The baptized, therefore, must no longer be concerned with the trivial
matters of this life but must direct their attention to the important matters

1 of heaven; for it is there that Christ is, risen and **seated at the right hand of God**. The right hand of God is the symbol for God's activity in power among men, and the ascension to the right hand of God was the early Church's symbolic way of describing how Christ shared in the sovereignty of God and yet remained distinct as a person. The Church was being led towards the formation of the doctrine of the Trinity.

In a true sense, through repentance, faith, baptism, and the receiving of the Holy Spirit, we have already shared in Christ's resurrection; and the Christian lives, not just in imitation of Christ, but motivated and guided by the resurrection life of Christ within him by virtue of his spiritual union with God in the power of the Spirit. Just as Christ's once-for-all death and resurrection in history foreshadowed the future baptismal death-and-resurrection of Christians, so it also foreshadows the future resurrection of the whole personality of the Christian beyond his natural death. The Christian's baptism, therefore, looks forward to 3 the fulfilment of that resurrection beyond the grave: **You died; and now your life lies hidden with Christ in God.**

Paul based on this teaching his insistence that the moral conduct of the Christian would demonstrate this risen life of Christ within him. **God's dreadful judgement** (*orge*, wrath, the reaction of a personal God 6 against sin and evil) **is impending.** Paul's list of sins and his injunctions may be a form of catechetical instruction given to converts before their baptism. Expressions such as 'putting to death', 'laying aside', 'discarding' and 'putting on' originated in this kind of teaching and were ritualized in the putting on of the white robe of the chrism in the later Christian rites of initiation. The apostle teaches in this passage that through baptism man is renewed in that image of his Creator which was his in the beginning, but which has been spoilt by disobedience and sin. Paul 10 conceived of this as a continuous process **(is being constantly renewed).** With that restored image the social distinctions between men and the sexual distinctions between men and women disappear, as all are one in Christ.

* John 11. 17–27
Lazarus had been dead four days. Perhaps there was a hint of folklore in this detail. The soul was supposed to hover around the body for three days and then depart; a change set in and decomposition began. The body was wrapped in linen and placed on a shelf in one of the thousands of cave-sepulchres that are found in Palestine, like the one the body of Jesus was laid in. The supposed tomb at Bethany is still to be seen by the modern

pilgrim. A visit of mourners at this time was a pious duty. Martha, the sister who liked to be up and about busying herself with the things to be done (Luke 10.40), came out to meet Jesus when she knew he was coming. Their dialogue reveals the truth about Jesus and the gradual acceptance of that truth by the woman.

21     Her first words were half-reproachful, half-hopeful, **If you had been here, sir, my brother would not have died. Even now I know that whatever you ask of God, God will grant you.** Jesus told her that her brother would rise again, and she interpreted this as meaning that he would rise again at the general resurrection on the last day; but at this point Jesus replied with a revelation of the truth that he is the incarnate Logos, the principle of life in whom all things and person exist. He did this in one of the important 'I am' sayings of the fourth Gospel, the words

25 echoing the revelation of God to Moses: **I am the resurrection and I am life.** Jesus had come to fulfil the Father's purpose that all men should attain to eternal life through faith in him. He is the one who raises believers from the dead, and those who believe in him have passed from the spiritual death of sin into the Spirit-filled life of Christ. Physical death can no longer have any hold over them.

    The question put to Martha by Jesus was not unlike the question put

26 to catechumens before their baptisms. **Do you believe this?** It is the question which evokes the faith of the convert as he prepares sacramentally to share in Christ's death and resurrection. Martha replied with a

27 confession in faith of Jesus as **the Messiah, the Son of God who was to come into the world.** In response to her faith, Lazarus was raised— the triumph of the resurrection foreshadowed in him as a promise to believers.